THE SHAPE OF THE LAND

THE SHAPE OF THE LAND

TOPOGRAPHY & LANDSCAPE ARCHITECTURE

EDITED BY MARC TREIB

ORO EDITIONS, NOVATO, CALIFORNIA

Publication of this book was supported by generous grants from the Hubbard Educational Foundation and the Richard and Rhoda Goldman Distinguished Professorship, University of California, Berkeley.

Book Design: Marc Treib
ORO Project Coordinator: Jake Anderson
Proofreader: Alicia Moreira

First Edition
Library of Congress data available upon request.
ISBN: 978-1-957183-24-4

International Distribution: www.oroeditions.com/distribution
10 9 8 7 6 5 4 3 2 1
First edition

World Rights: Available

Color Separations and Printing: ORO Group Ltd.
Printed in China

For

Marcella Eaton

&

Alan Tate

CONTENTS

PREFACE

Winston Churchill famously observed, "we shape our buildings; thereafter buildings shape us." With only slight modification, that pronouncement could apply equally to the influence of topography as the foundation for all landscape architecture. We shape the land; thereafter, it shapes how we live upon it. Transforming the earth is the primary act in realizing any landscape design—whether an act minimal or momentous, whether applied to unspoiled natural terrain or a polluted brownfield. It provides the base and basis for all subsequent planting and paving; it is the ground from which all buildings rise. Most commonly, the acts of digging, piling, and reshaping first address issues of function and performance. At other moments, however, the earth is altered for purely aesthetic reasons, at an extreme making sculpture of the land. In real estate, it is said that the three most important factors are "location, location, location." That adage applies in equal measure to the reconfiguring of the earth, as on location depend soil composition, its stability and fertility, and the vegetation that thrives there.

Held at the University of California, Berkeley, in March 2020, the symposium The Shape of the Land: Aesthetics and Utility gathered a select group of twelve landscape architects and historians hailing from eight countries, who presented their thoughts on the place of topography in their own work and in the works of others, both contemporary and historical. The range of scales represented by these projects was staggering, spanning the intimacy of backyard gardens to the grandeur of major infrastructure—here represented by the reworkings of the Don River in Toronto and the River Aire outside Geneva. One might humorously suggest that as an opening foray exploring the subject of topography, this book can only "scratch the surface." It is intended to question, inform, and provoke rather than provide an exhaustive study. Together, the chapters confirm topography's elemental and exquisite significance, whether in the design of an urban fountain or a "renaturalized" river.

The subtitle of the symposium, Aesthetics and Utility, emphasized the importance of the actual terrain, its forms, spaces, and materials—and that aesthetic concerns remain crucial, even in designs focused on social and/or environmental issues. Intended or not, all modifications to topography have an aesthetic consequence, a consequence that should be considered in the design. This is true even for landscapes we judge unsightly or blatantly deleterious, such as the toxic tailings of mineral extraction. Making form always has consequences.

Fewer than half the talks at the symposium originated as complete texts, which made producing chapters from the presentations a considerable challenge. For those talks without texts, the videos of the presentations were transcribed and substantially rewritten. For others, the original texts were heavily reworked, augmented by missing information and transitions, and in some cases even introducing issues I felt necessary to render the essay more focused or comprehensive. The speakers/authors then reviewed the suggested revisions of their talks, commenting and correcting as needed. The final form of the chapters represents a version mutually agreed upon as final. The book's fourteen commentaries reflect particular and personal points of view as well as the broader factors, constraints, and ideas that bear on their authors' own work. As no attempt was made to impose any standard template on all the texts, considerable variety is evident in the approaches and structures of the essays.

Despite the differences in discourse and terminology, each of the authors has positioned an aesthetic regard for topographic design within a greater social and environmental context. I would offer that most of the projects, despite their focus on ground form, are ecologically based and socially aware—and beautiful, if in varying ways. All began with topography, a consideration of the ground itself, the shape of the land.

Marc Treib
Berkeley, December 2021

1. REFORMING TERRAIN

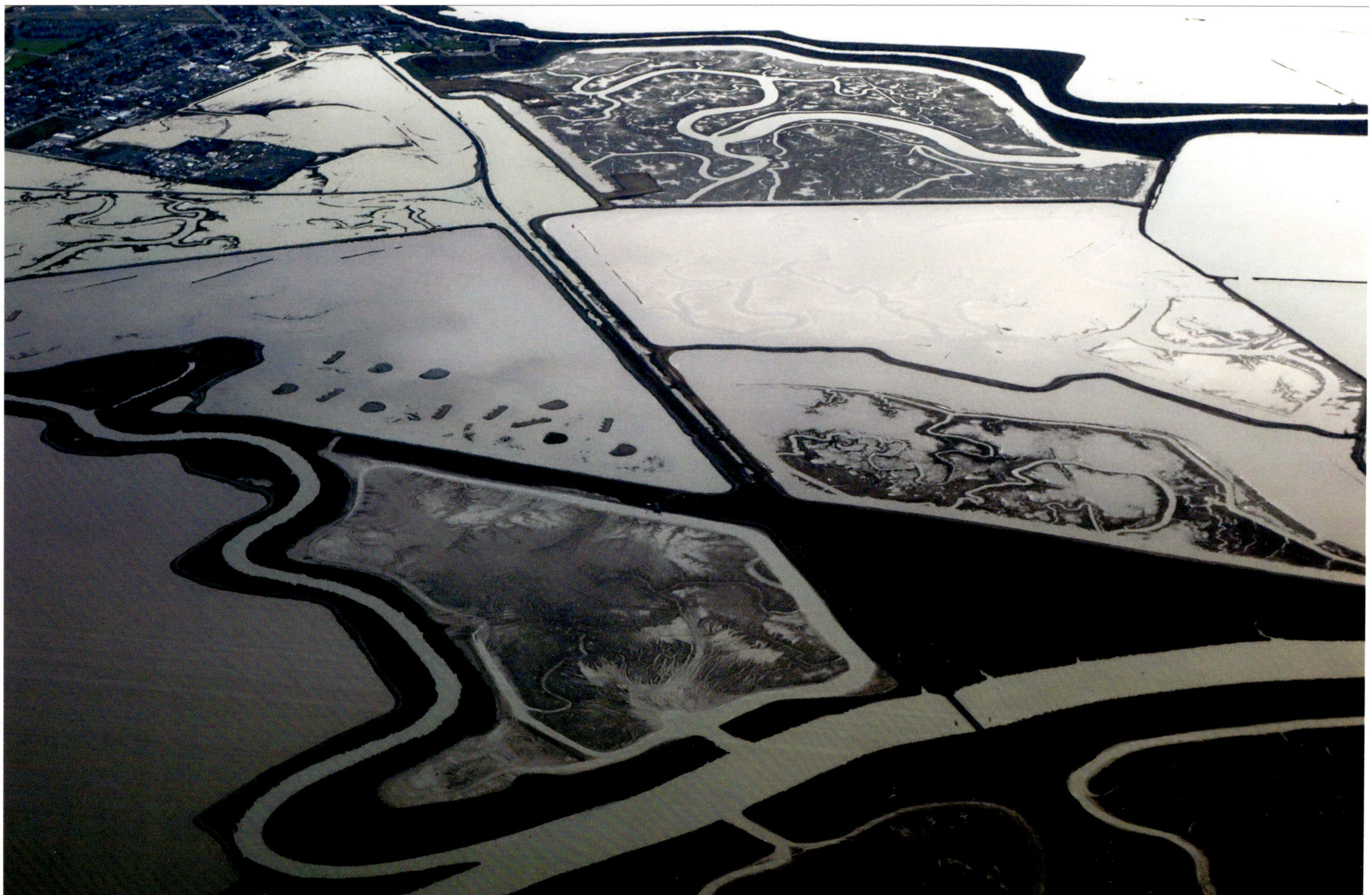

MARC TREIB

In Genesis it is written, "Let the waters under the sky be gathered into one place, so that the dry land may appear. . . . And it was so" [1-1].[1] Although water is said to still occupy two-thirds of our planet's surface, we live primarily on the land, on terra firma. In making landscape architecture, this land–topography–is primary in all but the most unusual of commissions. Earth is the surface upon which we work, and earth is the material with which we begin our designs. As soil, it provides the nutrients necessary for vegetal life. As a medium for landscape design, it is shaped, excavated, piled, and graded into varied levels and specific forms. Cutting and filling are primary acts in making almost every landscape. Although perhaps instigated by pragmatic concerns, grading inherently constitutes a sculptural act enfolding both need and expression. Today's landscape architect emulates what in the Beginning represented only divine intervention. As proclaimed in George Frideric Handel's *Messiah*, modeling the land was part of the Creation: "Every valley shall be exalted: Every mountain and hill made low, the crooked straight, the rough places plain." If not quite to the same extent, the landscape architect also intervenes by reshaping the land, according to a plan.[2]

At times humans do play God and make their own land, however; Venice and much of the Netherlands provide excellent examples of this form of creation. When asked what plans had been made for the architecture and landscape of the recently constructed Ijmeer housing development in Amsterdam, Dirk Sijmons responded. "We don't have any specific plans as yet; we have to finish designing the land first."[3] A related story involves Máxima, or Leidsche Rijn Park designed by West 8, also in the Netherlands, whose construction began in 1997. On a bicycle tour on the park's loop path when construction was still underway, West 8 principal Adriaan Geuze pointed to the sand and earth piled where the then-dammed river would eventually flow and told me: "The Rhine will be over there, but we haven't finished making it yet" [1-2].[4] Or consider the seemingly natural landscape of New York's Central Park that in actuality demanded the complex conversion of diverse terrains to shape a landscape to

1-1
Salt evaporation ponds. San Francisco Bay, California. [Marc Treib]

accommodate social use, traffic, address environmental demands, and provide water storage. The Olmsted-Vaux design for the park bundled all those needs within a landscape that appears to have survived from some primordial era, long before Manhattan was settled by Europeans. Not so, not at all. From these historical references and contemporary anecdotes we understand that land can be made as well as remade, and that the form of that land is consequential.

While we often consider land a static entity, it is in fact an active material continually reshaped by environmental forces and human efforts. Sand dunes, whether those of the great African deserts or the anomalous Grand Dune du Pilat in southwestern France, are always on the move [1-3]. Mountains erode; their sediment and debris fill estuaries and rivers or are carried to the sea. Displaced by glaciers, uncounted tons of rock, soil, and rubble may travel hundreds, even thousands of miles. Ultimately, then, we recognize that land is created through explosion, erosion, and sedimentation, by building up and wearing down, by inorganic and organic processes—and through human intervention. The Grand Canyon in Arizona may be America's most dramatic exemplar of erosion, but it has resulted from forces and processes that act upon all land, although their resulting forms are rarely so spectacular [1-4].

Animate yet nonhuman activities also remake the land. Animals dig holes to bury food, others make burrows for habitat, or some, such as ants and termites, build structures that can rise meters above the ground. A beaver dam can instigate the inundation of vast areas of territory, modifying local ecosystems to a significant degree. The human transformation of the land, then, is but the culmination and perhaps most rapid and consequential of the geologic and animal processes. Humans possess the means to effect major transformations in a short period of time; occasionally, we determine the need and exert our will. We do not always make these decisions wisely, however, as the 1930s attempt to build the Cross-Florida Barge Canal clearly revealed: an unfortunate example of bad digging.[5]

Humans reshape the land for environmental management by blocking the wind; trapping the sun; and storing, stifling, and redirecting the flow of water. By modifying the land we address functional needs such as transportation and defense, and spiritual needs such as worship, burial, and remembrance. While the scales of these applications may vary to an exponential degree, the acts remain basic: digging, piling, and shaping—singly or in combination.

1-2
West 8.
Leidsche Rijn (Máxima) Park.
Utrecht, the Netherlands,
1997–2012.
[Marc Treib, 2011]

1-3
Dune de Pyla, France.
[Marc Treib]

1-4
Grand Canyon, Arizona.
[Marc Treib]

Digging

The Bingham Canyon copper mine, sited on the outskirts of Salt Lake City, Utah, is said to be our planet's largest excavated void; it is also said to be visible from space without the aid of optical instruments [1-5]. Before mining began the topography was shaped as a hill, but after decades of mineral extraction that hill became a hole, and in time that hole became a chasm. Since the copper ore mined there is only of low grade, extensive earth movement has been necessary to turn a profit. In response to low economic return, mining operations ceased at one point, but the arrival of more effective processes and larger-capacity excavation equipment resulted in a profitable undertaking. Because the copper ore is of low grade its toxicity, I am told, poses little or no threat to human and animal life.[6] Yet in terms of disturbance to the prior landscape, the consequences of mining have been horrific. Mining equates with extraction, and paired with excavation, always generates a consequent by-product that requires disposal: waste that itself at times produces entirely new landscapes. At the Bingham Canyon Mine we readily see the interrelation of digging and piling evidenced in the ever-deepening excavations into the earth and the unavoidable growth of hills and tips whose slopes glow in the afternoon sunlight as if made of gold [1-6]. The Law of the Conservation of Energy states that energy can neither be created nor destroyed. Similarly, site interventions do not actually destroy earth but can only modify and displace it.

Mines produce ore; quarries yield stone. Their operations, also rooted in removal, are largely the same, but their products may differ significantly. The quarries of Carrara and Pietra Santa in Italy are famous for the quality of their white marble, historically and internationally prized by sculptors and architects. As mechanical equipment extracts stone from the quarry walls a new landscape emerges, regardless of whether that resulting topography has been consciously considered. Whether planned or not, a certain beauty is found in the contrast between the geometric, human-made cuts into the stone and the remaining source areas not yet worked—as well as the natural contours of the landscape that surrounds the quarry. Once human effort or the product has been exhausted, natural processes return and act upon the abandoned work site. At times with human intervention, at other times free of it, bold landscapes

1-5
Bingham Canyon copper mine. Salt Lake City, Utah. It began as a hill. [Marc Treib, 2006]

materialize, especially when water collects in its voids or pioneer vegetation takes hold. As ready-made landforms, many former quarries have been converted to parks, for example, the former basalt quarry that is today the Poço da Pedreira on the island of Santa Maria in the Azores, where the collected water at its base enhances the stone surfaces with their reflections [1-7].

Although mining is only one of the topographic operations that modify the stuff of the planet, its effects can be brutal. Irrigation ditches, canals, reservoirs, and other watercourses may transform miles of land, significantly altering the surrounding terrain and the patterns dependent on it. Constructing a ditch of any length, like mining excavation, produces a corresponding volume of spoil requiring disposition or distribution. The French dreams of building the Panama Canal as a sea-level passage between the Atlantic and the Pacific—free of locks—ended in failure and financial ruin.[7] With the American resumption of construction enormous amounts of soil were loosened and displaced, efforts augmented by six sets of locks constructed along the forty-mile passage that joins the oceans. In their wake the Isthmus of Panama was completely transformed: mountains were leveled, lakes purloined, rivers deepened, and their courses modified. Cutting was the primary operation, requiring the redistribution and regrading of vast tonnages of soil and rock [1-8].

Canals begin with excavations at the surface; tunnels begin below the ground and leave immense amounts of spoil to be removed and distributed—not unlike gophers working at colossal scale. In some cases the products of these excavations are sufficient to create entirely new land, as in the mid-strait island between Denmark and Sweden created by the construction of the Örebro Bridge. In other instances soil must be pilfered off-site: for Osaka's Kansai Airport the material to build its site was appropriated from neighboring islands in the Seto Inland Sea. When constructing a new subway line in the 1970s Stockholm's transit authority created a distinctive architecture while simultaneously reducing construction costs by leaving exposed the surfaces of the granite bedrock and inviting artists to intervene upon their surfaces [1-9]. Much of the granite residue was used for aboveground roadbuilding.

In the American Southwest, the Pueblo and Hopi peoples constructed networks of check dams that retained rainfall from the storms that inundate the land on late summer afternoons. To confront the strong winds that

1-6
Bingham Canyon copper mine.
Salt Lake City, Utah.
Tailings seen from outside.
[Marc Treib, 2006]

1-7
Poço da Pedreira.
Santa Maria, Azores, Portugal.
[Marc Treib]

1-8
Culebra Cut.
Panama Canal, Panama, 13 June 1912.
[Library of Congress]

plagued their cornfields, they also constructed ridges or small depressions to shield the nascent seedlings, which capture and hold the limited rainfall as well. To a far greater extent, earthen dams manage the landscape as if the products of super-strength beavers who still the river and spread its waters over the adjacent acres. Even when used for purposes primarily aesthetic, efforts to move the earth can nonetheless involve the transposition of significant amounts of soil. At the seventeenth-century imperial villa of Shugaku-in in Kyoto, a huge earthen dam withholds hillside seepage and rainfall to create a pond for boating and aesthetic reflection [see figures 7-2, 7-5, 7-6]. To disguise the magnitude of the dam its makers planted large hedges along its slopes, staging them in tiers to reduce the apparent scale for an earthen wall several stories in height.

Piling

It is obvious that to pile one must first dig—or at the very least, displace. The cores of mounds used for burial have often involved composites of stone and spoil, thereafter covered with earth—at the royal burial mounds at Kivik in southern Sweden, for example. The mounds built by native peoples in Cahokia, Illinois, and other locations across the American Midwest and South transposed huge amounts of earth and rock into truncated pyramids of impressive dimensions [1-10]. Some mounds served as the bases for wooden structures constructed on their upper surfaces, vulnerable constructions that have long since succombed to the effects of wind, rain, and rot. Yet their topographic bases remain, illustrating the potential longevity of earthworks. Not all mounds assumed purely geometric form; others have been given animistic shapes configured as emblems or representations of creatures and life forces, as with the celebrated Serpent Mound in Ohio [1-11]. In creating the *Effigy Tumuli*, in Illinois, the artist Michael Heizer referenced these historical works when reconfiguring areas of an exhausted mining landscape as part of its remediation and conversion to a park.[8] Admittedly, Heizer's insect and animal figures are illegible from ground level, and it is obvious that truly identifying them would require a view from above. Whether the figures can be discerned without an elevated view is of less consequence, however, than the amelioration of the land following the havoc caused by decades of extraction.

1-9
Per Olof Utveldt, artist. Kungsträdgården metro station Stockholm, Sweden, 1975. Excavation left exposed, stabilized, and painted. [Marc Treib]

Burial mounds and hill tombs are but two examples of topography reconfigured for religious purposes, be it to exclude the unholy or

1-10
Cahokia Mounds.
Collinsville, Illinois,
800–1300 CE.
[Marc Treib]

1-11
Serpent Mound.
Near Locust Grove, Ohio,
ca. 1000 CE.
[Marc Treib]

(opposite) **1-12**
Gunnar Asplund and
Sigurd Lewerentz.
Woodland Cemetery.
Enskede, Sweden, 1915–40.
Memorial knoll seen from
the urn burial garden.
[Marc Treib]

protect and preserve the sacred. The *kofun*, the circular or keyhole-shaped burial mounds of seventh-century Japan, still dot areas of the Yamato plain between Kyoto and Osaka. Constructed in staged layers, the mounds have served to protect the imperial remains while their impressive elevation above the ground plain in itself bestowed significance on their sacred deposits. Soil was thus a medium to ensure a presence in eternity. The pyramids at Giza in Egypt, or those constructed by several cultures in Mesoamerica, represent the extreme efforts in this class and call into question at what point piles of earth faced with stone are more fairly regarded as architecture rather than earthworks.

On a smaller scale is the memorial knoll at Woodland Cemetery in Enskede, outside Stockholm, the work of architects Sigurd Lewerentz and Gunnar Asplund [1-12; see also 7-10, 7-11]. Much of the power of this moving landscape, whose design spanned 1915 through 1940, results from the subtle management of its grading. The ground of the cemetery's central meadow is formed as a single sweep of earth and lawn, while the architecture of the three chapels at its limit appears to stiffen the edge of the pine forest, almost as if a retaining wall. These sites demonstrate that the two basic acts of adding and subtracting—acts that always reform and transform—govern all our interventions on and into the surfaces of the Earth.

Shaping

Piling and digging are inherently interrelated acts. Between them, though to some extent requiring both, is the reshaping of the land. Many works in this topographic category are functionally based: terracing a hillside for building construction or cultivation, or flattening hills to facilitate urban development, as was the case in making Seattle or Rio de Janeiro in the modern period. At the eighteenth-century Middleton Place plantation outside Charleston, South Carolina, the existing riverbank and slope were recontoured as a series of terraces to more smoothly link the plantation's main house with the Ashley River, the principal point of arrival and departure [1-13]. Two earthen moles embraced plots of river land converted to rice growing, while providing the transition between water and land. It should be noted that at the time of their construction mechanical earth movement had yet to exist, and as in innumerable related stories throughout history from around

1-13
Middleton Place. Charleston, South Carolina, late eighteenth century. Terracing seen across the former rice fields. [Marc Treib]

1-14
Terraced vineyards. Maia, São Miguel, Azores, Portugal. [Marc Treib]

the world, conscripted or enslaved people comprised the primary source of labor. Even the lawn mower was yet to come—and grass and grains were cut with a scythe, light tasks only when compared to the digging and hauling of earth and the removal of rock. This is the darker side of earth movement in history and illustrates that changes to the land may often require massive amounts of human effort.[9]

At larger scale are the hillside terraces of Southeast Asia, whose construction provides the level land required for the wet cultivation of rice. Here the slopes have been stepped into trays of earth and water that balance the operations of cut and fill. In the Azore islands of Portugal, as in the Douro Valley in the home country, the proportion of height to width signals the epic struggle to steal land from the steep slopes converted to vine cultivation [1-14]. While aesthetics were perhaps of little or no consideration to the makers of these productive landscapes, the order and variation of the resulting forms are strikingly beautiful—certainly to the modernist eye.

Topographic displacements also serve military functions, most often for defense, and at Machu Picchu in Peru we find terraces acting as both protection and cultivation. Whether the ringed mounds of the tenth-century Viking camps in Denmark or the networks of the horrid World War I trenches that scarred the battlegrounds of Belgium and France, embankments and depressions have been used to establish and control territory and moving troops. Their simplest form is the foxhole, a classic illustration of cut and displace if not fill. In his classic memoir *All Quiet on the Western Front*, Erich Maria Remarque comments on its power: "To no man does the earth mean so much as to the soldier. When he presses himself down upon her long and powerfully, when he buries his face and his limbs deep in her from fear of death by shell-fire, she is his only friend."[10] At times fortifications have grown to heroic dimensions embracing hundreds of acres of land, for example, at seventeenth-century Japanese castles like the White Heron at Himeji [1-15]. Here, defense derived as much, if not more, from the labyrinthine system of pathways that zigzagged up the slope than from the monumental keep or the use of rifle and bow. Cultivation follows in times of peace and in its own way transforms the land, sometimes almost as conclusively. When its incline exceeds its soil's angle of repose, some form of reinforcement must strengthen the slope against erosion. Like the walls and configurations of terrain terraced for cultivation, these patterns of geometricized contours can

1-15
White Heron Castle.
Himeji, Japan, ca. 1601–18.
Extensive earthwork was required to construct the convoluted defensive paths.
[Marc Treib]

1-16
Thomas Church.
Donnell garden.
Sonoma County, California, 1947.
A stone wall retains the former slope to create a terrace garden of a single level.
[Marc Treib]

1-17
Hargreaves Associates.
Byxbee Park.
East Palo Alto, California, 1992.
Former trash dump reformed as park.
[Marc Treib]

completely transform the character of the landscape and influence the animal and plant life that dwell upon and within it.

Road building habitually requires the displacement of enormous amounts of soil and rock, and in its wake scours a line that traverses all kinds of terrain. Where the conditions are not severe, embankments and causeways rely on piled earth to bridge depressions in the land; in gaps with more extreme dimensions, bridges and trestles are demanded. The interstate highways that today span the United States gobbled hillsides and sealed valleys, surpassing the transposition of earth needed to build the railroads in the prior century. Considerations of stability, turning radius, banks on curves, maintenance, and longevity—among many other factors—determined their dimensions and forms. As in *Messiah*, "every mountain and hill [was] made low, the crooked straight, the rough places plain."

Land movement has also channeled and even displaced the sea—the creation of the Dutch polders being our leading example [see chapter 3]. Dikes resist the intrusion of water and control wetness; levees lining the banks of rivers and shores of lakes harness and direct threatening environmental forces to prevent flooding. Although triggered by functional demands, river management at its best generates landforms with considerable aesthetic merit, as SUPERPOSITIONS' renaturalization of the River Aire in Geneva aptly attests [see chapters 12 and 13].

Aesthetics & Utility

The management of topography—whether by digging, piling, or sculpting—is as basic to landscape architecture as foundations are to buildings. It is the landscape's foundation for the design that follows. Whether the leveling of a slope for recreation, as in Thomas Church's 1947 Donnell garden in Sonoma, California; the reshaping of a hill into an amphitheater, as at the eighteenth-century garden at Claremont, or the Red Rocks Amphitheater in Colorado; or the recontouring of decades of trash into a park [see chapter 9], landform alone plays a consequential role as the project's opening act [1-16, 1-17]. At one extreme, soil serves as the material of an artwork in and of itself. In 1933 Isamu Noguchi proposed what could arguably have been the first work of land art, *Monument to the Plough*. For an unspecified location in the Midwest, as a monument to its rumored inventor

Thomas Jefferson; its first fabricator, John Deere; as well as the American farmer; Noguchi envisioned a three-sided pyramid capped by a gigantic stainless-steel sculpture of a plow [1-18]. The project never advanced beyond a single sheet of drawings now lost, however. Almost a century would pass before Noguchi's design for *Play Mountain*, also conceived in 1933, was realized on a landfill in a suburb of Sapporo, in northern Japan [1-19]. In the intervening years this seminal idea reappeared in many of his landscape projects proposed or realized along the way.

Beginning in the late 1960s, a small cohort of artists left the gallery to, as they put it, work at large-scale and deny the artwork a status as commodity. On sites primarily in the deserts of the American Southwest, Michael Heizer, Nancy Holt, and Robert Smithson, among others, most often relied on the simple acts of digging and piling to create identifiable figures on or in the landscape.[11] Using tons of basalt to conjoin land and water, Smithson's celebrated 1970 *Spiral Jetty* at the Great Salt Lake in Utah configured a spiral whose reflection engaged water and sky [1-20]. Early on, Heizer incised lines in the desert's desiccated surface to produce a topographic work "drawn" by removal.[12] His *Double Negative*, executed at virtually the same moment as *Spiral Jetty*, aligned two deep bulldozer-made cuts across the ragged edge of Mormon Mesa in Nevada [1-21]. As one descends into either of the cuts, the space created by the work emerges, the alignment between the paired cuts strengthens, and the sense of the distant geological past becomes lucid. As illustrated by Heizer's *Effigy Tumuli*, cited above, earth movement has also acted in conjunction with the remediation of despoiled land; Robert Morris's regrading of *Johnson Pit #30* south of Seattle provides an additional illustration [1-22].[13] Opinions on such works have been divided: some regard them as positive transformations of ruin into habitable or even pleasurable settings; others view them as disguising the remnants of evil industrial practices behind an attractive façade or as unfortunate disturbances to the landscape and the natural processes by which it has been governed. Both points of view are valid, at least in part.

We might rightly ask at what point topographic modeling becomes architecture. Perhaps when a roof hovers over the land? But would this also apply to the tunnel? In the end, as evident in many of the examples cited, the line between architecture and landscape can be a rather fine one. In the early decades of the 1900s Baldassare Forestiere, an immigrant from Italy, began to

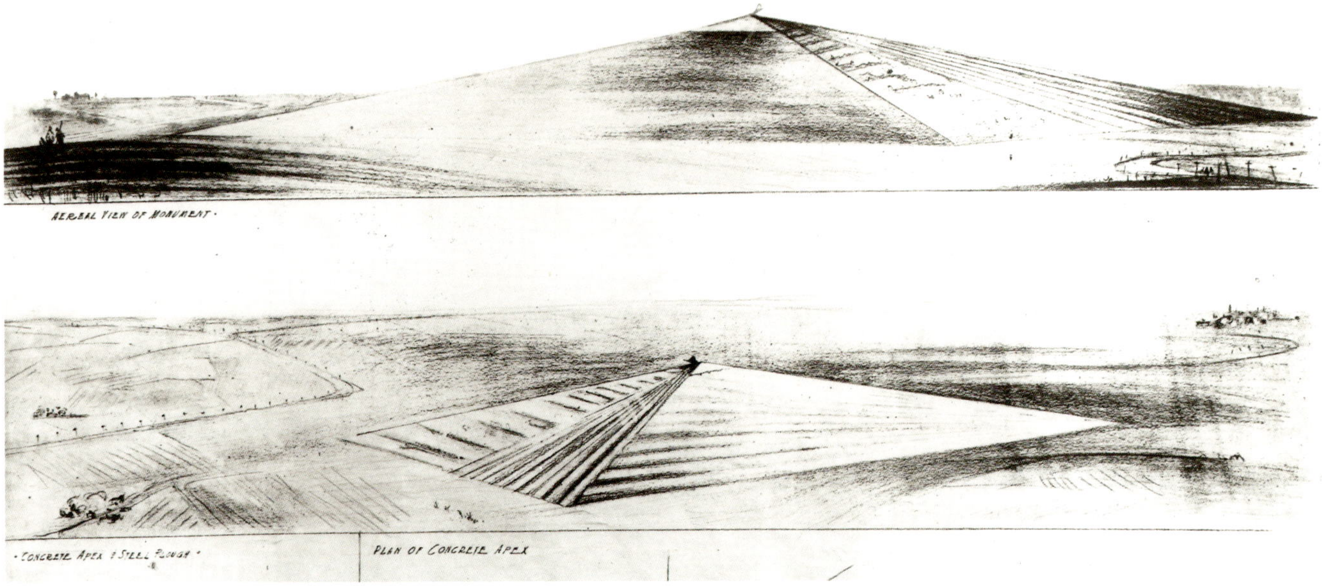

1-18
Isamu Noguchi.
Monument to the Plough.
1933.
[Isamu Noguchi Museum]

1-19
Isamu Noguchi, conception;
Shoji Sadao, Junichiro
Kawamura, Architects 5,
realization.
Moerenuma Park.
Sapporo, Japan, 1998–2015.
[Marc Treib]

dig a cellar beneath his house outside Fresno to escape the intense summer heat of California's Central Valley [1-23].[14] He was pleasantly rewarded for his efforts by a space far cooler than the temperatures encountered above ground, so over the years he kept digging. In the end, he produced some forty-odd subterranean rooms extracted from the hardpan and open to the sky. More monumental was the mortuary temple of the Egyptian queen Hatshepsut dug into the hillside circa fifteenth century BCE, accompanied by three terraces built in the very same material as the land itself—a product of addition more than subtraction. At Taliesin West, Frank Lloyd Wright modeled the desert landscape and built with materials garnered from it, with building forms and plans reflecting the plain of the desert and the profiles of the mountains beyond [1-24].

With the other factors that define and guide landscape design—among them social program, vegetation, and environmental forces such as wind and precipitation—the capture or remaking of topography is basic. Efforts today include the piling and shaping of waste and garbage into vital landscapes, solving functional problems such as drainage and flood control; the restructuring of riverbeds to direct, modulate, or impede the flow of water; and the purely aesthetic acts that employ earth as a sculptural medium. From these actions and interventions the shape of the land results.

Notes

1 Genesis 1:9, King James Version; https://www.biblegateway.com/passage/?search=Genesis%20 1:8-10&version=KJ21.

2 The oratorio *Messiah*—libretto by Charles Jennens and music by George Frideric Handel (HWV 56)—premiered in Dublin on 13 April 1742. While originally composed for an Easter performance, it has become a staple of Christmas choral performances.

3 Dirk Sijmons, in conversation with the author, Amsterdam, 1990s.

4 Adriaan Geuze, in conversation with the author, 14 May 2011, Leidsche Rijn (today Máxima) Park, designed by West 8, while still under construction.

5 Partway through construction, it was understood that completing the canal would cataclysmically alter the flow of water throughout the state, and might have resulted in the complete ruin of the Everglades; https://en.wikipedia.org/wiki/Cross_Florida_Barge_Canal.

6 Told to me by staff on site. I have not been able to verify this claim, however.

7 David McCullough, *The Path Between the Seas: The Creation of the Panama Canal* (New York: Simon & Schuster, 1977).

8 Douglas McGill, *Michael Heizer: "Effigy Tumuli"; The Reemergence of Ancient Mound Building* (New York: Abrams, 1990).

9 It is said that thousands of military and civilian workers died in the course of constructing the palace and gardens of Versailles.

10 Erich Maria Remarque, *All Quiet on the Western Front* (1929; New York: Random House, 1987).

11 John Beardsley, *Earthworks and Beyond* (New York: Abbeville, 2006); Philipp Kaiser and Miwon Kwon, *Ends of the Earth: Land Art to 1974* (Los Angeles: Museum of Contemporary Art, 2012); William L. Fox, *Michael Heizer: The Once and Future Monuments* (New York: Monacelli, 2019).

12 Julia Brown, ed., *Michael Heizer: Sculpture in Reverse* (Los Angeles: Museum of Contemporary Art, 1984); Marc C. Taylor, *Double Negative: Sculpture in the Land* (New York: Rizzoli, 1991).

13 Richard G. Hess, ed., *Earthworks: Land Reclamation as Sculpture* (Seattle: Seattle Art Museum, 1979).

14 Jan Wampler, *All Their Own: People and the Places They Build* (New York: Oxford University Press, 1979).

(above left) **1-20**
Robert Smithson.
Spiral Jetty.
Rozel Point, Utah, 1970.
[Marc Treib, 2016]

(below left) **1-21**
Michael Heizer.
Double Negative.
Mormon Mesa,
Nevada, 1970.
[Marc Treib, 1996]

(above right) **1-22**
Robert Morris.
Johnson Pit #30.
SeaTac, Washington, 1979.
[Marc Treib, 2008]

(below right) **1-23**
Baldassare Forestiere.
Underground Gardens.
Fresno, California,
ca. 1901–46.
[Marc Treib]

1-24
Frank Lloyd Wright.
Taliesin West.
Paradise Valley, Arizona,
1938+.
[Marc Treib]

2. REPTON FOR REAL: THE PRACTICAL AND PICTORIAL

STEPHEN DANIELS

The trade card of Humphry Repton (1752–1818), the leading English landscape designer of the later eighteenth and early nineteenth centuries, has become an emblem of the landscape profession [2-1]. It currently illustrates the Wikipedia entry for landscape architect, which describes a person whose practice includes "site analysis, land planning, planting design, grading, storm water management, sustainable design [and] construction specification."[1] As seen in the inscription on the tree in the image, Repton identified himself as a "landscape gardener," although his practice included designs for buildings of various kinds, as well as gardens, parks, and pleasure grounds. John Claudius Loudon first used the term "landscape architecture" in the title of his posthumous collection of Repton's published works.[2]

Repton attached the trade card to a circular advertising his business, explaining how "respectable friends" had persuaded him to transform his "amusement" of "laying out ground" for "picturesque effect" by making "sketches for the improvement of their places," to "plan and to pursue professionally his skill in landscape gardening." Repton claimed to have invented the term "landscape gardening" in order to "advance and perfect the united powers of the landscape painter and the practical gardener." He insisted that the "luxuriant imagination of the painter must be subjected to the gardener's practical knowledge in planting, digging and moving earth." Moreover, "the artist must possess a competent knowledge of surveying, mechanics, hydraulics, agriculture, botany and the general principles of architecture." Repton sought to combine beauty and utility in landscapes to be lived in and not just looked at. One of his sayings that has echoed down the years was written in a letter from a patron, which he included in his first published book: "Places are not to be laid out with a view to their appearance in a picture, but to their uses, and the enjoyment of them in real life."[3]

2-1
Thomas Medland. Trade card of Humphry Repton. Engraving after Humphry Repton drawing. 1789. [Stapleton Collection, Bridgeman Images]

As a sign of his professional expertise, on his trade card Repton portrays himself at a theodolite surveying an extensive parkland. Yet

Repton didn't abandon sketching; on the contrary, watercolor views formed a key component of his famous Red Books of designs and as aquatints in his published works; moreover, in his illustrations Repton often included an image of himself sketching. Although he had purchased a theodolite and level at the outset of his career, within a few years he seems to have largely forsaken surveying the sites himself, instead relying on the services of others. But he continued to use the same card throughout his career, pasting it in the frontispiece of the Red Books to convey the precise, practical, and prudent aspect of his profession: in every way a measured view.

The depiction of laborers in Repton's trade card, and their efforts to shape the lakeside, is part of his public acknowledgment of the role of social relations in the making of designed landscapes, an acknowledgment dating to the start of his career. While the theodolite that the foreground figure of Repton operates is a modern instrument, or rather a new model of an instrument that had been in use since the early eighteenth century, the laborers in the middle distance work with tools that had been used for earthmoving of all kinds since time immemorial: picks, spades, and wheelbarrows. Not until later in the nineteenth century did more advanced technology play a role, and even that was employed more for maintaining such landscapes—in the cutting of grass and rolling the ground—than in their making. There is some evidence of the use of horses and wagons to cart away barrows of earth, and wagons with mechanisms for transplanting mature trees, but the work was primarily achieved through human muscle and sweat. The techniques of grading slopes are now not well understood, however. Workers on projects by Repton's forbear Capability Brown would tip barrow loads of earth down terraces planned for that purpose; trees were then planted to stabilize slopes.[4] Repton travelled with pegs and ribbon to stake out ground, and on the trade card a Repton-like figure among the laborers points to the lakeside. But neither Repton's plans, nor accounts of the places where he worked, nor publications of the time, provide greater insight into how his designs were actually realized.[5]

The trade card represents some of the realities of site work, although in Repton's highly staged version of laying out grounds it is no less a performative image than his other self-portraits that display the repertoire of his practice: drawing on a sketch pad; peering through a telescope; peeping over a fence; directing work with a large umbrella; and in one Red Book, playing his flute under an oak tree as part of his clients' family music making. Repton's card recalls other depictions of surveying as a patriotic act, part of the progressive improvement of the nation, in an image evoking lines from Milton's *L'Allegro*:

Straight mine eye hath caught new pleasures
Whilst the landscape around it measures
Towers and battlements it sees
Bosom'd high in tufted trees.[6]

While Repton's trade card, then, is no less a cultural image than his other illustrations, it is a representation that signals some of the down-to-earth realities of his practice that have often been overlooked. Repton's Red Books, like his publications, are compelling. But they provide only partial evidence of his practice, and increasingly Repton researchers are looking beyond them to other, less graphic and literary sources to better understand the scope of his commissions, their geographic extent, the many people involved in their transformation, and the degree to which the designs as drawn were realized on the ground.[7] In this essay I will focus on the landscape on which Repton's trade card was based and consider the Red Book designs in terms of a more mundane but richly revealing source: the diary of the land agent who oversaw the business of estate improvement.

Repton at Welbeck

The scene on Repton's card is adapted from an image in a Red Book for an early, prestigious commission: Welbeck in Nottinghamshire, the seat of William Bentinck, 3rd Duke of Portland, a leading national statesman twice prime minister and major landowner. Under Portland's ownership Welbeck expanded to become the fifth largest estate in England, graced by a park of over a thousand acres and a lake over a mile in length. Welbeck became a showpiece of design and land management that involved an extensive and highly expensive campaign of improvement in farming and forestry as well as architecture and landscape design. The labor costs alone greatly surpassed what most great landowners would have dared to spend. These sums were separate from those spent on building and maintaining the estate housing offered to attract and retain families in a part of the country that had been remote and barely cultivated only a century before. The net result, far beyond the prospect of a return on his investment, was to run up massive debt—a familiar aristocratic practice—but in this case one that put Portland's very property at risk.[8]

2-2
Humphry Repton.
Welbeck.
Nottinghamshire, England.
Lake view with Repton
at the theodolitc.
First Red Book for Welbeck,
1790.
[Portland Collection,
Bridgeman Images]

The Welbeck commission not only secured Repton regular work for more than fifteen years—he reckoned that he spent ten days there each year and produced three Red Books for its design—but through Portland's influence it also generated many other commissions, both regionally and nationally. As Repton put it, the first Red Book for Welbeck established the "ground work" for his earliest published volume, *Sketches and Hints on Landscape Gardening*, which drew extensively from its text and graphics to illustrate the landscape gardener's principles and practice.[9]

Repton's trade card samples a portion of the panoramic drawing in the Red Book that depicts the complete lakeside survey, from Repton at the theodolite to a figure under a far tree positioning the ranging rod [2-2].[10] The published version of this drawing in *Sketches and Hints* was used to illustrate the chapter "Concerning Water." The figure on the right side of the tree holding a parasol is balanced on the left by a seated figure looking over the lake while holding a plan or large sketchbook. In the published view Repton also added one of his trademark overlays or "slides" to picture the scene before and after his proposals were realized, showing how a relatively small physical change to such a large landscape would transform the scene. In this case the landscape design benefited from the redistribution of earth taken from the bankside to increase the slope from the house and extend the water in the distance to run past the house [2-3, 2-4, 2-5]. Repton notes that,

> *the water at Welbeck had acquired the character, and indeed the name of a lake: but as a large river is always more beautiful than a small lake, the character has been changed, not only by continuing it beyond the house, but also by altering its line, and taking off those projections which were inconsistent with the course of a natural river.*[11]

A map in the first Red Book displays the proposed extension of the lake, while another in the second Red Book, produced three years later, shows the full extent of the lake in the park as a whole [2-6, 2-7].

It is fortunate that the diary of William Gould, the land agent for the Portland estates, survives and covers the early period of Repton's commission.[12] A land agent was a key figure, managing the business affairs of the estate, supervising its various operations—particularly those involving major spending or income generation—collecting rents and negotiating land sales and purchases as well as overseeing improvements, and mediating between various parties and their interests. Welbeck, like many great estates, had a large labor force, many members of which were accommodated in estate houses. Landscaping provided valuable work for the workmen, particularly in winter, when farming and forestry were less labor-intensive. But as we will see, the execution of Repton's designs required external sources of labor as well. Gould's diary documents the complex relations between designs on paper and operations on the ground, revealing the at-times contentious social and economic transactions in the process of a landscape in the making.

Groundwork

The first mention of Repton in Gould's diary occurs in the entry for 15 December 1789. After breakfasting with estate auditor William Heaton and riding with him to check on newly sown tree plantations across the land, Gould returned to his office at 3:00 p.m., "and found a Mr Repton had arrived here in order to lay out some pleasure ground. I furnished them with a map of Welbeck, fetched Mr [William] Speechly down with his spirit level, and left them at seven o'clock." Repton's first meeting with Portland about the commission had taken place at the duke's London residence, Burlington House, at which time Portland told Repton what he wanted done at Welbeck. However, Gould was evidently informed in advance neither of the commission nor of Repton's visit, which required a 145-mile, three-day coach journey from the landscape gardener's home.

Although the following day was wet and stormy Heaton and Repton rode out "to view the prospects and places about Welbeck." Speechly joined Heaton and Repton on their excursion the second day. On the third day Gould joined them for a walking tour, where they "viewed the different situations respecting the taking of views to particular places and objects on both sides of the lake." Still, he could "learn but very little of Mr Repton's designs." One day thereafter Gould received a letter from Portland asking him to accompany Repton and Heaton on a walk near the proposed new head of the lake as well as the dam that lay below. Gould recorded that on the following day Heaton and Repton traveled on horseback to view those neighboring great estates that featured similar topography and improvements; in the evening they were joined by surveyor James Dowland and his son from Mansfield Woodhouse, and the York-based architect John Carr, who was advising on alterations to the mansion at Welbeck, alterations that would be affected by Repton's proposals.

Repton took ten days, from 27 December to 5 January 1790, to produce the Red Book for Welbeck. Clearly mindful of Portland's precarious financial affairs, a fact that Heaton and Gould had impressed upon him, as well as the kind of careful accounting that might appeal as a matter of principle to more prudent clients, Repton listed "Estimates of Expenses" in the Red Book, and in great detail itemized on a sketch map where the sums would be spent. Many of the estimates concerned earthmoving: excavating an extension to the lake to pass by the family rooms of the house, widening the banks, removing a dam, and regrading the lawn in front of the house. Earthmoving was computed at a total of 39,373 cubic yards, which at three or four pence per cubic yard would cost some £670, twice the amount of all other expenses combined. This was a considerable sum—over £300,000 ($420,000) in present-day valuation—but nothing like the costs of more comprehensive earthmoving used to reshape entire parks. The latter could run to over £100,000 pounds, which is more than £40 million in today's money.[13] Repton reckoned his costs were far less than for a design less mindful of major landscape effects created by only modest changes.[14]

Not only in their mathematics but in another vital aspect, the estimates proved so severe a miscalculation they nearly cost Repton the Welbeck commission—and given Portland's influence perhaps the landscape improver his career. Repton failed to fully appreciate at this time that for his patron high spending and great debt were not to be avoided but rather an aristocratic badge of honor. "When I presented my plan and drawing to the Duke I saw his countenance change and he returned the papers with these words, 'I thank you Mr Repton, but when I receive a hint from you, I do not expect to find any second best expedient.'" Only the duchess's intercession saved the day by persuading her husband to adopt Repton's plan. "Thus did I save him a very considerable sum of money," Repton recalled in his memoir, "by my economy: a word he detested, when applied to his own concerns."[15] As it turned out, Portland spent a prodigious amount on Repton's plans over the next six years, with earthmoving alone vastly exceeding Repton's estimates, totaling £3,000—the equivalent of more than a million pounds at the time of this writing.

On 30 January Gould recorded in his diary that he had received Repton's "plan of the intended improvements," which he had then forwarded to William Speechly for plotting on the ground. Thereafter, Gould became involved in Repton's designs, attending closely to earthmoving and drain laying before Repton arrived on 30 March: "He appeared to be satisfied with what

2-3
Humphry Repton.
Welbeck.
Nottinghamshire, England.
First Red Book for Welbeck,
1790.
House with proposed
slope created from
earth moved from lake
in the background.
[Portland Collection,
Bridgeman Images]

2-4
Humphry Repton.
Welbeck.
Nottinghamshire, England.
First Red Book for Welbeck,
1790.
Proposed extension
to the lake
(overlay down).
[Portland Collection,
Bridgeman Images]

2-5
Humphry Repton.
Welbeck.
Proposed extension
to the lake
(overlay up).
[Portland Collection,
Bridgeman Images]

The Ferry boat.
a Chain across the Lake
Sheep Walk.
Deer Park.

2-6

Humphry Repton.
Welbeck.
Nottinghamshire, England.
Map showing excavation for extension of the lake.
First Red Book for Welbeck, 1790.
[Portland Collection, Bridgeman Images]

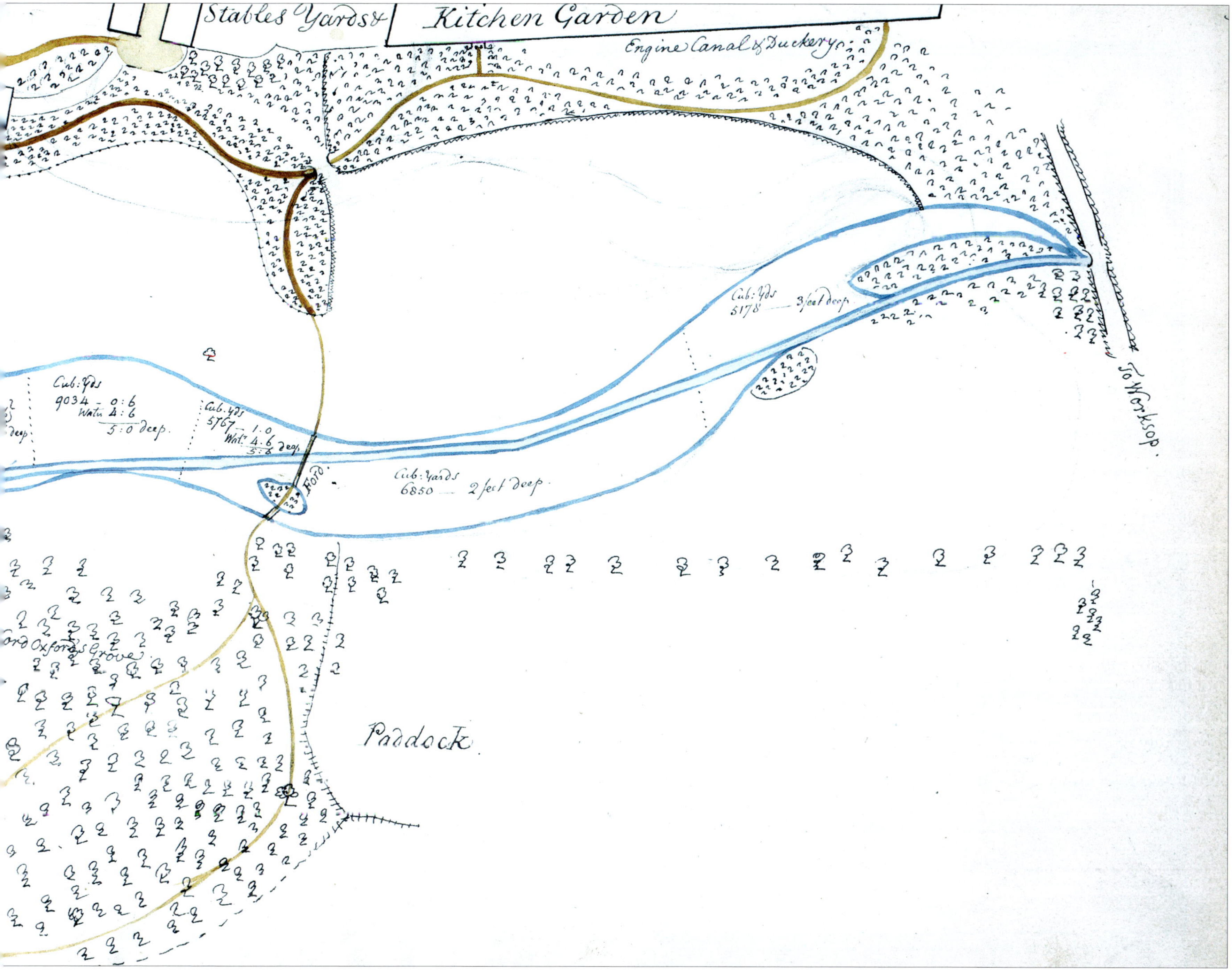

WELBECK PARK.
with the Roads Drives & Walks
either finished in 1793 & 4.
or proposed to be made.
Scale of 40 Chains, or half a Mile
10 20 30 40

we had done." On a horse loaned from Gould, Repton spent the day with Dixon "to view the different locks and reservoirs belonging to the Canal from Chesterfield to Stockwith." Repton observed some lessons on water management that would be long-lasting, as well as specific operations for the hydrography at Welbeck—human as well as technological—notably employing "navigators," gangs of often migrant canal workmen.

Part of the following week Gould accompanied Repton on his inspections of the work. The duke and duchess made their arrival, meeting Repton and Gould in the garden and having long, separate conversations over the next few days with each of them. Repton's recollections of his walks through Welbeck with Portland are those of an artistic man following deer and sheep tracks to find scenes of "beauty or interest," pointing out their resemblance to Old Master landscape paintings, and expressing delight at observing groups of laborers at rest, a "cheerful smile on their countenance." When Repton visited Welbeck again in August 1790 he sent Joseph Wright, his foreman from Romford, to superintend the work.[16] By the end of September, Wright was directing earthmoving at the top of the lake, accompanied by Repton and a laborer named John Smith. Gould attended to the workmen wheeling the earth in barrows to raise the ground about the mansion, which he considered "a wild scheme."

In the nine months since his first visit to Welbeck, Repton had run up expenses of £184.14, in addition to the costs of producing the Red Book. Gould continued to wonder at Portland's extravagance; his "finances being in a very deranged and complicated state," the expensive alterations represented "madness in the extreme." In addition to being what he considered a more sensible scheme, some elements of Repton's designs actually helped the estate's finances, for example, by thinning woods and hedgerows for their timber. Elsewhere, however, the costs mounted.[17]

Gould died two years later, in 1792. In a series of fragmentary entries written before then, he made his usual sardonic observations on the execution of Repton's designs. In January 1794, for example, he recorded that, unable to penetrate ice and frosty ground, the enterprising navigators working on the lake decided to down their tools, borrow a wagon, buy coal, and then sell it to locals. When Portland's wife died in 1794, the duke transferred the estate to his newly wedded son. Repton continued to make annual visits until his death in 1809.

2-7
Humphry Repton. Welbeck. Nottinghamshire, England. Second Red Book for Welbeck, 1793. Map of park showing full extent of lake. [Portland Collection, Bridgeman Images]

Repton Revealed

The park at Welbeck remains in Bentinck family ownership, and many aspects of Repton's design still survive, accompanied by documentary records of the estate and the manuscript of the land agent's diary.[18] Unfortunately, such continuity is not the case for most of Repton's commissions, many of which were smaller properties for minor gentry, merchants, and professionals, and as such were attended and supervised for shorter periods than Welbeck. For these families we have far fewer records than for the aristocrats. Their sites were often near towns and main roads, and many of them were soon sold and subsequently redeveloped. Repton's designs were more delicate and ephemeral than the large-scale projects of his forbears, and even in his lifetime were vulnerable to the vagaries of nature, sale, redevelopment, and the realization of his designs supervised by others. This is the primary reason that toward the end of his life Repton regarded his works on paper, and not his works on the ground, as the lasting monuments to his art.[19]

The vignette for August 1808 in the *Polite Repository* has long been thought to picture a place where Repton was not involved: Lambeth Palace, the Thameside residence of the Archbishop of Canterbury [2-8]. On close viewing, however, the vignette reveals—in the foreground, hidden in plain sight—the possible site of a Repton commission, the garden of Charles Abbot, the Speaker of the House of Commons in the Palace of Westminster.[20]

Repton's plans for the Speaker's Garden were part of a larger program involving other figures, notably James Wyatt, the architect who converted St. Stephen's Chapel to accommodate the hundred Irish members of the House of Commons added following the passage of the Act of Union of Britain and Ireland. The need for the expansion of the Speaker's House reflected both the increase in the body's volume of business and the ambition of Charles Abbot—appointed to his office in 1802—to renovate and enlarge the premises with suites of state and private rooms built over new foundations that would address the chronic problems of damp and drainage.

A series of difficulties arose with staff on-site, including the clerk of the works, his assistant, and the team of laborers they employed. Repton appealed to the clerk of the works, writing him personally to "describe their difficulty, perhaps I could remove it before I come to town which will not be till late next week." He explained:

2-8
John Peltro. View from the Speaker's Garden. Engraving, after Humphry Repton drawing. Headpiece for *Peacock's Polite Repository*, August 1808. [The Gardens Trust]

Notes

1 https://en.wikipedia.org/wiki/Humphry_Repton.

2 J. C. Loudon, *The Landscape Gardening and Landscape Architecture of the Late Humphry Repton* (London: Loudon, Longman & Black, 1840).

3 Humphry Repton, *Sketches and Hints on Landscape Gardening* (London: W. Bulmer & Co, 1794), pp. xiii, 156. The phrase "in real life" is reprinted as a motto in Thomas Church, *Gardens Are for People* (New York: Reinhold, 1955).

4 Information from John Phibbs, personal communication, 27 February 2020; see also his *Place-Making: The Art of Capability Brown* (London: Historic England, 2017).

5 At times in Repton's career, labor loomed large in his landscape designs, when labor relations more widely were a pressing issue. Thus, in the panoramic designs for Sheringham, of 1812, figures with a pickaxe, spade, and wheelbarrow depicted in a portrait-like rendering, albeit in the shadow of their excavation, occupy the foreground, while, in a compression of before-and-after scenes, carriage folk speed down the road they have made, in the sunlit distance. The text of the designs frames the social relations in view, explaining that work here was scarce and times were hard, local farmers treated their laborers harshly, "and whether the poor slave is driven by the lash of the Negro-driver or the dread of confinement in a Workhouse, he must feel that man is not equal, though he may be taught to read he is so." On the Sheringham estate, by contrast, landscape design was a matter of social reform, laborers were valued, and their cottages were to "be marked by neatness and decora-

The General principle is thus to hollow the ground between the house & terrace that the water may fall from each towards the centre where drains may be concealed & this would be so gradual a fall as to be imperceptible to the eye—tho it would keep the house and the Terrace perfectly dry.[21]

Repton also noted that he had found "a gang of blundering Irish Labourers" who looked:

to take a month doing what they ought to finish in a week . . . but since the Union, I suppose it is quite right to employ Irish Labour altho they get in each other's way . . . I have directed them to finish the ground near the house & leave the Centre to the last—by this means we shall be able to form the margins to be planted & have a depot of good mould for the shrubs on the spot, although I think very little planting will be required—if by any good fortune I could have five minutes conversation with you on the Spot, I could explain the matter—I know exactly your wishes—I believe.[22]

Repton's remodeling of the Speaker's Garden was part of a scheme to compose a river frontage with "the finest possible picturesque effect," viewed by spectators from Westminster Bridge or boats passing on the Thames. The scene did not survive the nineteenth century.

On 16 October 1834 the Houses of Parliament caught fire; St. Stephen's Chapel was largely destroyed. Luckily much of Repton's garden, silhouetted against the flames in the many views of the event, survived the fire, only to be later demolished for the foundations of the new Palace of Westminster, designed by Charles Barry and Augustus Pugin. Today, only faint traces of Repton's garden can be detected, as the Commons Terrace had been built on an extension of the embankment. Although archaeology seems out of the question, as does restoration, we should still recognize Repton's long-lost contribution to the picturesque landscape in an urban setting in Britain's very center of national power, not just for the site, but for the view. The church on its site has been converted to house the Garden Museum, where Repton's bicentenary was commemorated in 2018 with an exhibition of his work.[23]

ted with ornamental shrubs and creepers." Humphry Repton, *Fragments on the Theory and Practice of Landscape Gardening* (London: T. Bensley, 1816), p. 205.

6 Stephen Daniels, *Humphry Repton: Landscape Gardening and the Geography of Georgian England* (London and New Haven: Yale University Press, 1999), pp. 11–13. On the symbolism of surveying images see John Bonehill and Stephen Daniels, "Designs on the Landscape: Paul and Thomas Sandby in North Britain," *Oxford Art Journal* 2 (2017). pp. 223–48.

7 Tom Williamson, *Landscape Design in an Age of Revolution* (London: Reaktion, 2020); Sally Bate, Rachel Savage, and Tom Williamson, eds., *Humphry Repton in Norfolk* (Norwich: Norfolk Gardens Trust, 2018); Susan Flood and Tom Williamson, *Humphry Repton in Hertfordshire* (Hatfield: University of Hertfordshire Press, 2018); John Phibbs, *Humphry Repton: Designing the Landscape Garden* (New York: Rizzoli, 2021).

8 Daniels, *Humphry Repton*, pp. 149–66.

9 Repton, *Sketches and Hints*, p. 16.

10 Humphry Repton, *Plans, Hints and Views for the Improvement of Welbeck* (1790); private collection. At the time of writing, this Red Book is accessible as a digitized copy on the Harley Gallery website: https://www.harleygallery.co.uk/whats-on/the-portland-collection-museum/.

11 Repton, *Sketches and Hints*, p. 29.

12 The Diaries of William Gould (1739–95), University of Nottingham, Manuscripts and Special Collections, MS 736.

13 Roderick Floud, *An Economic History of the English Garden* (London: Penguin, 2020), p. 12.

14 These included a cheaper option for a foot crossing from the lake to the duchess's garden using planks cut from the timber of one of Welbeck's famed oak trees, inset in an iron frame, rather than constructing an expensive arched bridge. "I have ever been of the opinion that where I can suggest great improvements with the least expense I am more effectually doing the duty of my profession." Repton, *Plans for Welbeck*.

15 Anne Gore and George Carter, eds., *Humphry Repton's Memoirs* (London: Michael Russell, 2005), pp. 33–34.

16 Wright was not paid by Repton but by the Welbeck estate, and he became an increasingly important figure on-site in sustaining Repton's commission.

17 Gould notes, "the money arising from the sale of timber to be applied to the discharge of debts at and about Welbeck which at this time is very considerable."

18 The current, 7th Duke of Portland occupies part of the house.

19 Repton, *Fragments on the Theory and Practice*.

20 Abbot assisted Repton in his search for other publicly funded commissions, such as the Royal Pavilion, Brighton, and an estate to commemorate Admiral Lord Nelson; it also helped that at the time the prime minister was the Duke of Portland, Repton's longstanding patron, and that Repton was involved in remodeling Portland's London residence, Burlington House. The following account is condensed from Stephen Daniels, "Repton's Designs on Westminster," *London Gardener* 23 (2019): pp. 74–84.

21 Daniels, "Repton's Designs," p. 82.

22 Daniels, "Repton's Designs," p. 83.

23 Stephen Daniels, "Landscapes of Memory," *Garden Museum Journal* 35 (Winter 2018).

3. THE ART OF LANDMAKING

ADRIAAN GEUZE

Systemic Approach

This book's title, *The Shape of the Land*, suggests multiple readings such as "shaping the land" and "landshaping," operations highly relevant for conceptualizing and constructing landscape architecture. In today's world, where the notion of climate change forces us to rethink the ways in which humanity has exploited the planet, landscape architecture is uniquely positioned to adopt a systemic approach to the production of responsible and engaging landscapes. One prominent school of thought believes that our park systems and gardens sprouted from the pairing of a narrative approach with the beaux arts tradition. At the same time, the professional as well as academic realms of landscape architecture have also benefited from a strong legacy of polytechnical subjects and those drawn from the life sciences. The need for understanding the broader context for our interventions, for considering the physical realms of geology, water, ecosystems, and the metabolism of the metropole, distinguishes landscape architecture from other fields and spheres of design.

At West 8 the systemic approach—our prevailing method—has resulted in projects that have challenged the status quo. The education specific to where I was born reflects the long-standing Dutch tradition of sublime and pragmatic landmaking. In the Netherlands, where Western Europe's three largest rivers converge as a delta, spatial planning is inherently linked to the pumping and movement of water, and to the creation, movement, and shaping of land at grand scale. This perspective and lifelong experience, combined with approaches to landscape architecture both systemic and tactical, have been the driving forces behind the projects discussed in this essay. Through systemic thinking, landscape architecture and engineering become more closely intertwined, resulting in the emergence of new, beautiful—even poetic—topographic realities, each infused with a strong identity.

3-1
West 8.
Espenhain Brown Coal Mine.
Lake Strömthal,
Leipzig, Germany, 1994.
The Schaufelradbagger
looms over a terrain
of despoiled land.
[Adriaan Geuze, West 8]

The Phoenix of the Espenhain Brown Coal Mine

Shortly after the fall of the Berlin Wall and the reunification of Germany, many of the large open-pit mines around Leipzig underwent a serious environmental and political reevaluation. As they extracted coal from the land, the Schaufelradbaggers—colossal excavation machines armed with revolving wheels and miles-long conveyor belts—had literally devoured terrain the size of provinces [3-1]. In their wake the machines eradicated medieval cultural landscapes, streams, and even entire villages, leaving in their place piles of contaminated soil unfit for any practical purpose. Surreal moonscapes arose, landscapes where the cooling towers of the power plants hung from the skies, while slow, mechanical dinosaurs never stopped eating away at the layered edges of the quarries.

The dependency on open-pit mining for labor, economy, and energy in North Rhein Westfalen and Sachsen in the former East Germany was not easily abandoned. Although it was understood that the mines had caused vast environmental ruin, shutting them down had become a taboo subject for politicians. It became clear that any cessation of mining would only be achieved "sometime in the future." Nevertheless, in 1992, using research conducted by a team led by professors from the polytechnic universities of Berlin, Aachen, and Leipzig, a new generation of democratically elected political leaders debated the inevitable halt to mining and the initiation of further research regarding the reclamation of Espenhain, a mine located directly south of Leipzig.

In 1994, West 8 was asked to consider the potential forms and uses for this derelict land and to produce a master plan to direct its future. Due to the troublesome nature of the site, visits were possible only by helicopter. Development was also hampered by several site conditions, the most challenging being its steep and unstable edges, and the erosion of the softer geological strata of the 150-foot-deep pit. From constant drainage over time the geologic water of the mines had acquired a toxic acidity. In places where management stopped pumping, small toxic lakes and surface water had formed and stymied the evolution of any kind of healthy ecosystems. The depth of the coal layer suitable for extraction measured only 15 feet; the remainder had been backfilled with debris to form a new landscape whose composition prevented any new soil from developing. In addition, the gargantuan and spectacularly athletic mining equipment had to be dismantled. Our master plan focused on introducing a water purification plant to clean and refill portions of the old mine pit and transform it into a lake [3-2].

An innovative ecological soil-engineering program guided the conversion of the ground that would stand above the future water level. Compost and pioneer plant species provided the materials for successional vegetation, rejuvenating depleted soils by means of a woodland ecology. The eons of forest life dating to Mesozoic times that had formed the brown coal were somehow reincarnated as a new identity for the revivified landscape. Planted as a regular grid, this forest restored the soil biotopes that supported the growth of a healthy woodland in the future. Forest vegetation, which grows rapidly in the region, will acquire its own expression over time.

The steep, unstable slopes of the pits, on the other hand, were unable to sustain life, and the cliffs lining the eastern side of the mine were therefore treated in a radically different manner: they were regraded into terraces. The upper portions were shaped more broadly to accommodate future urban leisure and entertainment facilities, waterfront development, and preserve the remnants of the tall Schaufelradbagger equipment for display. In contrast to the newly made landforms, we proposed keeping the sharp, irregular, and somewhat eerie ridges of the backfill at the base of the slopes as a series of re-wilded linear islands in the future lake.

The West 8 master plan resulted in a unique place, where the landscape's identity would be reincarnated and facilitated by embodying the metabolic process of mine regeneration. Unlike the successional and ecological processes of the lake and strip islands, the leisure and entertainment zone sited on the new upper terraces would develop by appropriating the dramatic mine topography and machinery as mediators [3-3]. The resulting waterfront engaged in an active dialogue with the violence of the reclaimed mine. Much of the surrounding land continues to be rejuvenated with woodlands and agriculture: the Phoenix of Espenhain has become a reality [3-4].

3-2
West 8.
The Phoenix of Espenhain Brown Coal Mine.
Lake Strömthal, Leipzig, Germany, 1994.
Master plan depicting intervention, restoration, and future development.
[West 8]

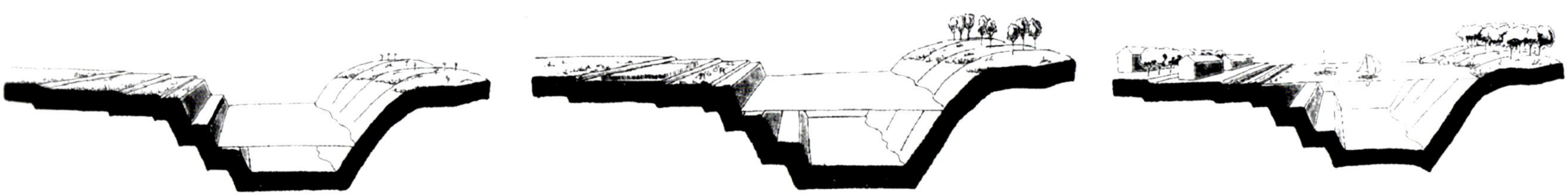

3-3
West 8.
The Phoenix of Espenhain Brown Coal Mine.
Stepped sections showing increasing urbanity.
[West 8]

3-4
West 8.
The Phoenix of Espenhain Brown Coal Mine.
Contemporary condition of the site, highlighting the lake, the reclaimed island strips, the woodland forest, and agricultural land.
[© euroluftbild de / Robert Grahn]

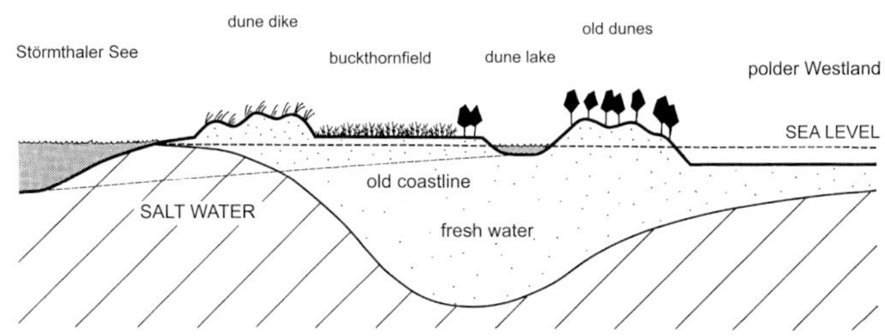

3-5
West 8.
Buckthorn City and
Dune Apocalypse.
Hoek van Holland,
Rotterdam,
the Netherlands, 1995.
Sections showing three
types of dunescape:
shallow and salty beach,
brackish ecology, and
freshwater lake.
[West 8]

Buckthorn City and the Dune Apocalypse

In response to an urgent request to study the urban extension of Rotterdam and The Hague, West 8 proposed the creation of new land using sand reclaimed from the nearby seabed. Our proposal combined a concern for protecting the land from rising water with the urban and ecological extension of the existing terrain. In response to sea-level rise the vulnerable shores of this segment of the Dutch coastline had been granted priority for the construction of new seawalls. Applying an approach that replaced hard walls with natural forms, the budgets demanded by aggressive engineering works could be employed more beneficially to create a massive dunescape that promoted ecological performance and urban use.

The state of scientific thinking at the time provided the starting point, while the most advanced technological knowledge and innovations utilized by the dredging industry were applied to the project. At the coastal edges we proposed raising the land to five meters above sea level and to protect that new land with a series of dunes. To foster spontaneous ecological activity the new terrain would be retained at a suitable distance from the existing land, enclosing a freshwater lake in the space between as a new ecological reservoir. The resulting sequence of spaces that moved inland from the sea comprised three types of dunescape: shallow and salty beach, brackish ecology, and freshwater lake [3-5]. The next layer of the design involved planting dune grasses on the salty side of the site and seeding the brackish side with fields of buckthorn. The geometric layout of the buckthorn reflected the irregular if orthogonal grid of the future streetscape. For the first time, urbanity was designed as a phase of succession, earning the project the name: Buckthorn City [3-6].

The master plan would require a time horizon of twenty years. Creating four-by-fourteen miles of land—the exact area of Manhattan island—would demand four years of dredging, 24/7, its yield blown onto the shore. The next step, which would require an additional three years, involved the realization of a four-stop subway line connecting Rotterdam and The Hague to address basic transit needs as well as stimulate the site's adaptation to mass tourism. The double waterfronts introduce two types of urbanity that anticipate the diverse conditions of the newly born land. The southern portion of Buckthorn City will develop as a modern city with a downtown, boulevards, plazas, and

(opposite above left) **3-6**
West 8.
Buckthorn City and
the Dune Apocalypse.
Buckthorn City master plan
with three successive phases:
existing, buckthorn planta-
tion, and urbanity.
[West 8]

(opposite above right) **3-7**
West 8.
Buckthorn City and
the Dune Apocalypse.
The dune becomes the
identity for the new city.
[West 8, 2006]

(opposite below left) **3-8**
West 8.
Buckthorn City and
the Dune Apocalypse.
The dancing dune.
[West 8]

(opposite below right) **3-9**
Rijkswaterstaat.
Zandmotor.
Hoek van Holland,
Rotterdam,
the Netherlands, 2011.
The initial fetal shape
of the lagoon, moving
and growing over time.
[Joop van Houdt /
Rijkswaterstaat]

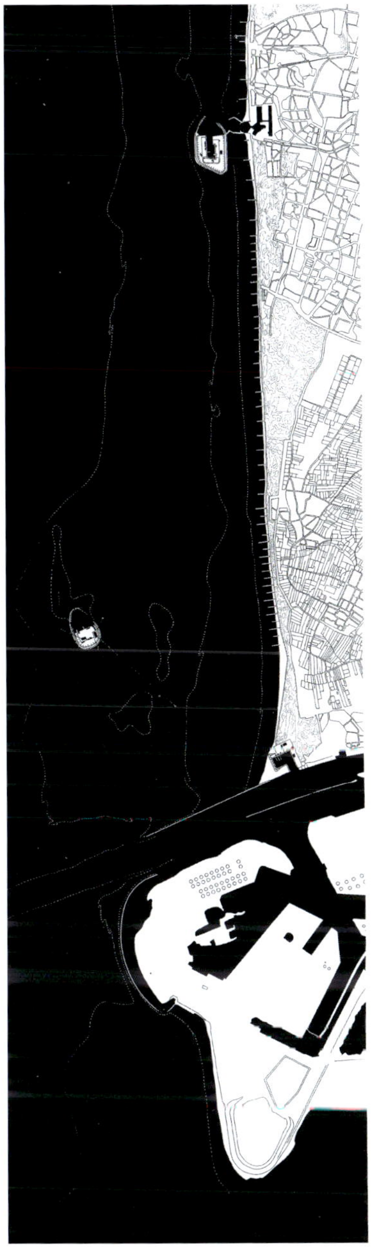
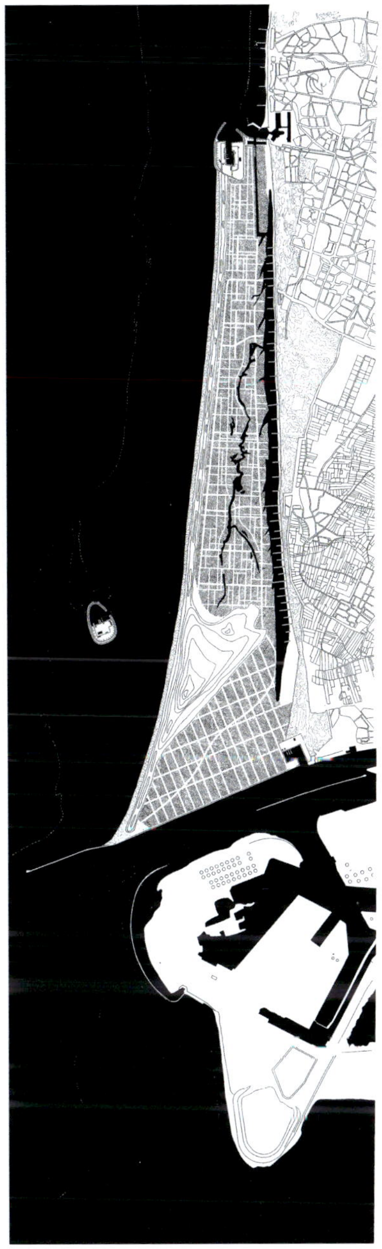
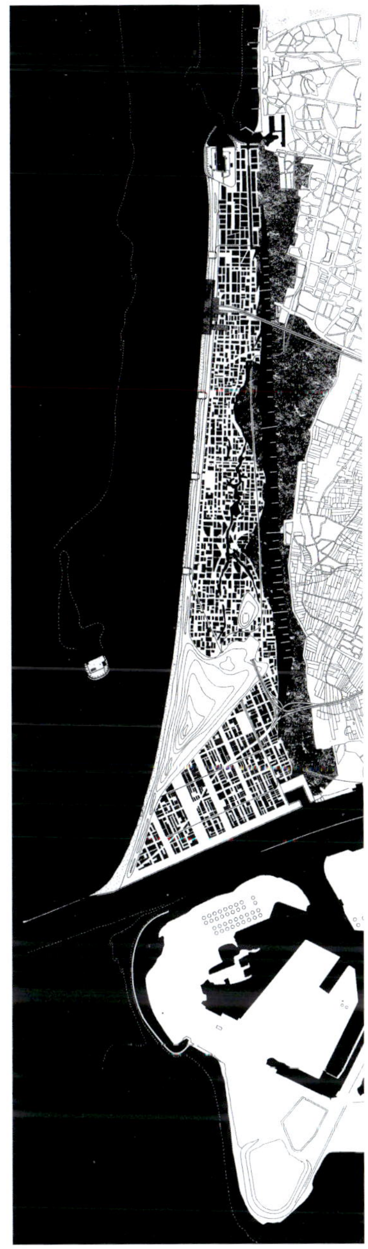

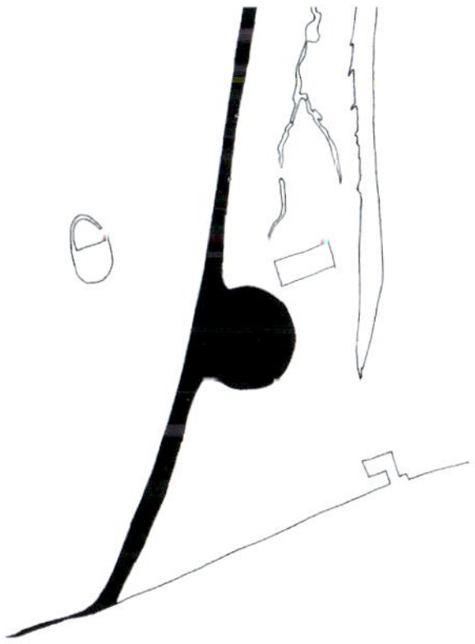
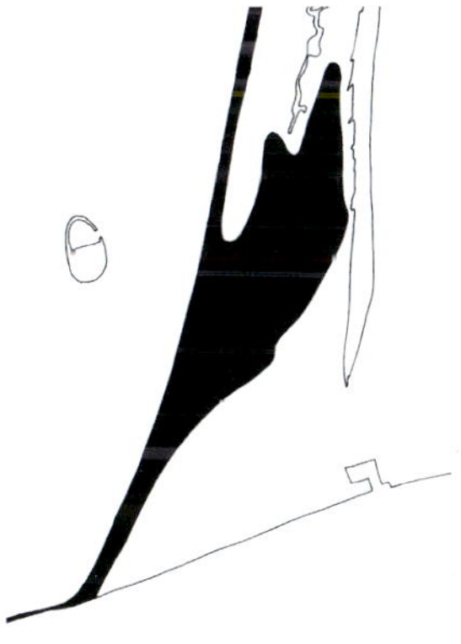
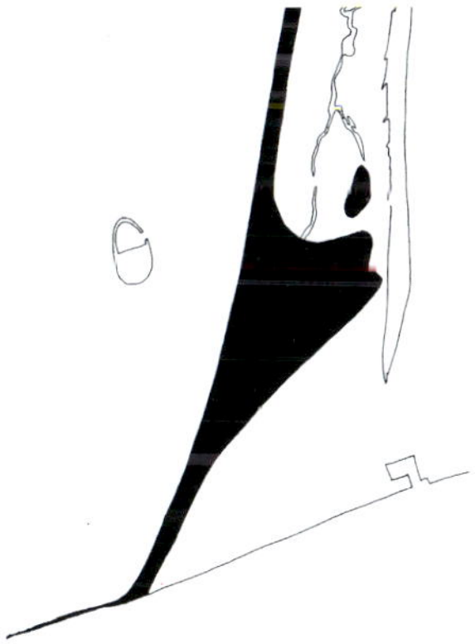

dense high-rises. In contrast the northern portion will pioneer an environmental lifestyle: low-rise, in harmony with nature, with no cars, and public transit and bikes the only forms of transportation.

In its early years, Buckthorn City combined seeded buckthorn woodland with developing urbanity. As an ultimate gesture of place-making and building with nature, we proposed raising one of the dunes as a 300-foot-high knoll, to become the silhouette seen from every street in downtown Buckthorn City [3-7]. The dune also adds intimacy and a sense of direction within the windswept new cityscape, giving the newborn urbanity an image and identity. The most compelling aspect of the knoll is its existential nature, determined by the wind. We regarded this human-made dune as a greeting to Poseidon and the forces of nature, an offering of land to be sculpted into its "final" shape by natural forces. This process may require a decade to crystallize, its form shaped into a playful Aeolian geology by the dominant southwesterly winds, with the dune meandering over the newborn land [3-8].

Computer modeling and laboratory wind tests demonstrated that as sculpted by the diverse winds, the dunes would assume either parabolic or elliptical forms over time. Beyond designing with nature, the plan introduced a degree of play and lightness. Using physical models we researched the dialogue and relation between urbanity and shape-shifting sandscapes. The outcome of this research was remarkable and promising: no one could exactly predict the final form or the magnitude of the drifting sand. In other words, the plan speculates on uncertainty. Will the land become joyful, playful, euphoric—or apocalyptic? Can a city exist with a dancing dune of this magnitude?

The plans became the subject of a 1996 exhibition at the Architectural Biennale in Venice that was called "Claiming the Void" and garnered extensive media attention. Ten years later, one of the plan's strongest DNA strands was brought to life by testing a key component of the project in reality. On the site of the future Buckthorn City, 30 million cubic yards of sand were "rainbowed" onto the site, producing a giant artificial reef that rose high above sea level: a pilot of the build-with-nature concept to be shaped by real wind and water currents. The most playful and delightful aspect of the design, however, the feature that captured the temporal and Aeolian character of the sand-Matterhorn, achieved reality under the technocratic, nonpoetic name

Zandmotor (sand motor). Since the project's realization, the artificial dune has grown in a northerly direction and has defined an ever-changing coastal lagoon [3-9]. At the same time, the metro line connecting Rotterdam and The Hague has been realized and the construction of a second line, linking Rotterdam with the Hook of Holland, is underway—the first coastal-beach metro station in the country.

Climate Adaptation for the Twenty-first-century Delta

Serious flood threats in 2009 forced the Dutch government to produce an action plan for the Netherlands known as Ruimte voor de Rivier (Room for the River), a twenty-seven-nation project to extend portions of the floodplains while creating bypasses in the Rhine delta to accommodate times of high water. Noordwaard, a bypass at the downstream portion of the main river—and the largest of the projects—was assigned to the dredging industry. As the sub-consulting landscape architect of record, West 8 devised an alternative plan based on controlled inundation. Instead of buying all the precious farmland on which to excavate a permanently swampy bypass arm of the river, we proposed the construction of an advanced but low-tech levee system in which dedicated farmland could serve as a periodic bypass when needed. Under this plan, farmers retained ownership of their land and would be compensated for the seasonal losses of harvest resulting from any periodic flooding.

The project commenced with research on the progressive escalation of water quantities during floods. From the data we collected, paired with climate-change projections, four distinct flood scenarios emerged: regular seasonal flooding; a five-year flood; twenty-year flood; and an extreme, hundred-year flood [3-10]. In response to these parameters the area was engineered using four types of levees, each corresponding to one of the scenarios. The farmhouses themselves were relocated onto newly built artificial hills (terps) that rose above the highest flood level [3-11].

The second component of the project was to reveal the engineering and the effects of flooding. Multiple circuits of trails connected by forty bridges allow citizens living in the area to discover the landscape on foot or by bicycle. The position of the trails on the inundation dikes and levees ensured that all these circuits are fully accessible, even in times of high water.

3-10
West 8.
Ontpoldering Noordward.
Noordward Polder,
Dordrecht, the Netherlands,
2011–15.
Flood levels across different scenarios, including accessible route in high water (pink);
100-day flood;
100-year flood;
1,000-year flood.
[West 8]

3-11
West 8.
Ontpoldering Noordward.
A spectacular landscape produced by an advanced but low-tech levee system.
[West 8, 2021]

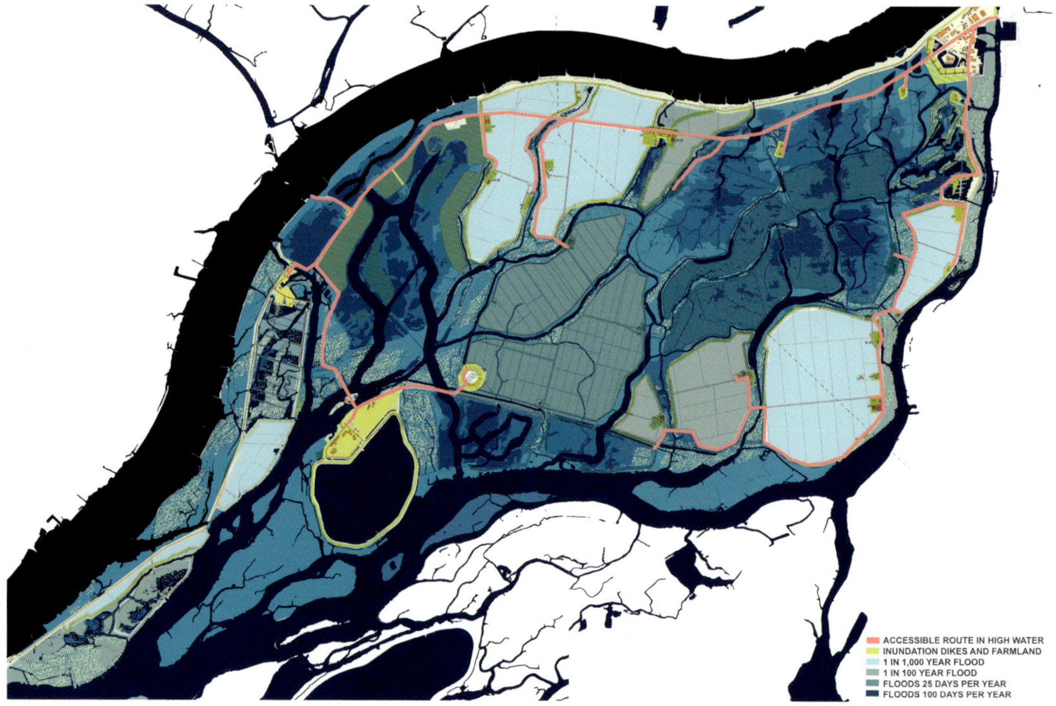

3-12
West 8.
Ontpoldering Noordward.
A network of waterways,
enjoyed by kayakers and
canoeists year-round.
[West 8]

3-13
West 8.
Ontpoldering Noordward.
Natural landscape and
accessible route during flooding, including pump houses
made from bricks reclaimed
from relocated farmhouses.
[West 8]

The interlinked paths have even formed a new infrastructure supporting "flood tourism," complemented by a network of waterways for use by kayaks and canoes year-round [3-12]. The structures housing the pumps required at times of peak flows are elegant cubes of bricks recycled from the farmhouses relocated by the project [3-13]. Their panoramic decks create new outlooks from which to view the landscape, with the old bricks retaining the record of past high-water levels on their surfaces. The plan's uniqueness resides not only in the new climate-adaptive approach for bypassing floodwaters, but also in the preservation of the cultural landscape that binds community and farmland to achieve cultural protection while working hand in hand with environmental solutions.

Floodplain and Cosmos: The New Grand Egyptian Museum

In designing the landscape for the new Grand Egyptian Museum in Cairo, one of our most important projects to date, we drew upon many of the lessons learned from prior efforts that had also applied a systemic approach to landscape design. The first Grand Egyptian Museum was built in 1902 on Tahrir Square in Cairo, a colonial-style building housing an extensive collection that spanned the Predynastic to the Greco-Roman eras. It is home to some of the ancient world's most magnificent works. Over the years since its founding, the old museum had been packed and filled to capacity, a problem exacerbated by the 300,000 new archaeological fragments and artifacts found in Egypt each year and acquired by the museum. Archaeology of this magnitude, combined with scientific research, the housing and display of the World Heritage Collection, and mass tourism, demanded a large-scale intervention and a major rethinking of the nature of the museum. With support from UNESCO, the Egyptian Ministry of Archaeology conceived and funded a new museum with sufficient space and facilities for the processing and display of the priceless cultural legacy from the Pharaonic dynasties that had been uncovered at sites such as Karnak, Giza, and Luxor.

From these studies, and with UNESCO's support, the Ministry of Archaeology developed a brief for the new Grand Egyptian Museum (GEM), a document that outlined a logistical tally specifying the amenities and programs involving science, preservation, and the accommodation of millions of international visitors. An appropriate site was found two miles from the pyramids,

3-14
West 8.
Grand Egyptian Museum (GEM).
Cairo, Egypt, 2004.
Site model of the museum, demonstrating the positioning and integration with the plateau.
[West 8]

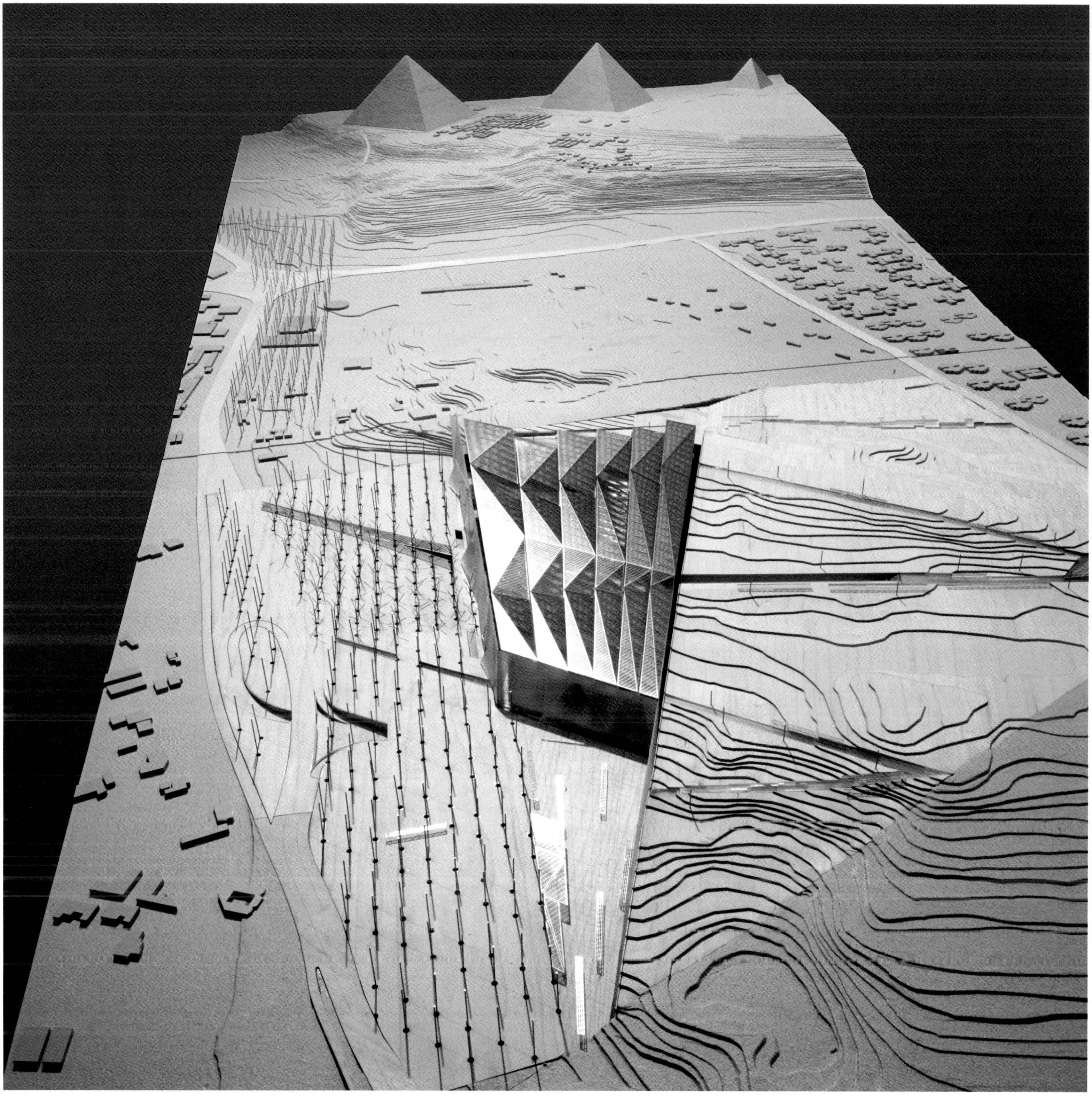

on the edge of the Giza plateau and the fertile grounds of the Nile floodplain. The largest-ever international architectural competition was held in 2002. It was won by heneghan peng architects, a young, Dublin-based office, who proposed a remarkably efficient building situated along the geological edge of the plateau. Their design successfully accommodated the gargantuan program entirely within the site's topography, sunken beneath the level of the desert; only the building's façade would be visible, as a replacement for the existing cliff face [3-14]. This concept was the building's sole architectural aspiration.

The geometries of the planning, sections, and elevations all facilitated long, conical views of the three Giza pyramids; the architecture of the museum itself yielded to their grace. From every position within and outside the GEM at least one of the ancient pyramids remained visible. The resulting planning coerced the architecture into a triangulated grid focused on a vanishing point, as if to achieve cosmic resonance by speculating on the astronomical logic of the space surrounding the pyramids. The terraced museum galleries share the building's triangular section, where on its north side the planning logic resulted in a ceiling height of nearly 240 feet, a dimension that could easily absorb the overwhelming monumentality of the largest Pharaonic statues displayed within. As originally proposed—but not executed—the triangulated, half-mile-long façade would be built of alabaster, in reference to the ancient cladding of the Great Pyramid. In all, the design resulted from a negotiation between site and topography that would camouflage the building within the geology of the plateau.

West 8 joined the heneghan peng design team after the competition, working to finalize the GEM design and prepare a broader master plan for Giza—which encompassed the pyramids themselves, the museum, and the rapidly growing urbanity on the edge of the site. Our first task was to accurately site the museum at the level of the Nile floodplain and bond the building with the topography of the plateau. The integrity of the edge and the interface with the floodplain were crucial for reclaiming the river's identity as the source of fertile civilization. Historically, shaping the land had been a key element of the Egyptian built environment. The agricultural society of Pharaonic Egypt devised and employed well-organized water management governed by an institutionalized bureaucracy that distributed the precious liquid over the fertile alluvial plains. Temples and monuments, like the farmlands, were positioned along the borders of the river. Siting the museum building in this way was therefore key to the public's understanding of the Nile, the pyramid-building process in ancient times, and the location of the pyramids. Large, heavy stone blocks mined from southern quarries were shipped to the Giza plateau edge during the river's flood stage. From its banks thousands of workers pulled sledges up ramps to install the stones on successive levels.

How did the beautiful floodplain landscape function so well in a hostile desert climate that it could be maintained over 3,000 years by succeeding dynasties? To better understand the natural conditions of these historical landscapes, we consulted with scientists. Analysis of ancient evidence of this landscape of paddy fields, water runnels, and canals explained the evolution of farmland, channels, temple gardens, papyrus basins, fishponds, and gardens filled with herbs used for mummification, and successfully introduced their use as a part of the GEM program and visitor experience.

The most complex aspect of the project was the master planning of the larger site. A city in itself, the GEM employs thousands of people and includes a scientific center, security offices, police and surveillance, emergency services, a VIP area, an education center, restaurants and shops, hotels, and facilities for buses and other forms of transit, accompanied by chaotic and ad hoc vendors and merchandising. Two to ten million visitors per year—numbers equal to the Louvre—will arrive in dedicated time slots for their visits to GEM, but before entering the museum they will have to walk serious distances, queue in lines, suffer a consistent flow of vendors and guides soliciting their services, and somehow resist the burning sun. The sites bordering the museum have a long history of leisure uses that include golf courses and a military shooting range, activities that could not be sustained in the future reality of millions of tourists.

Our master plan successfully limited the encroachment of the Cairene urban fabric and diverted the arrival of buses and taxis from the plateau edge to a boulevard the scale of a modern highway, Alexandria Desert Road, which links the museum with the pyramids. Taxis and buses north of the site were rezoned to reduce, if not completely eliminate their noise, chaos, and pollution from the visitor experience. This created a clear division between Cairo's street culture and the museum's forecourt, where visitors can experience contemplation, quiet, comfort, and safety distanced from the commotion of

Alexandria Desert Road. A robust antiterrorist security fence for visitors is part of this strategy. The scientific research and preservation center, where all new artifacts enter the museum, was given its own domain and entrance facing the desert, away from the masses of tourists [3-15, 3-16].

The forecourt was also intended to be a green zone that visitors would intuitively relate to the geologic history of the site, set at the level of the former Nile floodplain and paddy fields, and extending over the entire length of the museum to provide an authentic "green identity." The scientific research center, the Pharaonic Thematic Temple Gardens, the forecourt, and the welcome plaza contained within, all follow the building's triangulated planning, giving it the beauty of a rhythm rather than a style. Angled green slopes with thousands of palm trees, planted as a field of green planes that somehow abstracts and echoes the shapes of palm leaves, welcome visitors. The triangulated gardens outside extend the museum shop and restaurant on the north side within: the sole element of the project where the vegetation features color and flowers. The forecourt will have a permanent exhibition of Pharaonic artifacts able to endure outdoor exposure.

After queueing in the shade of the palms, visitors enter a sloped welcome plaza that passes through the façade and enter directly into a covered courtyard the scale of an aircraft hangar. Comprising one-third of the forecourt, the welcome plaza slopes downward toward the museum, guiding visitors into the building using topography in place of signage. The vast courtyard is entirely dedicated to the monumental, monolithic granite statue of Ramses II on permanent display, whose triangular pedestal is surrounded by water from the Nile shaped in abstracted form. Our team proposed the statue's symbolic return to the river from its historical location on Cairo's railroad station plaza, where it stood as a result of colonial discovery and placement. The divine monarch now appears as the centerpiece of the gigantic courtyard.

Inside, the museum's three interior galleries terrace upward toward the pyramids, joined by outdoor spaces sheltered by extending the gallery walls outdoors and cantilevering the roofs above them. From the shaded courtyard, one can either enter the museum to experience the exhibits on the chronologically organized terraces that present the progression of Egyptian dynasties or continue outdoors to enter the Land of Egypt exhibit. Under the

3-15
West 8.
Grand Egyptian Museum (GEM).
Cairo, Egypt, 2004.
GEM master plan, integrating the pyramids, surrounding development, and the Alexandria Desert Road.
[West 8]

3-16
West 8.
Grand Egyptian Museum.
Area site plan.
[West 8]

Egyptian sun, the sunken landscape demonstrates the region's ancient farming methods, landscapes, and crops—all informed by extensive data gathered through field and laboratory research.

Other outdoor components of the museum house the Pharaonic Thematic Temple Gardens, created using state-of-the-art pollen research that provided a clear picture of which plants were historically cultivated. The gardens also exhibit sacred practices relating to plants and water, raising fish, papyrus, and other plants for ceremonies and mummification. These gardens were the last elements of the design-and-construction process, which culminated in a grandiose procession of the sculpture of Ramses II through the streets of Cairo in its ceremonial deliverance from the traffic and congestion of the city to its cleaning, preservation, and display in Giza.

Then, the Arab Spring arrived. The Tahrir Square revolution directly impacted the old home of the GEM, halting the work of the original design team, management, and consultants. Several years later, however, the new government resumed the process with a renewed focus, transferring the design to a new team and assigning management to an international consortium supervised by a state-appointed group. At the time of writing, the forecourt and entry garden largely reflect the years-long design process of the original designers, including the installation of the Ramses II statue and the arrival sequence [3-17]. The fish and papyrus ponds of the Pharaonic Thematic Temple Gardens have also been constructed and the façade and Land of Egypt exhibition have found new resolution. Despite these departures the generating idea to have the museum explain the meeting point of the floodplain and the desert-edge plateau endures. Rooted in clay and water on one side, and desert and drought on the other, this simple narrative makes the GEM a literal reflection of this systemic diagnosis on the geological scale.

The time periods of many of our projects span decades, and in turn influence decades of development. This longevity is only possible when supported by an understanding of the historical transformation and contemporary possibilities for shaping the land. Research and design using a systemic approach support the understanding of the layers of a site and enable the creation of authentic, beautiful, and unexpected landscapes.

3-17
Grand Egyptian Museum,
Cairo, Egypt, 2019.
[West 8]

4. THE STARTING GROUND

BAS SMETS

Inspirations

In the fifteenth century, the term "topography" still reflected its origins in the Greek *topographia*: the description of a place. Its original English meaning, as given in the *Cambridge Dictionary*, refers to the physical appearance of the natural features of an area of land, especially the shape of its surface. In France, even today, they say *faire le topo*—to "make a topography"—which in that application describes an exhaustive inventory of a certain subject. So the word "topography" has had, and continues to have, a broad range of meanings: from the physical characterization of a place as registered in maps to written histories, inventories, and the statistics of a particular place. With this notion of topography being more about understanding than just describing a place, I will first introduce two men whom I find important to the notion of exploring and describing the characteristics of a geographic expanse.

Alexander von Humboldt (1769–1859) traveled through the Americas, noting what he saw while trying to comprehend the underlying systems of natural processes that had produced a certain geology or natural life form. Von Humboldt was among the first geographers to reveal the characteristics of a site by reading how multiple factors interacted. In his well-known diagrammatic section through the Ecuadorian volcano Chimborazo he related the geographic readings of temperature, air pressure, soil type, and plant growth to altitude [4-1]. That is to say, he attempted to truly grasp the forces and processes that shaped natural environments, and their role in producing their vegetation and terrain. This was the foundation for a new way of knowing, wide-ranging and encompassing, that already included the effects of climatic conditions in the evolution of vegetation around the world. He was the person who most inspired Darwin, and much of what Darwin presented in *The Origin of Species* could already be found in Alexander von Humboldt's own writings.

4-1
Alexander von Humboldt and Aimé Bonpland. *Géographie des plantes equinoxiales*, 1805. Considering all his observations simultaneously, Von Humboldt had the extraordinary capability to extrapolate them into general principles. [bpk / Ibero-Amerikanisches Institut, SPK / Ruth Schacht]

The second person of consequence to the field of topography is Eugène Viollet-le-Duc (1814–1879), who was recently brought to public attention when the spire he designed for Notre Dame cathedral in Paris collapsed during the 2019 fire. As a prominent architect Viollet-le-Duc was engaged in many important building restorations of his time, but on holiday he often explored Mont Blanc in eastern France. For more than ten years, in a Humboldtian manner, he described and drew what he saw. He measured the glaciers to understand the processes that shape them, how they form and grow, and how high temperatures and erosion work against them. He understood Mont Blanc as a primordial upheaval that eventually became granite and thereafter acquired its present form through erosion. Perhaps not surprisingly Viollet-le-Duc saw Mont Blanc as a giant piece of architecture, a kind of deliberate design that like a building could be restored to its original form to better reflect the forces that acted upon it.

In Viollet-le-Duc's fabulous map of Mont Blanc, the mountain appears as a crystalline rock depicted in two stages of evolution. The first view shows its state today after eons of erosion; the second shows the mountain's "restoration" to what Viollet-le-Duc believed to be its original state [4-2]. To him the processes of erosion were a degradation of an original concept, much like what happens to a building over time. As an architect and archaeologist he looked at nature as a version of built form.

To me these two great innovators, Von Humboldt and Viollet-le-Duc, provide major sources of inspiration. When we design, we try to remember their meticulous research of a site and their relentless pursuit of understanding what lies before them. From this starting point we try to determine how to intervene, how to restore, or how to create a new landscape.

I was neither born in the Swiss Alps like Georges Descombes, nor below sea level like Adriaan Geuze, but instead in a strange country called Belgium. Satellite imagery clearly reveals the endless sprawl that characterizes much of Belgium, a messy urbanism resulting from the lack of urban planning [4-3]. At the border with the Netherlands the differences in national policies are evident and easily discerned in aerial photographs. Dutch planning yields urban space organized and ordered; in Belgium there seems to be a lack of resistance to any kind of planned development, whether a new freeway, the extension of a city, or the replacement of agricultural land by urbanization.

4-2
Eugène-Emmanuel Viollet-Le-Duc. *Le Massif du Mont Blanc*, 1879. For Viollet-Le-Duc there was no essential difference between human constructions and mountains produced by natural forces. [Département des cartes et plans, Bibliothèque Nationale, Paris]

PAR
D'APRÈS
et des levés de Mr MIEULET
1876

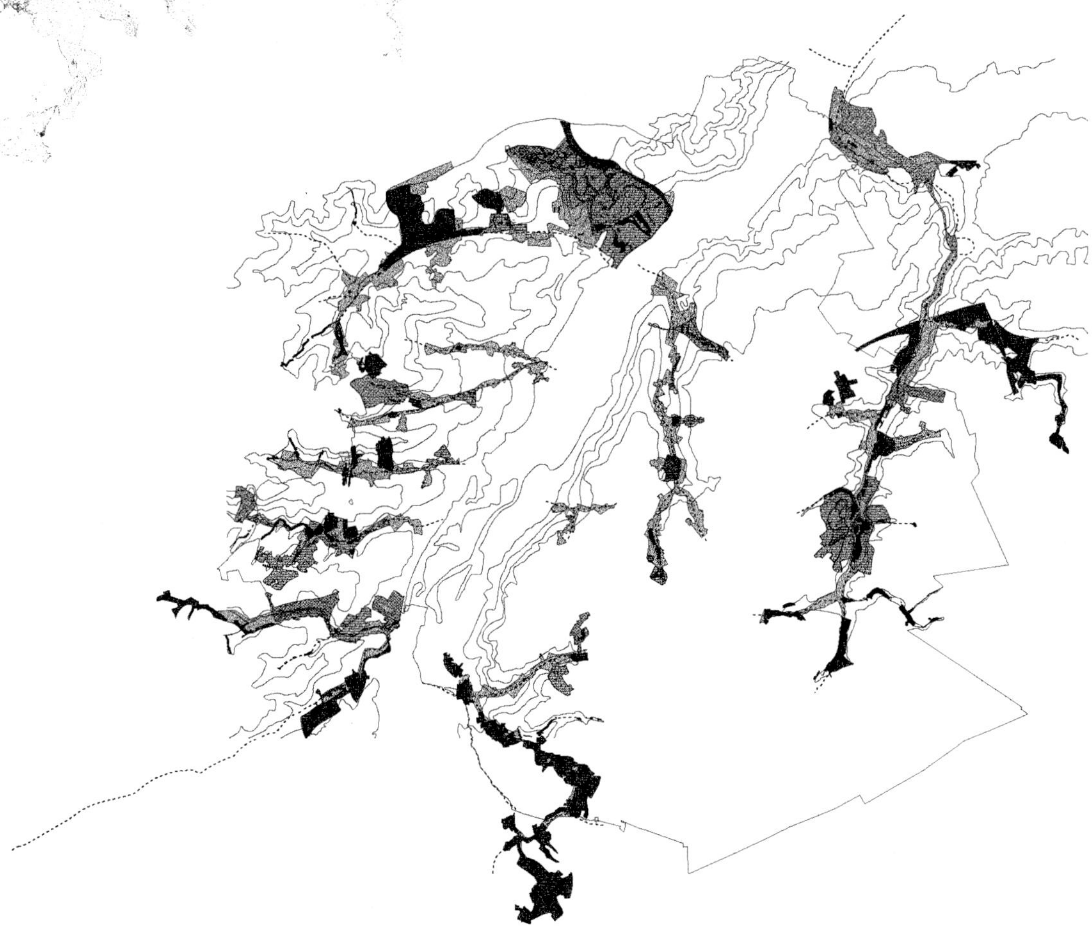

4-3
European Environmental Agency. Population Density Map of Europe, 2017. The flatness of the Belgian terrain provided no resistance to development and has resulted in an endless urban sprawl, visible even from space. [GEOstata]

4-4
Bureau Bas Smets. Brussels 2040: City of Tributaries, 2012. Brussels as the city of secondary valleys. The reinforcement of Brussels's eight tributaries creates a new landscape structure that guides development and captures rainwater along the length of large urban parks. Bureau Bas Smets [hereafter BBS].

If one overlays the built space of Belgium on the map of the country's existing rivers, their lack of correlation is shocking. However, when you look at those waterways in greater detail you understand that these are not major rivers. Our rivers are perhaps 200 kilometers long—less than one-tenth of the Rhine or the Rhône, each of which flows through 3,000 kilometers. Their difference in the fall of their land is about 3,000 meters, while in Belgium the difference is perhaps only 100 or 200 meters at most. In conducting our research we came to appreciate what geologists have always known: that in Belgium we mainly have what are called "rain rivers," that is, rivers with significant flow only during seasons with significant rainfall. In flat terrain any small difference in height becomes significant. The effect parallels that of pouring water onto a glass table: the little cracks in the tabletop determine where the water goes and how it moves. Our office has become obsessed with topography, especially with changes in level as a starting point for developing design. The following five projects illustrate our continually evolving methods and ideas.

Rain River

In 2010 the Brussels government asked our office to produce a vision for the city's form in 2040. We began with topographic readings, inventorying the elements of the urban fabric to better comprehend what currently existed. In the nineteenth century the city's main river, the Zenne, was diverted into a subterranean culvert running beneath the center of Brussels. The result: the city lost its river; there was no longer an iconic natural feature to mark Brussels, as the Thames does for London or the Seine for Paris. After uncovering traces of the original waterways we then mapped the city's green spaces. Our findings puzzled us; there seemed to be no systemic logic behind the locations of these green spaces. However, recalling the larger-scale river study we had conducted, we realized that these open spaces reflected a kind of a capillary system of rain rivers that carry runoff to the North Sea.

Under these conditions the tributary becomes almost as important as the primary river. After we traced Brussels's eight tributaries on a map it became clear that 80 percent of the city's green spaces were directly linked to the same system of flow—something that geologists know, of course, but that urban designers, architects, and landscape architects seem to have forgotten. From the lessons learned from mapping we proposed a scheme for Brussels 2040 that would reinforce these eight tributaries traversing the city's nineteen municipalities [4-4]. We thought it would be beneficial to invest in these eight linear water systems to store water and reduce the risk of inundations while simultaneously creating terrain for urban forests. We imagined a new "landscape structure" as a contemporary version of the park systems devised by Frederick Law Olmsted Sr. in the United States. The difference between the two was that Olmsted's designs were made a priori, before urban sprawl, while we were acting a posteriori, within the urban sprawl that already existed and with more of a "make do" attitude. In response, our scheme was based on the physical reality of the eight tributaries running through Brussels which respond ed perfectly to the city's decentralized governmental power structure.

Valley

Around the same time that we were conducting the study for Brussels 2040 a developer asked our office to design a park on the site of Tour & Taxis, adjacent to the canal and the River Zenne. Historically, the site was one of the world's first multimodal freight platforms to integrate water, road, and rail transport. Long ago, to create level ground for the railroad tracks a gully had been excavated to shape a horizontal trajectory not unlike a tributary of the secondary rivers that brought water to the city. Based on an understanding of the historical urban patterns, we conceived the park as a dry valley replacing the railroad tracks running beneath the bridges that once crossed the site. Our primary goal for this emblematic site was to create a large park to guide future development. Starting with the idea of retaining elements of the 10-hectare site's industrial heritage—the bridges, stations, warehouses, and platforms—we proposed a transition from wilder spontaneous vegetation along the gully to a more organized landscape that connected to the city center [4- 5].

The park was to be the first designed by our office, and in preparation we studied great Brussels parks from the nineteenth century. This set the standard. We felt that we must do at least as well for our time as they did in theirs—not an easy task considering that our predecessors had at their disposal far more money per square meter relative to their time.

4-5
Bureau Bas Smets. Tour & Taxis Park. Brussels, Belgium, 2017. The park is conceived as a dry river valley with different atmospheres created by the spontaneous vegetation on its slopes, open lawns, and the rows of trees that connect to the city center. [BBS]

4-6
Bureau Bas Smets. Tour & Taxis Park. Sections through the site trace the contour of the ground plane. [BBS]

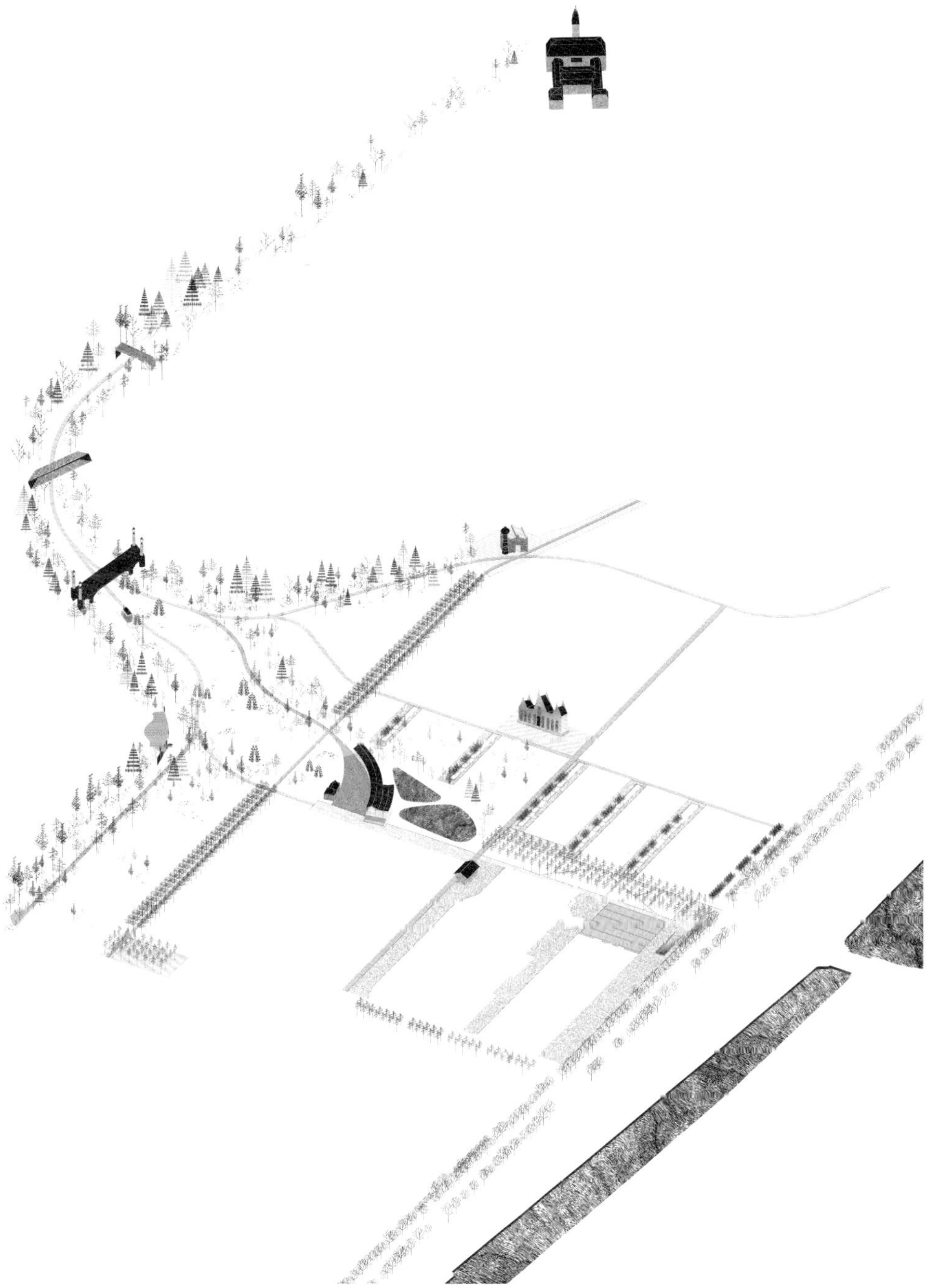

An additional challenge was that to accommodate the railroad tracks, the terrain had been flattened, with an 80-centimeter (approximately 3-foot) layer of ballast added to support the tracks. As our budget was limited we determined that we could bring no new earth to the site nor haul any away. The top layer of the soil was scraped, stored, and later used to create a natural valley—in this case, one that had never existed before. The site was then planted with 3,000 small pioneer trees and 300 mature climax, or long-lived, species. Over the first three or four years the pioneer trees would grow quickly and form a screen concealing the development on either side of the park, while over time the trees from the climax species would gradually replace them and transform the site into a robust environment.

Since we had to work with what existed on-site, the sections through the site were continually redrawn to reflect the new conditions we encountered there. No calculations were sufficiently accurate to establish how much ballast and how much topsoil actually existed, and what vegetation could be expected to thrive in these new conditions. The design came to reflect a play between an abstract design concept and the specifics determined by the material found on-site. At some point we became desperate about what to do with all the ballast: stones usually large and strong, the properties required for supporting railroad tracks. Then came an idea: if we sorted the stones into their various sizes, perhaps we could reuse them in an underground cistern for water storage. After testing on-site we discovered that by excavating a pit at the bottom of the valley and filling it with the excess ballast, we could store more than one million liters of water beneath the park. We negotiated with the developers and showed them that by creating the underground cistern, there would be no need to divert water from the site, and that in fact all the water could be stored within the park and even used for irrigation. Water management thus became an integral component of the development as a whole, with the park becoming a performing landscape in the process. The ballast was scraped, removed, and filtered into different sizes; larger stones were used in the water reservoir while the finer soils were used in the mix of the surface layer. The medium-size rocks became the foundations for the paths [4-6].

In response to the severe financial constraints, we wondered how nature could work for us. There was neither money to bring in topsoil

4-7
Bureau Bas Smets.
Tour & Taxis Park.
Brussels, Belgium, 2017.
The transformation of an industrial site into an undulating valley by reusing materials found on-site.
[Michiel De Cleene, BBS]

nor to sow a lawn. Working with a botanist we determined that planting clover enriches the soil and that over time a lawn would develop on its own, as indeed it did in less than three years. In this sense the lawn chose to live on the site all by itself; we never planted it. Today it thrives and does just what it is supposed to do.

We envisioned a similar principle for the pioneer trees. Willow trees grow very quickly both above and below ground, bringing air and water to this thick clay soil that benefits long-lived species such as the oaks and beeches that were planted. Curiously, in talking with historians after the design and much of the work had been finished, we were told that the railroad had been built in that location because an existing river tributary provided a relatively easy path for the engineers to follow. By imagining the park as a valley we had in fact re-created a preexisting tributary [4-7].

Plaza

Saint-Gilles is one of the nineteen municipalities that comprise the city of Brussels. Since 1865 a daily market had been held on its beautiful plaza, one of the oldest uninterrupted markets in Belgium [4-8]. The arrival of the automobile significantly changed the character of the place, however. It still functioned as a marketplace in the morning, but for most of the day parking prevailed. As a result, the cafés and restaurants with their beautiful, curving façades were struggling to prosper, further hidden by the trees planted to screen the parking spaces. To improve this unfortunate situation the city decided to ban cars from the plaza and hold a competition to convert it to pedestrian use.

Topography was a major concern, as the site dipped about two meters from one end to the other, a distance of fifty meters. We proposed reorganizing the plaza through a series of flat curbs in natural stone, lines that would reveal the building façades while facilitating water drainage [4-9]. Diverging toward the church, the lines restore the building's role as the focal point of the plaza. They also help signal the plaza's diverse functions, which include delivery and available market space. In winter they mark single terraces and in summer, double terraces.

To determine the appropriate hardscape we looked first to the existing plaza and found that half the site had been paved with Belgian

(above left) **4-8** Saint-Gilles Parvis, Brussels, Belgium. Post card, 1881. Since 1865 the plaza has uninterruptedly housed a daily market [Dexia Banque Postcard Collection]

(above right) **4-9** Bureau Bas Smets. Saint-Gilles Parvis. Brussels, Belgium, 2018. Diverging lines of bluestone reveal the curved plaza, organize its uses, and collect water runoff. [BBS]

(center) **4-10** Bureau Bas Smets. Saint-Gilles Parvis. The existing pavers were cut in two and installed on edge. [BBS]

(below) **4-11** Bureau Bas Smets. Saint-Gilles Parvis. The density of the reused pavers increases toward the valley, creating a giant mosaic. [Michiel De Cleene, BBS]

Bruxelles-Saint-Gilles.
Brussel-Sint Gillis
Parvis Saint-Gilles
Sint-Gillis Voorplein

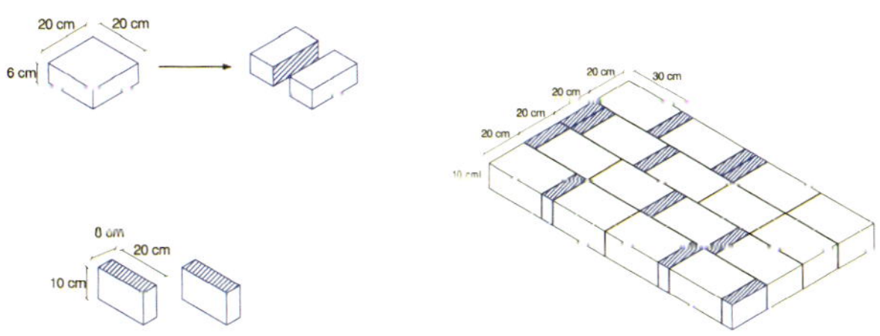
20 cm
20 cm
6 cm
20 cm
30 cm
20 cm
20 cm
20 cm
8 cm
20 cm
10 cm

L'ATLAS

bluestone, the country's dominant quarried stone. Rather than discarding this valuable resource we felt it should be reused, although its 6-centimeter thickness was insufficient to structurally support contemporary market activities. To address this problem we cut the stones in half and reinstalled them on edge, an operation that yielded about one-quarter of our paving materials at almost no cost [4-10]. We expressed our fascination with topography by varying the number of reused elements in each strip, so that as one moves toward the valley the frequency of the "pixels" increases. The position of each reused stone was drawn one by one in the manner of a giant mosaic [4-11]. The surfaces of the recut bluestones were more brilliant and reflective in both sun and rain than the new granite pavers alongside of which they had been set.

The diverging bands of stone enhance the reading of the plaza as one continuous space, while effectively demarcating the spaces assigned to the outdoor terraces. Seven different species of trees have been strategically planted to further organize the functioning of the plaza and work in concert with the terraces to create a single uninterrupted, flexible space [4-12].

Beach

Himara is a beach town of 11,000 inhabitants on the Albanian side of the Ionian Sea, opposite the heel of Italy and frequented mainly by Greek and Albanian tourists. In 2015 Atelier Albania invited us to participate in an international competition for the refurbishment of the Himara waterfront. Although the beach was the city's biggest attraction, the town was very poorly connected with the sea. Only a few small staircases, set perpendicular to the beach, led down to the water. The two-meter-high seawall had been backfilled after construction, with its surface used for parking, awkwardly planted with olive trees, and decorated with an old millstone. From seats along the waterfront only parked cars were visible, with not even a glimpse of the water [4-13].

On our first visit to the site it was cold outdoors, cold in the hotel, and cold in the restaurant. The conditions were so poor it was hard to believe the competition was authentic. Was this for real? Atelier Albania had received funding from the European Union to organize the competition, but would they really build the winning entry? At the same time, so much uncertainty

4-12
Bureau Bas Smets. Saint-Gilles Parvis. Brussels, Belgium, 2018. The stone bands, the trees, and the terraces form one continuous space adaptable to many different uses. [Michiel De Cleene, BBS]

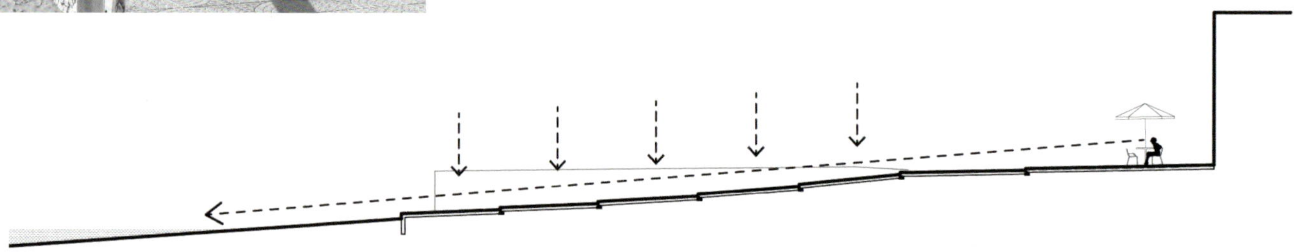

granted considerable freedom, and I decided to imagine the best, even most utopian scenario. I started dreaming of a coastal pine forest and a beach shaped by erosion, like the Turkish Steps in Sicily.

We began looking for a way in which to reorganize the entire space by applying the logic of a natural system. Our proposed solution was simple: demolish the retaining wall and address the level difference with a sequence of stepped platforms that, in addition, would absorb the impact of the waves more effectively than the existing vertical wall [4-14]. Our competition entry was based on the transformation of the beachfront primarily through its section then applied and extruded along more than 300 meters of coastline. And we won.

4-13
Existing Waterfront. Himara, Albania. Prior to the new construction a high seawall blocked both the access and the view toward the beach. [BBS]

4-14
Bureau Bas Smets. Himara Waterfront Himara, Albania, 2017. A series of stepped platforms better absorb the impact of the waves, while providing full accessibility. [BBS]

4-15
Bureau Bas Smets. Himara Waterfront. The platforms continue the sandy beach as if they are made of solidified sand. [BBS]

A linear grove of Italian stone pines (*Pinus pinea*), imported from nurseries in Italy, was planted on the higher terraces, where their roots would grow above sea level and be less threatened by salt. The platforms were made of concrete using carefully washed sand from the beach, thus appearing almost as solidified sand. Daily tidal changes deposit sand on the terraces and blur the line between the beach and the buildings along the waterfront. The grove of pine trees has since matured and become a shaded promenade where people shelter from the sun [4-15] .

The municipality demanded that the street fronting the beach remain open to traffic. We countered that the waterfront should be pedestrian and proposed paving the street with the same material as the promenade so that if desired, it could be closed for special events. Time has proven us right. At first the street was closed only on weekends, but today traffic is completely banned. There is full access to the waterfront, and the sea is always visible from the terrace. An additional benefit is that from the water, the unremarkable buildings that line the promenade are no longer visible, and that you only see the pine forest that screens the buildings and grants them only a secondary role [4-16].

Park

Arles, which lies between Montpellier and Marseille, was among the greatest cities of the Roman Empire, second only to Rome itself. The city center is characterized by a network of small public spaces—all very mineral. Adjacent to the center lies

a former industrial site, the Parc des Ateliers, an open space somewhat similar in size to our Tour & Taxis park in Brussels. Once a railroad yard used to repair locomotives, the site was carved from the bedrock to be perfectly flat. There is no soil, no water, only rocks [4-17].

Maja Hoffmann from the LUMA Foundation asked us to design a landscape for this barren space, destined to become a new center for creating and exhibiting art. Annabelle Selldorf would convert the old industrial buildings; Frank Gehry would build the centerpiece: a tower for the arts. The lack of obvious landscape features troubled me when I first arrived on-site. In Belgium we often bemoan that we're neither artificial enough to be exciting nor natural enough to be beautiful; we are stuck somewhere in between. But this sterile site seemed even worse than the typical Belgian situation, requiring a new attitude and approach to discover qualities of beauty and interest.

After intense study, we determined that three types of landscape comprised the site, each marked by dramatically different geographical conditions: the Crau, the Camargue, and the Alpilles. The Crau is the bed of a former glacier, today strewn with rocks and lined with an impenetrable layer of clay, a landscape where no tree can grow. The Camargue occupies the estuary between the turbulent Rhône and the Mediterranean; the Alpilles are the southern extension of the Alps. One landscape is very wet, one is very dry, one is very mineral. Seen on a map it appeared as if those three landscape types were reaching out toward our site. How could we utilize the foremost characteristic of each to bring nature back to this sterile land? We spent considerable time exploring those geographies that are, perhaps ironically, one of the richest environments in Europe for both plants and animals.

The site had been, in part, carved from bedrock, and built atop a Roman necropolis. Due to its historical significance we were not permitted to dig, and instead sealed the ground before installing a garden above it on a new layer of soil. Other constraints such as fire-engine access and underground services determined the places where we could model a new topography to support vegetation growth. In Arles another consideration is the mistral, a northerly wind that blows straight from the Swiss glaciers that follow the Rhône and brings with it ice-cold temperatures. There is a saying that when the mistral blows, it makes

4-16
Bureau Bas Smets.
Waterfront.
Himara, Albania, 2017.
A grove of pine trees provides shade. Seen from the water, the trees form a coastal pine forest.
[BBS]

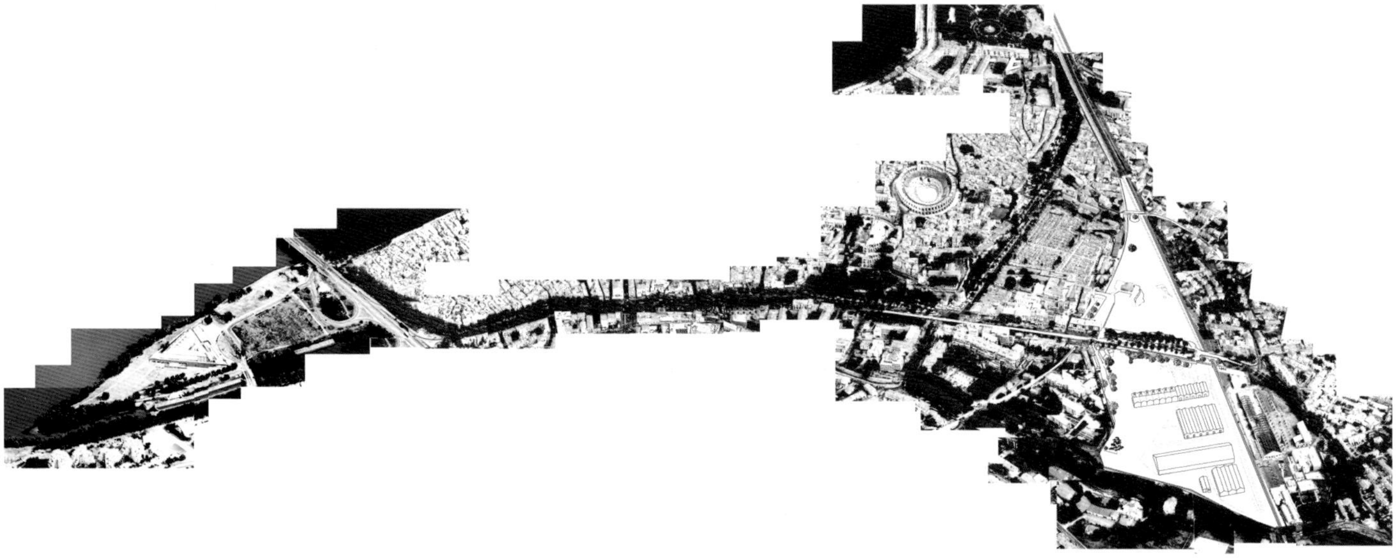

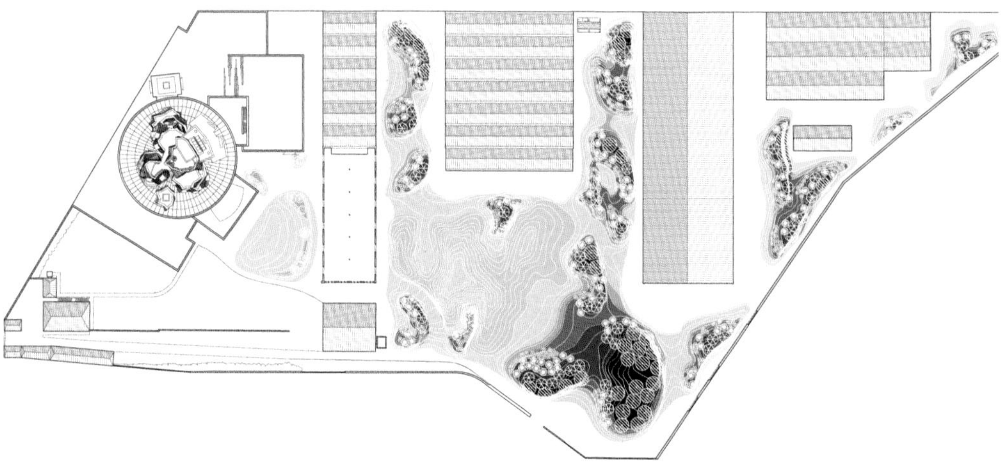

+1.50
+1.20
+0.90
+0.60
+0.45
+0.30
+0.15

4-17
Bureau Bas Smets. LUMA Arles Parc des Ateliers. Arles, France, 2021. The Parc des Ateliers had been carved from the bedrock to create a level terrain. Graced with neither earth nor water, the site was barren. [BBS]

4-18
Bureau Bas Smets. LUMA Arles Parc des Ateliers. Site plan. The design is based on accelerating natural processes. [BBS]

4-19
Bureau Bas Smets. LUMA Arles Parc des Ateliers. The depth of soil brought by the mistral wind reflects varying types of vegetation, planted as a spatial version of ecological succession. [BBS]

you crazy; and when it arrives with a velocity of about 100 kilometers per hour, everyone stays indoors.

Drawing on what we learned in designing the Tour & Taxis park we questioned how we could use the forces of nature to transform the site. What would happen if we didn't do anything on the site for ten years, one hundred years, two hundred years? How would nature appear and how would it develop over time? Studying the wind patterns, we understood that wind, particularly the mistral, would bring sediment over time—and when deposited, sediment creates topography. The new terrain would create different environmental conditions, which would in turn support the growth of various types of vegetation. That exercise was much like science fiction, of course: you establish the rules and then you follow these rules, rules of your own making. We modeled how the landscape would be formed when interacting with the buildings. We imagined that the strong winds, when diverted by the buildings, would first scour a depression for a lake and then deposit sufficient sediments to create a dune. The resulting ground would have an asymmetrical section that, coincidentally, would create a comfortable climate: in summer people could relax on the soft slope in the shade of the trees; in winter they could walk along the steeper slope, protected from the wind by plants growing on the dune [4-18].

Topography was a major concern, as the soil needed to be sealed to ensure that no roots entered the archaeological site. Pioneer trees that grow in very shallow soil were planted, to be followed in an ecological succession by pine trees requiring at least one or two meters of earth [4-19]. In terms of experience, a walk through the space would become a walk through time—one that could potentially illustrate 200 years in succession. All the levels on which the trees had been planted were maintained. A walk on the site reveals the pine trees growing on one level, the oaks on another, the maples on yet another. This logic was applied to the entire six hectares of the park [4-20].

Although there was neither sufficient soil nor sources of water on-site, those problems were mitigated by an adjacent sixteenth-century canal, which brings irrigation to the Crau. An agreement was struck with the company that manages the canal to allow us to pump its water into a new pond. After filtering, the water is used to irrigate the newly planted vegetation.

The mounds were constructed layer by layer, guided by GPS and then planted with vegetation. In total more than 1,100 trees and shrubs have already been planted, from large to small. First the pine trees, then the oaks, then the remaining species—as if following an inversed ecological succession. More than 80,000 smaller plants introduced more than 140 different species to the site and completed the scheme. Even while still under construction, animal life started to return to the site. Birds seem to smell the changes, and new species have been spotted. The evaporation of the pond and the evapo-transpiration of the leaves have already created a new microclimate. The semidesert conditions of this former industrial site have already transformed into those of a Mediterranean climate.

In closing I would like to return to the idea of the section, and expand the understanding of topography with the same notion that Vladimir Vernadsky once used to describe the biosphere: that in the end, the space in which life occurs is quite constricted: 300, 400, or 500 meters wide in an atmosphere only about twelve kilometers high. For Vernadsky the biosphere is the composite of all living things combined with all the former organisms that have died. Fossil fuels, most minerals, the entire layer in which plants and animals grow—all are a part of this biosphere. The living entity that draws on both the atmosphere and the ground is, of course, vegetation. This is the topographical layer in which we live, the interface between a stable geological reality and an uncertain meteorological evolution.

4-20
Bureau Bas Smets.
LUMA Arles
Parc des Ateliers.
Arles, France, 2021.
By planting some 1,200 trees and 80,000 plants, the semidesert conditions have transformed into a Mediterranean climate.
[BBS]

5. SCALED DOWN

JENNIFER GUTHRIE

The land is a storyteller, topography its essential narrator. The contour of the land informs and engages people with their physical world—wherever they are, wherever they have come from [5-1]. Born on the West Coast of the United States, I grew up along the coastal beaches, cliffs, and fault lines of Southern California. I spent summers in the high desert, in the Owens River Valley, among incredible rock formations, extinct volcanos, and places where water was a critical issue [5-2]. I now live in the Pacific Northwest, a landscape framed by mountain ranges and supplied by abundant quantities of water. These are interesting and important landscapes shaped by natural evolution, the movement of tectonic plates, the lift and lowering produced by volcanic activity, and the advance and retreat of glacial migration—as well as the human management of water to direct its flow and the growth of vegetation. To be an observer in these big, beautiful Western spaces—to be a part of these unique, natural, and topographically complex landscapes—has been both humbling and inspiring. Though wildly different and often impressive in scale, they provide us with only a small hint of their full geological story. We see and experience a moment in time, and perhaps then appreciate that we are only able to modify in small measure their potential physical and experiential effects. Their story far surpasses what our eyes can perceive—landscapes are expansive and deep.

Given the grand scale of the landscapes described above, you may wonder about their connection to the chapter title: "Scaled Down." When invited to participate in the symposium from which this book derives, I first considered the scale of the large, powerful, and familiar landscapes in which we may work as landscape architects. In reality, however, we more often work on sites of much smaller dimensions and marked by far less drama. The challenge, then, is how to achieve in projects of small dimensions at least some of the presence, interest, and beauty possessed by natural landscapes of much grander scale [5-3]. One answer: through an intelligent, informed, and artful shaping of the land we can remember that the land is greater than any individual site, especially an urban site—and that the land is also larger than us and what we do.

5-1
Gustafson Guthrie Nichol [today GGN]. CityCenterDC. Washington, DC, 2013. [GGN]

shade –
Utah Garden
rain garden
turf – flex space &
water collector (use ??)
4 seasons

From reviewing projects we have undertaken at GGN, I have identified three concerns that grant power to large topographical landscapes, and from them proposed the corresponding means by which they may be applicable to smaller urban sites.

Expansion: The topography, ecology, and engineering systems of urban environments extend broadly beyond a project's boundaries. This expansive, horizontal quality of the landscape is represented primarily by the plan view.

Depth: A site's story lies deeper than what is visible on its surface. As only the proverbial tip of the iceberg is normally apparent, we rarely "see" or understand the material narrative that guides most landscapes. The depth of the site, in contrast to its horizonal extent, involves the vertical dimension and is best represented by the section.

Perception: Expansion and depth are properties of the landscape. Perception concerns how we experience these properties, dependent to a large degree on their scale and the nature of their features—but above all, from the relationship between what was once present, how it has changed, and how people have or have not been considered in the process. The principal representation of perception is the perspective view.

5-2
Sierra Nevada Mountain Range. Upper Owens River Valley, California. [Jennifer Guthrie]

5-3
Jennifer Guthrie / GGN. Nu Skin Headquarters. Provo, Utah. Study sketch, 2015. The land is greater than any site with which we work. [GGN]

5-4
David Malda / GGN. Spring District. Bellevue, Washington, 2015. Understanding the greater landscape beyond the project site is critical. [GGN].

Expansion: A Landscape Has No Boundaries

<< Horizontal >>

In one sense, landscape is endless, a connective tissue with no limits; it joins all individual sites, natural or designed. In our effort to see and understand the landscape, we have imposed limits such as urban and territorial borders, and the property lines that circumscribe the sites on which we work. Although our contractual project may end at the curb or lot line, our responsibility demands that we see and regard the site without borders, to think far beyond them. The river continues its flow before and after it traverses our site; rainfall covers districts and regions, not merely the individual plot, seeds and pollen fly with no regard for the limits of ownership. Our duty is always to contemplate the greater context in which our site is only a small fragment and where appropriate, employ its topographical features as our guide [5-4].

Due to the limits set by property lines and contracts, we usually have only a block, a parcel, or an edge on which to work. Despite these artificial limits, we must take stock of the greater environment in which we are building to apprehend the site beyond the immediate confines of the given project. Among the first things to consider are the properties of both the historical and the contemporary city, understood by referencing historical representations such as territorial topographic maps and newer tools like Lidar and GIS mapping. From these we acquire a more comprehensive understanding of the site's evolution over time as part of the larger region. By better grasping the history of the land on which we are building, we can offer informed decisions that lead to more creative solutions. The product of this study results in what could be termed "contextual landform," a reworking of the existing contours to reflect prior conditions in accordance with the needs of the project at hand. The spirit of contextual landform is that landscape design begins with the topography of the existing urban systems and fabric to establish the foundation for the project's conceptual design and experiential goals. It is topography, vegetation, and social program —rather than property lines—that should trigger ideas and help them germinate.

India Basin Shoreline Park

The commission for the India Basin Shoreline Park in the Bayview–Hunters Point neighborhood of San Francisco presented GGN with the opportunity to repair and restore the broken connections that join people, land, and water. By absorbing the natural flow of the broader site topography into the park and intentionally constructing several prominent pedestrian features, the neighborhood could be relinked with the hill and the bay.

Over the years since settlement, following a pattern common to waterfront sites, the land had been manipulated to support maritime services, industrial uses, and limited recreational activites [5-5]. The resulting landscape was, and looked, engineered and alien. The study of historical maps supplied us with information concerning the more natural character of the land prior to development and the data needed to encourage a looser framework for the design. By extending the slopes of the surrounding hills to the water, softening the shoreline edge, and then sculpting the land to more strongly root it to its context, the design physically joined the park users to the authentic nature of the place and the rich past that had been lost.

The formal decisions that followed were deliberate. As one might choose to imprint a geometric form upon a piece of soft clay, we

5-5
India Basin Shoreline Park. San Francisco, California, Existing conditions. [San Francisco Recreation and Parks Department]

5-6
Shannon Nichol / GGN. India Basin Shoreline Park. Studying the imprinting of a geometric lawn upon the existing landscape. [GGN]

5-7
Gustafson Guthrie Nichol. India Basin Shoreline Park. Site plan. [GGN]

BEFORE

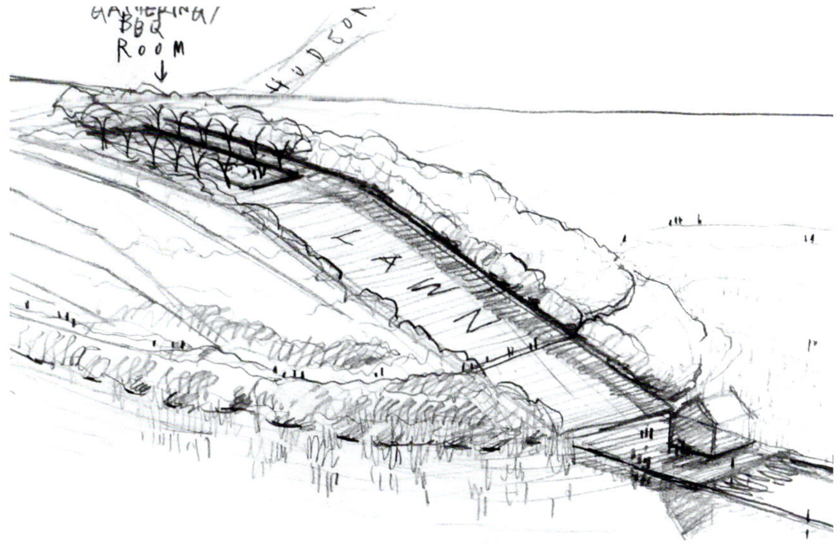
BBQ
ROOM
LAWN

disrupted the existing elements of the greater landscape with purposefully formed elements that strengthened the bond between the local community, the land, and the water. These connectors were inspired by the historical marine-way rails and took shape as hill-to-water walkways, crossings, docks, and a pier. A large lawn—admittedly an unnatural landscape feature—emphatically extended the upland neighborhood to the water's edge, a connection made obvious by the jarring shift in topographical form from organic to engineered [5-6].

At India Basin Shoreline Park, the land was molded and shaped to accommodate the programmatic features that modern neighborhood landscapes require: improved access to the water and the provision and integration of active-recreation facilities such as basketball courts, playgrounds with accessible pathways, flexible lawn space, and—most directly affecting our modeling of the topography—planning for sea-level rise [5-7]. Our greatest challenge has been to absorb and incorporate these multiple and competing demands within the larger context derived from the authentic character of the local landscape and its historical topography.

CityCenterDC

The intersections of the grand boulevards that resulted from the rigorous grid of Pierre L'Enfant's plan for the city of Washington, DC, created distinct, wedge-shaped parcels. While these produced inherently problematic sites on which to work, over time the shapes of the blocks have spawned some interesting architectural solutions. One of these bisected city blocks had been graced by monumental fountains on each of its two parcels, fountains that together marked the entry to the city's civic core. The CityCenterDC project, a nongovernmental initiative, took possession of one of these parcels; its goal was to restore the block as a civic space with an enhanced public presence.

The site, which is almost level, lies adjacent to one of the grand boulevards that radiate from the White House. While we respected the site by maintaining its essential flatness, we knew that a significant transformation of the existing topography would be needed to counter the dimensions of the adjacent boulevard and to create a comfortable space appropriately proportioned for its intended use. After reviewing historical city maps, we opted to elevate a portion of the land within the site as a reference to the monumental fountain that formerly occupied its center. The design embodies our idea that the fountain should be a landscape in itself, rather than just a heroic object that occupies a central position on the plaza [5-8].

Like the original fountain, this new water feature serves as the primary element of the design. In plan view, the substantial size of the fountain complements the grand scale of the adjacent boulevard; in section, however, its dimensions are more intimate, with the edges of the fountain set at a height appropriate for seating. These adjustments of the dimensions in plan and section establish the transition from the monumental scale of the boulevard to the pedestrian-oriented scale of the immediate neighborhood.

The fountain design drew its inspiration from the dynamic geometric shapes of the bisected city grid and relied on a series of radiating lines to condense the scale of the monument to that of the pedestrian [5-9]. The more organic surfaces within the fountain contrast with the hard boundary edges to create a sculptural presence even without the actual presence of water. Yet it is the flow of water over its surfaces that grants life to the fountain and the plaza. The fountain's "terrain" was designed by raising and lowering a series of blocks, and thereafter plotting by computer to model a surface coated completely by water that left no dry areas. From the initial block study, the forms were subsequently softened by overlaying a digital surface (similar to laying a soft blanket over a series of cubes) to smooth their edges and render the fountain as a single warped plane [5-10]. Computer Numerical Control (CNC) technology was then employed to shape the stone in forms determined by the use of mock-ups; these were configured to animate and increase the energy of the water flowing over their surfaces [5-11].

Depth: Sometimes We Have Only Six Inches

<< Vertical >>

In reality, landscape is endless, both horizontally and vertically. To truly understand the site, we thus also need to consider what lies beneath its surface. "What story does this larger landscape have to tell us about how our cities and landscapes were modified to accommodate growth and changing needs?" This theoretical question is part of the story of the land and is not bounded by pragmatic issues such as the foundations for the columns needed to support the parking garage above. At times, a site has been levelled or interrupted by prior interventions; at other times, a below-grade labyrinth of pipes and conduits determines the weight

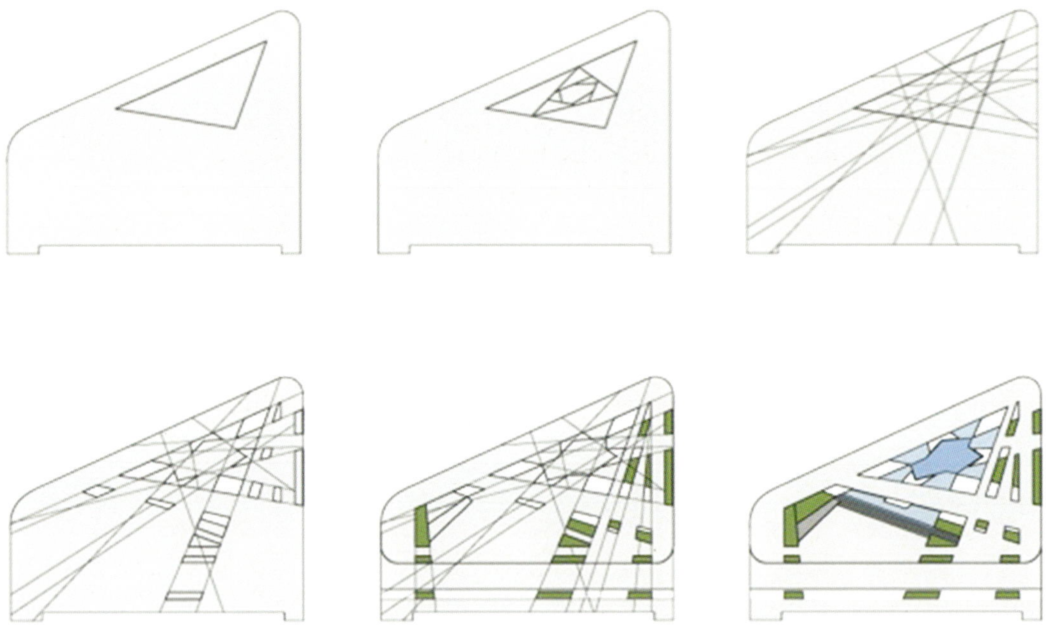

5-8
Gustafson Guthrie Nichol. CityCenterDC. Washington, DC, 2013. Exploring the shapes of the city's bisected grid to determine a comfortable pedestrian scale. [GGN]

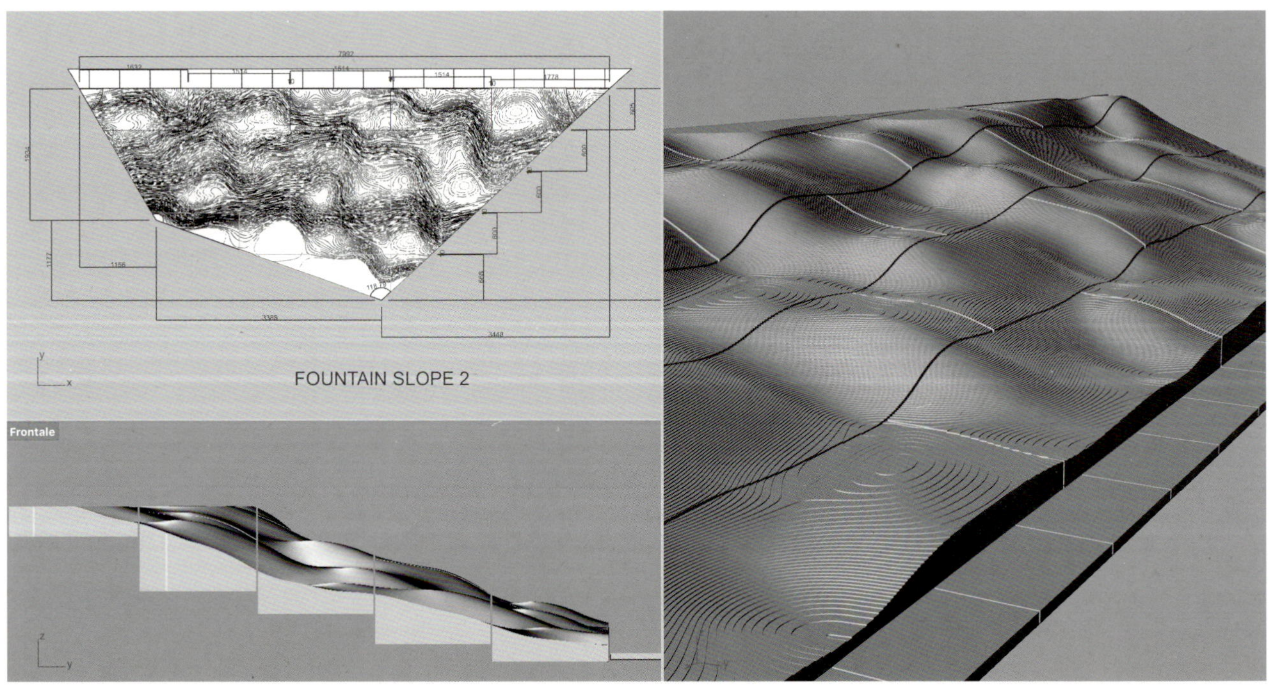

5-9
Gustafson Guthrie Nichol. CityCenterDC. To ensure the surface would be fully coated by water, elements were lifted or lowered in studies using Rhino. [GGN]

5-10
Gustafson Guthrie Nichol. CityCenterDC. After reviewing mock-ups, a rougher CNC carving technique was adopted to make the stone resemble topographic lines. [GGN]

5-11
Gustafson Guthrie Nichol. CityCenterDC. On the plaza side, the grand fountain was sculpted to reflect the pedestrian scale of the adjacent neighborhood. [Nigel Young, Foster + Partners]

limitation on any construction above it. In all cases, however, we must seek to reveal and express the original topographical and geographical narratives of the larger landscape. These are important aspects for considering the shape of the land. The vertical modeling of the land provides a great design opportunity. If you are granted only six inches with which to work, make those six inches count.

We often search for clues in the existing landscape by which to direct the project's design and identify the site's unique qualities, whether those that remain or those that previously existed on and around the site. When working in cities, significant relics of past uses—antiquated boundary walls or the remnants of railroad corridors, for example—commonly appear on maps and other historical documents. Such objects provide valuable sources for piecing together a narrative for the place. Perhaps the land was once marshland or tidal; perhaps there were once hills. Recognizing these historical features provides opportunities to elevate or depress the land and reshape it in accordance with the program and design ideas.

Bill & Melinda Gates Foundation Campus

GGN's conceptual site diagram for the Bill & Melinda Gates Foundation Campus in downtown Seattle acknowledged the need for the building's form to represent the organization's outreach to the world. We also believed that the landform beneath the project should represent the organization's deep connection to its locale and thus convey its humble roots in the Pacific Northwest. Over a 100 years ago the site had been bogland characteristic of the Puget Sound region, a history that inspired the design language for the project's stormwater pools and security walls. GGN's design objective was to cohere the character and depth of the dark, organic, marshy edges of a Puget Sound bog with the unpretentious language envisioned for the landscape [5-12].

After studying materials such as dark, mottled granites and weathered, rusty metals, the design team settled on a more modest use of concrete to meet the demands of water retention and possible vehicular crashes [5-13]. One benefit of concrete is that its color can be darkened to a tone and visual depth appropriate for the site design. Another is its malleability: poured and molded, its forms can allude to the historically marshy, vegetative language of the site's prior form as bogland. These resonances joined architecture and site, present and past.

5-12
Shannon Nichol / GGN. Bill & Melinda Gates Foundation. Seattle, Washington, 2011. Study sketches. The property's historical boglands inspired the features such as walls used to retain water or for security. [GGN]

5-13
Gustafson Guthrie Nichol. Bill & Melinda Gates Foundation. Concrete walls were molded using custom formwork and darkened with lampblack as a reference to the site's former state as a murky bog. [Sean Airhart, NBBJ]

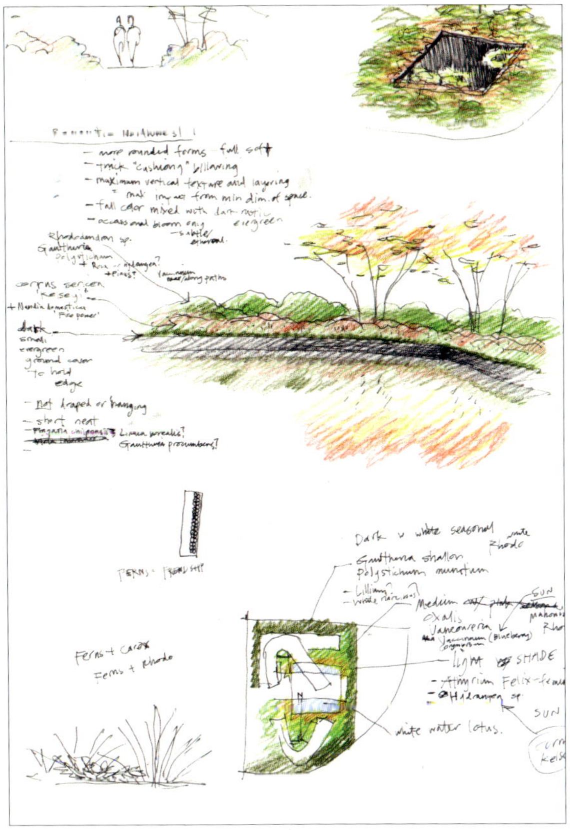

North End Parks

Severely constraining our design for Boston's North End Parks were restrictions on the loads placed upon the cover of a buried freeway, which permitted soil of only very limited depth. In response, we proposed small, sculpted earth forms to at least conceptually join the new parks—conceived as an elevated "porch"—with the city's prior topography. The linear central green protects children's water play and other amusements, while a sloped lawn accommodates visitors in small groups and those of larger numbers when attending special events. Constrained by being built on structure, with soil limited in depth, the lifting and lowering of the lawn with the shallow steps, walls, and walkways yielded parks that nonetheless offer visitors an experience of considerable richness [5-14, 5-15]. Although possessing neither the grandeur of the mountain nor the depth of the ocean, North End Parks demonstrates that in an essentially flat terrain, small gestures are consequential, somewhat related to the adage "In the land of the blind, perhaps the one-eyed person may lead."

Perspective: See the Land / Read the Land

<< Experiential >>

Our experience of the land is most often sensed and comprehended visually, in perspective, and haptically, through movement, no matter the size of the area we occupy and in which we move. Because we experience landscape in three and four dimensions (the fourth being that of time), designing topography solely in plan view can be restrictive. What one "sees" in plan from above rarely corresponds with the landscape as viewed at ground level, readings additionally colored by personal experience. From the ground, encounters with the terrain tend to be more emphatic: curved forms appear curvier, and the lifting and lowering of the land infused with greater drama. At times, the landscape also feels more engineered. To truly see and understand the land while designing, it is invaluable to toggle among plan, section, and three-dimensional model. Although this statement may seem quite obvious, I feel it is worth restating to reinforce my belief in its message. There are two classic and essential steps that must take place prior to building a three-dimensional model, possibly the most important steps needed when shaping the land. These practices should be learned and relearned because they are critical when designing topography.

5-14
Shannon Nichol / GGN. North End Parks. Boston, Massachusetts, 2007. Study sketch. A slight lifting and lowering of the ground integrated an elevated porch with a slightly lower water feature and created planters that frame pathways as a welcome entry. [GGN]

5-15
GGN. North End Parks. The subtle "folding" of the land to create elevated edges makes North End Parks feel more comfortable and safe. [GGN]

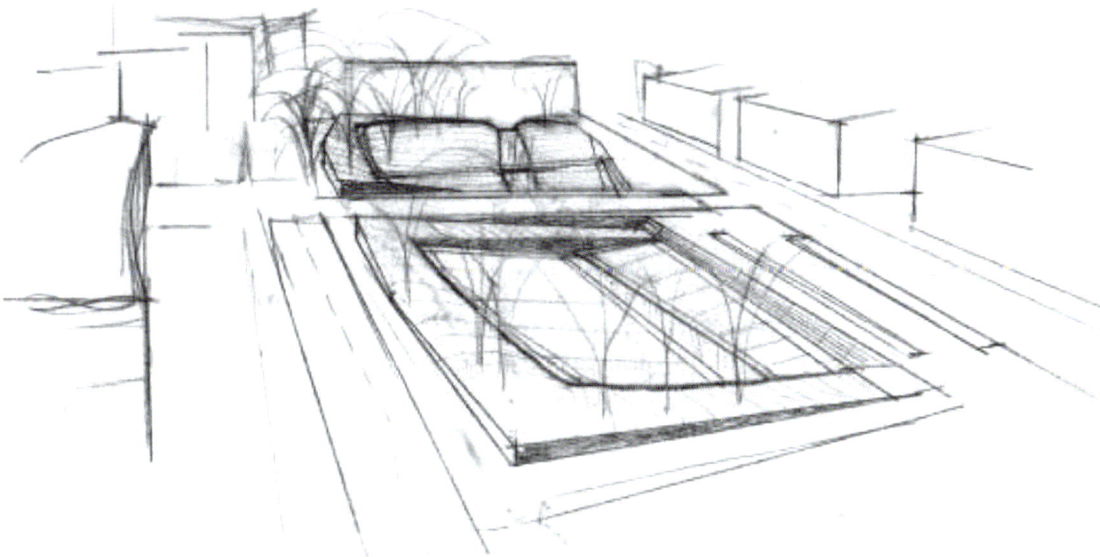

First: see the land. Draw both longitudinal and cross sections through the site; include representations of people as a constant indicator of relative dimensions, especially heights [5-16]. From these views, understand what the occupant and visitor will see and experience as determined by the new landform. This is among the best ways for beta testing the flow, or lack thereof, of both the topography and the spaces that result. Do the spaces feel comfortable, or are they oddly proportioned and unpleasant when inhabited?

Second: read the land. With your eyes as close to the level of the plan as possible, review the proposed contours and read the topography in perspective [5-17). That this is a low-budget method for viewing the movement of the landform does not diminish its value as a step prior to the three-dimensional model. Adjust the contour of the terrain while viewing it in perspective rather than when reverting to the plan or even the section.

The three-dimensional model—whether physical or digital—is an essential tool for studying and designing the land in an immersive way, a method impossible to achieve using two-dimensional drawings or simulations alone [5-18]. Too many built landscapes lose their sense of dimensionality and scale—as well as their emotional and experiential connection—by having been studied solely in two dimensions. Cardboard, tagboard, modeling clay, 3D printing, and virtual reality are effective tools for defining and crafting the contours of the land. The key point is to simulate the terrain in three dimensions as accurately as possible during the course of design. Shifting back and forth among the various drawing types while refining the design can help overcome the limits of each, while benefiting from their advantages. The goal is to understand the experience of the body within the bounded and unbounded spaces and places we design, and to configure the land in accordance with that understanding.

Even when working in constrained settings, landscape architects serve as the storytellers of the land. By training ourselves to see the landscape as expansive and deep, and to truly see it in perspective as well as apprehend it through senses such as sound and touch, we can narrate a story with a design that displays a reverence for the larger landscape. Even when limited by property lines and other physical or political restrictions, these landscapes can stimulate feelings of moving through/over/on the greater topography beyond the site, and thus help others understand the story of the place and strengthen their relationship to it.

5-16
Gustafson Guthrie Nichol. CityCenterDC. Washington, DC, 2013 Section taken through the grand fountain to study its scale relative to the human body. [GGN]

5-17
Gustafson Guthrie Nichol. Long Beach Civic Center. Long Beach, California, 2021. Reviewing and reshaping contours in perspective provides an initial understanding of the topography. [GGN]

5-18
Kathryn Gustafson / GGN. Lurie Garden. Chicago, Illinois, 2004. Clay study model. [GGN]

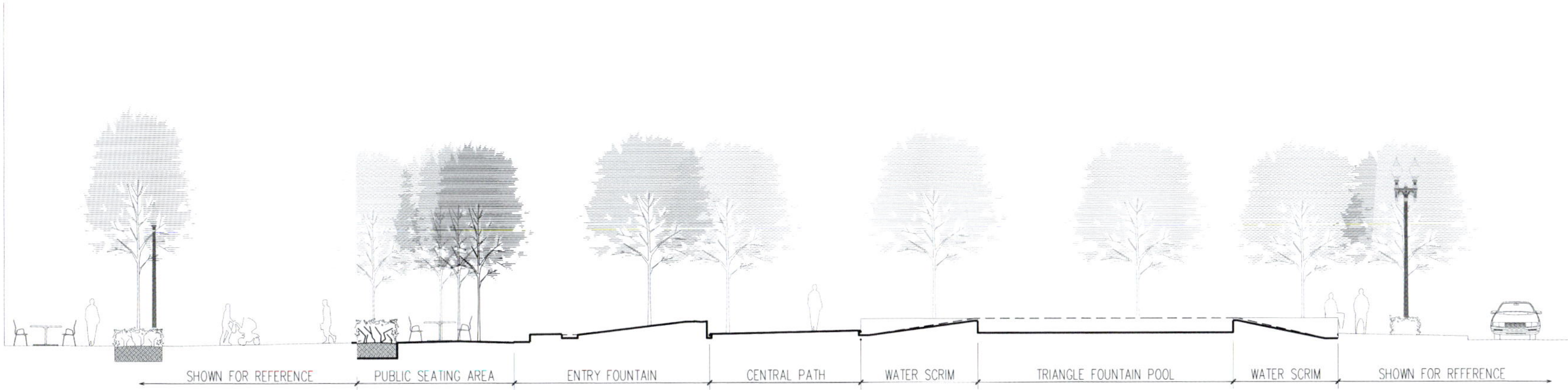
SHOWN FOR REFERENCE
PUBLIC SEATING AREA
ENTRY FOUNTAIN
CENTRAL PATH
WATER SCRIM
TRIANGLE FOUNTAIN POOL
WATER SCRIM
SHOWN FOR REFFERENCE

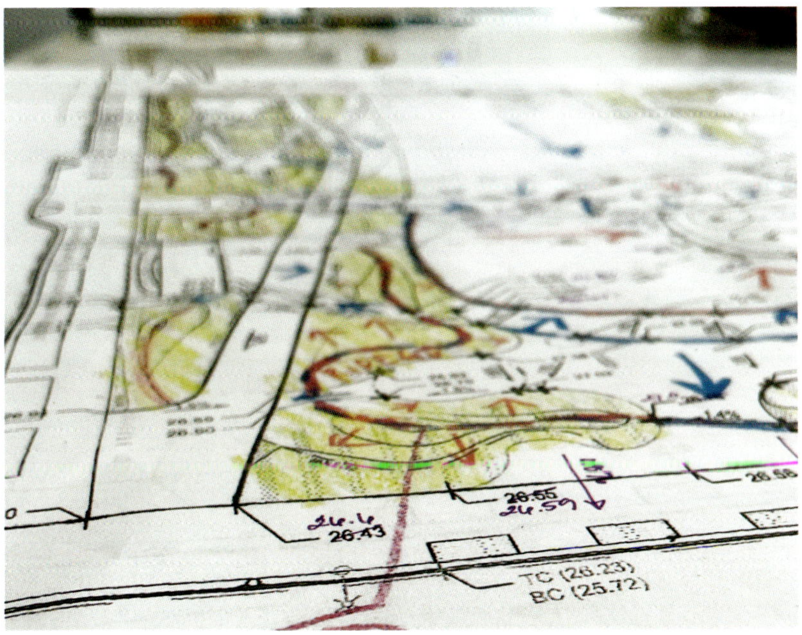
TC (26.23)
BC (25.72)

6. UNLEVELING THE LAND, ON SAND AND LAVA

KARL KULLMANN

We tend to use the word "topography" as synonymous with "landform," but topography as represented on a map usually includes other natural and cultural features evident in the landscape. The term "topography" derives from the Greek: *topos*, place, joined with *graphia*, to write, describe, or draw lines that capture a place, as does a map. To begin, I would like to draw some lines through places that have influenced my topographic thinking, as a background for the ideas to follow.

The field of landscape architecture is a bit off the main track of destination professions. Instead, it's a field that you somehow find or that somehow finds you. Three brief topographic origin stories will establish how it found me. The first of these landscapes is Kings Park and Botanic Garden in Perth, Western Australia, situated in the traditional lands of the Whadjuk people. My father was superintendent of the park, and my family lived on its 1,000-acre grounds for some thirty years. We lived in the gatehouse on the main avenue into the park, the only house on the highest hill, in the middle of the city [6-1]. As a recent immigrant from Germany who spoke no English, my father began work at the park by digging holes. Modifying topography became basic to him. One could say that he dug his way up in rank, first to become head nurseryman and eventually the park's superintendent. By necessity, he became an autodidact landscape architect with a drafting table prominently installed in his office. Whenever some part of the park needed improvement, he would draw it up, take it to the site, and instruct the work teams on how to implement it.

His style was unconsciously influenced by the wood turning that was his hobby, and his designs were reminiscent of those of the beaux-arts tradition. He most definitely had not received the modernist memo. Although it was called a park, 90 percent of the sandy terrain was—and remains—the natural remnant bushland originally reserved as a source of firewood, bushland that remarkably has survived in the heart of a sprawling city of two million people. As I grew up I drew my own lines through the bushland, with secret trails that followed the lay of the land and connected my home with the river, the city center, the primary school, the high school, and ultimately the university.

6-1
Perth, Australia, 1896. Bathymetric and topographic map of Perth's Swan River and surrounds. [State Library Victoria]

The second topographic influence derived from my family's extensive journeys into the Australian interior, the Outback. Taking one of Kings Park's Land Rovers, we would brave the dust, heat, and incessant flies in search of what I understand now to be remoteness. Looking to the endless horizon through the window of the Land Rover, I would imagine that we were headed to some place marked by dramatic topography and more evident signs of civilization. That we'd been going down the same dirt track for a week and hadn't encountered another vehicle—let alone a mountain or a townsite—should have been a clear sign that this was not the case. In this vast, ancient, worn-down landscape, the topographic rewards arrived in extremely small portions. Surrounded by 1,000 miles of scrub in every direction, a small, dry gully or a lonely outcrop is all you might get for your prolonged efforts. But while the terrain at first appeared to be featureless, in time one learned to appreciate and read its nuances, and to understand the forces that produced them.

My third formative topographic line involves the conversion of terrain-reading the Outback and Kings Park into a sport. From about age six I competed in orienteering, an athletic sport centered in the Nordic countries and involving "analog navigation," unaided by GPS (Global Positioning System). When orienteering one reads the map, uses the compass, and interprets the lay of the land to traverse the terrain in minimum time. Growing up amid the sandy topography of Kings Park, I had spent much of my life in an orienteering map. To know the logic of one's own terrain is the ultimate home-field advantage. But on the flip side, when orienteering in other parts of the world, one must quickly find one's bearings in new terrain. I competed with varying success on sand dunes, complex granite shelves, Karst limestone, alpine slopes, and—most challenging of all—the post-glacial terrain of Scandinavia.

These topographic experiences were formative to my understanding of the land; in particular, they heightened my interest in complex and nuanced terrain, how human activity has shaped the land, and how landform has shaped behavior. Landform's ability to shape behavior is wonderfully demonstrated by Gas Works Park in Seattle, where landscape architect Richard Haag reshaped a former industrial site into an unprogrammed topography available for multiple uses and interpretations. These are the "uncommitted plastic forms" that Kevin Lynch considered a necessary aspect of public space, although the landform

6-2
Lützow 7 Landscape Architecture.
Park Rabet.
Leipzig, Germany, 2000.
Cobbled desire path subtly impressed into landform.
[Karl Kullmann]

provides subtle clues to behavior on-site.[1] In that sense, Gas Works Park is a free and liberated landscape that allows us to perform as if on stage, in this case a stage with a rather grand view. Subtle landform that guides behavior through motion is also found at Park Rabet in East Leipzig, Germany. Derived from the desire lines worn over the years, the park's cross-paths are simply imprinted down into a ground elevated above the postwar rubble [6-2]. Setting the path slightly below grade reinforced the weight of human passage, with the contours themselves indicators of people's movement, much in the manner of a watercourse.

And if we think in terms of water, and how and where it flows, the projects and terrains discussed above all represent non-dendritic landforms that lack the converging, branching structure formed by moving water. We are more familiar with the dendritic landforms that emerge where rills merge with creeks, creeks with rivers, and rivers with the sea. Without the organizational structure of surface water flows, non-dendritic landform is more variable and unpredictable. It is a kind of terrain usually associated with porous substrata such as limestone and landfill, but also sand and lava, as addressed below. But first I will briefly discuss a garden project that used dendritic flow, although literally and figuratively reversing it.

The Garden of the Forking Paths was created for the International Horticultural Exposition in Xi'an, China, in 2011.[2] In the collective Chinese imagination, rivers flow from west to east, from the plateau to the sea, but the Chan-Ba River, upon whose floodplain the garden was situated, appears to flow in reverse—from east to west. In the garden, hydrological mythology was conceptually amplified. The water's natural tendency to converge was reversed through a system of divergent flows of both paths and runnels [6-3]. Read metaphorically as an allegory for life, the bifurcating flows question a worldview in which history coheres to form a meta narrative. The garden was entered through a single aperture in a bamboo grove, from which the choices escalated as one path metamorphosed into thirty [6-4]. Each path was accompanied by bifurcating water channels that fanned out and finally emptied into a lake. As we learned, it's quite difficult to divide paths of water because water molecules want to stick together and follow the path of least gravitational resistance. In response, and quite on their own, visitors found stones to use as makeshift sluices with which to rearrange the courses of the water.

From the divergence of water, the story now shifts to the divergence of lava on the Big Island of Hawai'i, most of which rests below the ocean as the accumulation of a million years of lava flow [6-5]. Sited above a "hot spot" the island remains in continual evolution, as demonstrated by the 1990 eruption above the residential neighborhood of Kalapana Gardens. As the lava flowed downward from the volcano to the sea, it was stopped by an existing ridge that caused it to pool laterally. Eventually, the entire neighborhood was buried beneath 50 feet of lava, while the coastline was extended by 1,000 feet. Although almost all its buildings were wiped out of existence, Kalapana Gardens as a community wasn't wiped off the map. The original topography of the homesites had been entirely effaced, but on paper the boundaries that marked land tenure survived [6-6]. What resulted was a radical superimposition of the old lot lines upon this newly formed and unruly topography. As the residents slowly returned to retake their property, vestiges of the old street lines were bulldozed through the lava. People have even reoccupied the land in a way that at first appears completely indiscriminate, but actually complies with the prior lot lines inscribed by law.

The new wave of homesteading that followed mixed tiny homes, converted shipping containers, old buses, flat-pack huts, and land-locked boats—anything that could be repurposed for habitation [6-7]. As the lava continued to cool, crack, and settle, each of these structures functioned as a life raft. Everyone and everything was self-sufficient because utilities were nonexistent. And it's all self-made because no agency will insure structures on the site; it takes a particular kind of lava pioneer to inhabit this basalt desert. Everyone builds light, ready to leave at a moment's notice when the lava flows inevitably return. The pull of the ground is compelling, however, and if they stay long enough the residents step off their life rafts and begin to modify and interact with the igneous terrain. They start by scraping, leveling, and reshaping the lava to form useful spaces on its surface. When they start fashioning gardens, you know these re-pioneers are really putting down new roots.

Halfway around the world, on a volcanic island in the North Atlantic, the work of two dedicated gardeners showed just how to put down roots in lava. Situated off the southern coast of Iceland and blessed with a magnificent natural harbor, the tiny island of Heimaey is home to one of Iceland's

6-3
Karl Kullmann. *The Garden of the Forking Paths.* Xi'an, China, 2011. Exploded axonometric. Layers from bottom to top: landform, paths, runnels, planting, trees.

6-4
Karl Kullmann. *The Garden of the Forking Paths.* Garden entrance with diverging paths visible in the foreground and diverging landform in the background.

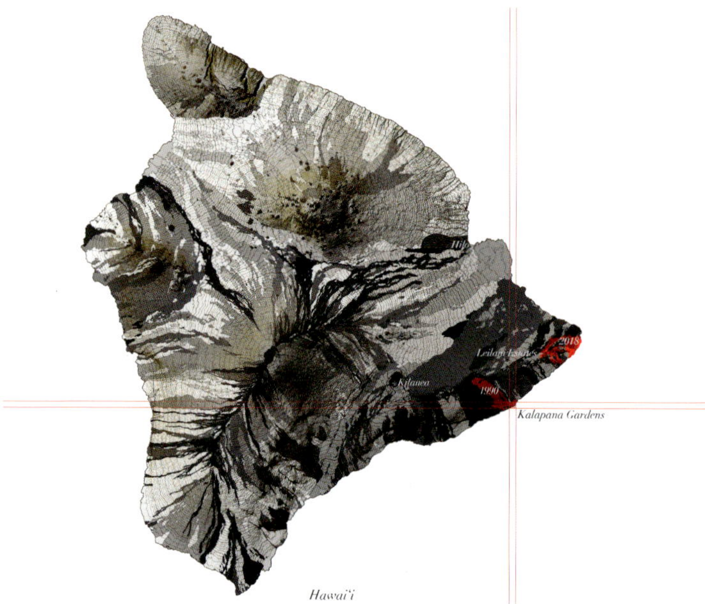

Hawai'i

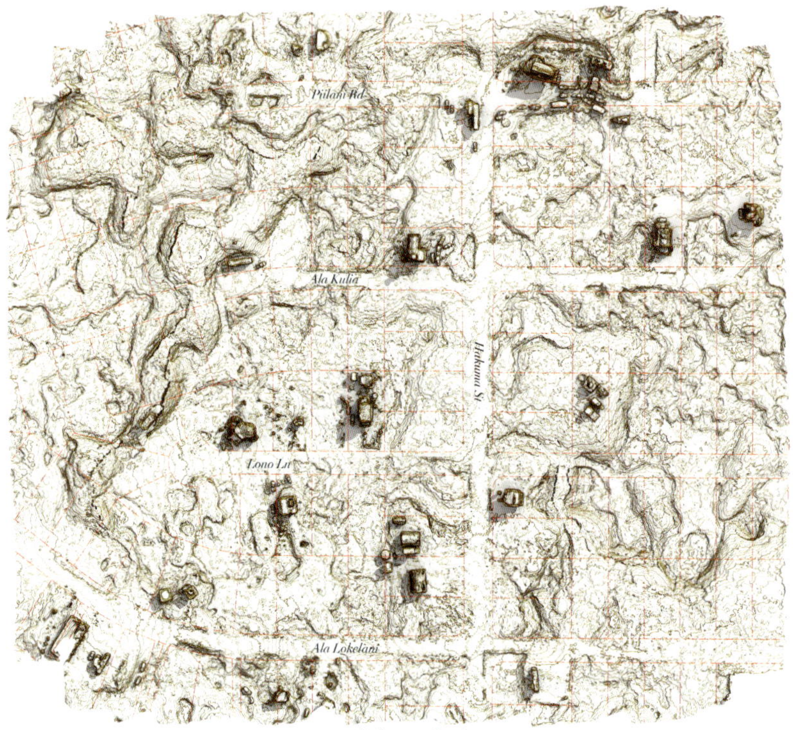

Kalapana Gardens

most important fishing ports. It also straddles the highly seismically active Mid-Atlantic Ridge, which, in the middle of one night in 1973, erupted without warning and opened a one-mile-long lava fissure across the island. Happily, within about five hours the boats of the local fishing fleet had safely evacuated all of the island's 5,000 inhabitants. Within a week, a cinder cone—later named Eldfell, or fire-mountain—grew in height to over 500 feet. As the eruption progressed, lava advanced at a rate of twenty feet per day and threatened to inundate the town and seal off the entrance to the harbor, rendering it a lake.

Instead of sailing away for good, a team of industrious "geological agents"—the term is Anne Winston Spirn's—dared to return and fight fire with water.[3] In what at first appeared quixotic, a plan was hastily hatched to hose down the advancing front of the lava with vast quantities of seawater to cool and redirect its path. Incredibly, it worked. By the time the eruption ended six months later, the island had expanded in surface area by one-fifth; the harbor had been saved. In fact, its amenities had been improved by a new lava breakwater that now sheltered the port's entrance from Arctic storms.

As displaced residents began returning to Heimaey, the question became what to do with all this new ground: a still-cooling and menacing, black mass of twisted topography. To help reestablish their sense of place, the residents were invited to adopt a patch of lava. After much searching across difficult ground, a local couple, Erlendur (Elli) Stefánsson and Guõfinna (Gauja) Ólafsdóttir, found a sunken dell flanked by a distinctively animistic rocky protrusion that they named Gaujulundur [Gauja's Grove]. Stefánsson and Guõfinna spent the next twenty years digging and reshaping the lava bed, propagating about a hundred species of plants, and introducing various garden features that included paths, a gnome, a fishpond, a gabled wooden shed, several follies, and picket fences [6-8]. While the recessed shape of the dell offered some shelter from the incessant northernly and southernly gales, Stefánsson and Guõfinna augmented this natural protection by constructing windbreaks to the east and west. Together, these features created a semipermeable frame around the garden: in part topography, in part fence [6-9].

The idea of the garden has expanded over the millennia with varied degrees of enclosure that have ranged from the cloistered garden of the medieval period to the open horizons of the seventeenth-century French formal garden. One of the beautiful things about Gaujulundur is that it combines

(opposite left) **6-5**
Accumulated lava flow map. Big Island, Hawai'i. The 1990 flows at Kalapana Gardens and more recent flows at Leilani Estates are shown in red. [Karl Kullmann]

(opposite right) **6-6**
Kalapana Gardens. Topographic relief map. Original property boundaries are shown in red. [Karl Kullmann]

6-7
Kalapana Gardens. Reinhabiting the lava. [Karl Kullmann]

Gaujulundur

both internal and external orientations, despite being to a certain degree carefully framed on all sides.

As opposed to just a rock, a garden affirms a human commitment to a place. Once the gardener plants a garden, he or she must stay and shepherd its growth or it will soon go rogue or die. And yet gardens always seem to get away from the gardener, never quite developing according to plan, though often for the better. As geological agents, gardeners are always modifying the topography of their place, reshaping hills and sculpting depressions. Much of the distinctive character of the Gaujulundur and Kalapana Gardens derives from this topographical manipulation that evolves over time, the product of hardy individuals working at a human scale on a labor of love.

When we get organized and start planning—and there is no threat of the lava's return—our geological labor reshapes landforms on an industrial scale, which is not necessarily a bad thing. Consider San Francisco, where the city's grid famously contrasts with the unruly topography below it. Florence Lipsky observes how San Francisco's urban quality resides precisely in the grid's basic incompatibility with the hills.[4] Or consider Hong Kong, where through sheer necessity construction continues even on severely steep slopes; exceptionally precipitous inclines are engineered to ensure their stability against landslides and mapped in a database thereafter [6-10].

This apparent equilibrium between nature and culture is an exception rather than the norm, however. Many cities have breached the natural limits of reason in their quest for level or stable land. In Central and South America it is often the people of the lowest socioeconomic stratum who are relegated to the steepest slopes, while closer to home it's more often the reverse: enabled by "mountain cropping" terracing techniques, the wealthy retreat to the hills and look over those in the flatlands [6-11].[5]

While the conspicuous excess and flat/steep binary of terracing characterizes many landscapes in the American West, elsewhere in the world it's not so dichotomous. In Nagasaki, Japan, for example, low-density suburban terraces have commandeered preexisting terraces formerly used for agriculture. The case of Nagasaki also illustrates how suburban terracing is not simply solved by urban densification. Even as the city's aging and shrinking population moves downtown from the surrounding hills, new terraced suburbs continue to

6-8
Erlendur Stefánsson and Guðfinna Ólafsdóttir. Gaujulundur. Heimaey, Iceland, ca. 1980–present. Sheltered lava garden with Dragon Rock visible in the background. [Karl Kullmann]

6-9
Erlendur Stefánsson and Guðfinna Ólafsdóttir. Gaujulundur. Topographic relief map of Gaujulundur. Constructed windbreaks to the east and west shown in red. [Karl Kullmann]

6-10
Mid-Levels neighborhoods.
Hong Kong, 2016.
Slope engineering database.
Stabilized slopes are shown
as dark-gray areas and
retaining walls as red lines.
[Karl Kullmann]

6 11
Las Vegas, Nevada, 2016. Terraced earthworks prepared for suburban development. [Karl Kullmann]

6-12
Nagasaki, Japan, 2015. Extreme suburban terracing in a new neighborhood on the outskirts of the city. [Karl Kullmann]

be created on the periphery. These newer developments feature massive terraces that hardly encourage a chat with one's neighbor without a cell phone [6-12].

Returning to Perth, where the underlying sandy terrain is continuously undulating, it's a similar story. There's no clear mountainous frame, no dichotomy of flat-versus-sloped land, just sand dunes of varying ages and topographic complexity. And due to decades of population growth and uninhibited suburban sprawl, the city has extended 100 kilometers up and down the coast from the center in Kings Park where I grew up [6-13]. Much of that expansion has been achieved by stripping away all the native coastal heath and remodeling the land into megalithic, terraced earthworks of retaining walls and perfectly flat building lots. Termed "land benching" by the local industry, this mining-derived practice clears the way for standardized tract housing to be plotted without respect for the local topography.

The contours that are ironed out of the terrain are stacked within the retaining walls that border each parcel, isolating each residence as if a stone fortress. The resulting streetscapes fail to meet basic urban-design standards for livable neighborhoods, and moreover also fail to create any sense of place. And yet the act of leveling itself is not necessarily the problem, since seeking or making level ground is a primal act of inhabitation. Throughout history we have actively levelled the ground to sleep for the night, to grow crops, or to found settlements. Viewed through this lens, level-building pads still have a place in architectural site works. As Norman K. Booth has observed, a building often appears most "stable and comfortable" when situated on level ground. In contrast, buildings set on columns to touch the ground lightly may appear to cling precariously to the hillside.[6] The catch is that while this may hold true for one-off dwellings on large lots, the impact of site leveling quickly escalates when repeated across many dwellings at suburban densities.

Suburban-style development in Perth predates the practice of land benching, which really began only about two decades ago. Until then it was normal for housing parcels to retain their natural, unlevelled topography and even to retain some native vegetation. So, what changed? First, as land values increased, the city expanded into areas of more rugged topography where development had hitherto been prohibitively expensive. Second, coupled with standardized construction techniques, the popularization of the modernist concept of indoor-outdoor continuity reconstituted the garden as an extension of the house's

6-13
Perth, Australia, 2014. Topographic map of the northern half of the city. The sandy coastal plain is bounded by the Indian Ocean to the west, and an ancient granite escarpment to the east. [Karl Kullmann]

6-14
Perth, Australia, 2014. Aerial view of coastal suburban development. The case-study sites for future development are outlined in red. [Karl Kullmann]

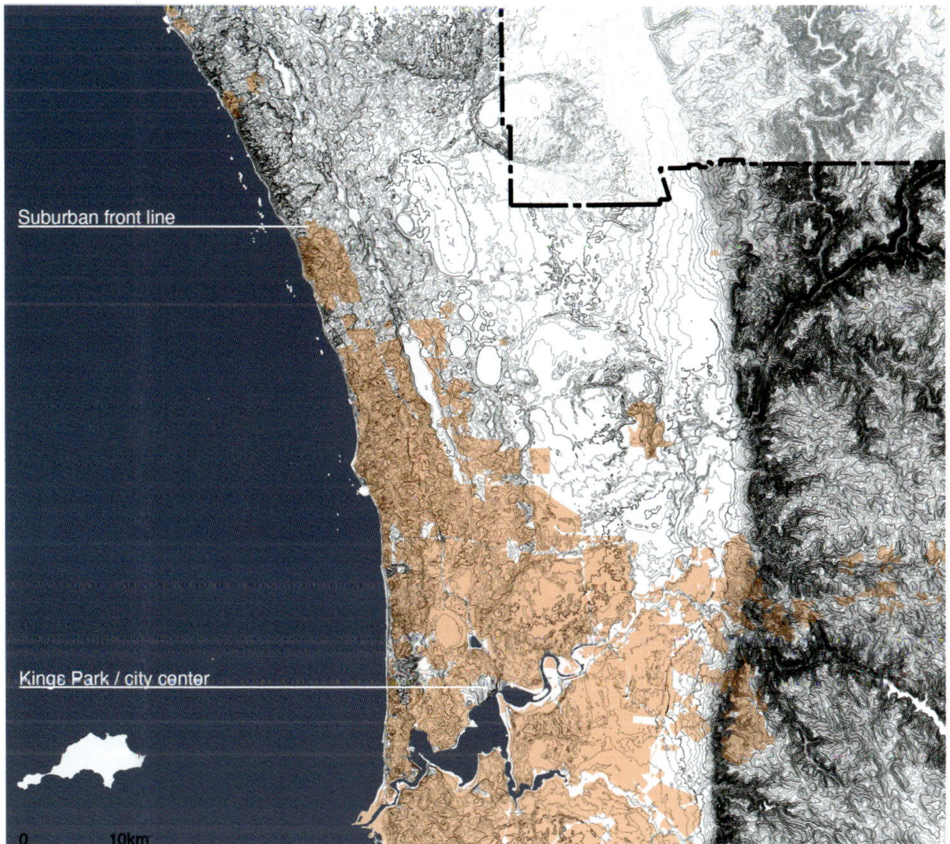
Suburban front line
Kings Park / city center
0 10km

floor plate. And third, Perth has witnessed a significant increase in plot ratios, that is, the relationship of the size of the building footprint to the area of the plot.[7]

Until the mid-twentieth century, a small house of roughly 1,000 square feet occupied a large lot with plenty of room for its stone foundation to accommodate any topographic nuance. By the 1970s, houses were growing in size and the lots were getting smaller, although the adoption of split-level residential plans absorbed some topographic differences. The functional yard of the suburbia of the past, with its place for drying clothes, housing chickens, and perhaps a well as a source of water, became a space for entertaining and other social activities. Since the 2000s, houses have grown to occupy up to 80 percent of the parcel. That is to say, the building footprint and lot size have been rendered almost congruent, with the retaining wall around the parcel boundary essentially serving as the foundation for the house.

So, why is terracing a bad thing? For one, it does not permit the keeping of remnant vegetation. Some new developments have tried to retain some trees, commonly species such as the locally endemic Jarrah (*Eucalyptus marginata*). As they don't like their roots trod upon, however, these trees often survive only about five years and have been retained primarily for marketing purposes. Also lost from terracing is the biotic layer that has required hundreds of years to accrue, even if it's only very thin. And there's also a loss of the phenomenological value of rough terrain converted to terraces, a loss of what Kevin Lynch called the "topographical gradients," by which we navigate and create a sense of place and identification.[8]

A series of case studies on a sandy coastal development site at Perth's northern suburban frontier explored how past approaches to the development of suburbs might be adapted to mitigate or reduce the impact of retaining walls and improve topographic expression in these suburban developments [6-14]. After modeling the existing layout on the current topography, I considered different ways to plot a community based on different historical models, only two of which can be illustrated here due to limited space. The studies matched the yield of the developer and worked with industry-standard low- and medium-density housing types. While it would have been easier to simply propose housing everyone in a single residential tower or to curtail urban expansion altogether, the study's aim was to be relevant to current practices.

One scenario adapted the grid-iron layout common to prewar suburbs and draped it over the terrain. While admittedly requiring more retaining walls, the use of split-level lots expressed the terrain as a pixelated form while maintaining good urban legibility and connections [6-15]. Another scenario referenced the earliest informal coastal fishing settlements and routed roads along the swale lines with dwellings set on columns on the surrounding slopes. This scenario exhibits a high degree of topographic expression but necessitates the rethinking of housing-construction methods, as well as accepting a layout less orderly than the typical one [6-16]. The final study retained a significant landform that bisected the site as a combination of public open space and very-low-density rural lots. While this scenario enabled a tangible area of natural topography to remain, the trade-off was the low topographic expression of the standard benching practices that were required elsewhere to reach the developer's total yield.

Several consistent themes emerged from these case studies. The first is that standard-issue housing design and construction remain a significant hurdle for creating more topographically expressive suburbs. While several Australian architects have designed houses that lightly touch the earth, they remain, for the most part, custom-designed residences for wealthy clients on large rural or bush lots. Thus far, few solutions have proven applicable to the more compact suburb. The second is that topographic expression is often not entirely compatible with contemporary urban-design doctrine that implicitly prioritizes orderly urban plans. This stance should be interrogated, and perhaps loosened, to allow a greater flexibility for planning streets, lots, and building types and forms. There's a compelling demographic reason for doing this as well: today, we live in far more diverse arrangements than standard-issue three-bedroom bungalows with 2.3 people per household. Designs that connect a diversity of housing types and sizes to a diversity of landforms would benefit both suburban life and topographic expression.

In this regard, sand could learn from lava. While the sandy suburbs of Perth are geologically and geographically half a world away from the lavascapes of Hawai'i and Iceland, they nevertheless offer transferable lessons. The eclectic tiny homes of Kalapana Gardens and the sunken garden at Gaujulundur demonstrate what is possible when communities are incorporated into unruly topographies rather than land that has been ironed out. And while both exemplify frontier exceptionalism, they offer tantalizing insights into how we might reimagine the historical relation between the building of cities and the process of clearing and leveling ground. In the unleveled city, topography becomes a medium through which to invest in one's urban environment—and be inspired: to shape a sense of place, both individually and collectively.

Notes

1 Kevin Lynch, "The Openness of Open Space," in György Kepes, ed., *The Arts of Environment* (New York: Braziller, 1972), p. 112.

2 Although designed with graduate students as a speculative exercise that was not intended to be built, the garden was–miraculously–realized. While the complex grading and hardscape were very well executed, sadly, the planting was never finished.

3 Anne Whiston Spirn, *The Granite Garden* (New York: Basic Books, 1984), p. 91.

4 Florence Lipsky, *San Francisco: The Grid Meets the Hills* (Paris: Editions Parenthèses, 1999).

5 "Mountain cropping" is a term coined by William Bronson to describe the earliest suburban terracing in California, which he interpreted as emblematic of environmental wastefulness in post–World War II industrialized society. William Bronson, *How to Kill a Golden State* (Garden City, NY: Doubleday, 1968).

6 Norman K. Booth, *Basic Elements of Landscape Architectural Design* (New York: Elsevier, 1983), p. 65.

7 These are Perth examples but US data is similar, given that Australian suburbanism is largely imported from the US with local adaptations.

8 Kevin Lynch, *The Image of the City* (Cambridge, MA: MIT Press, 1960), pp. 96–97.

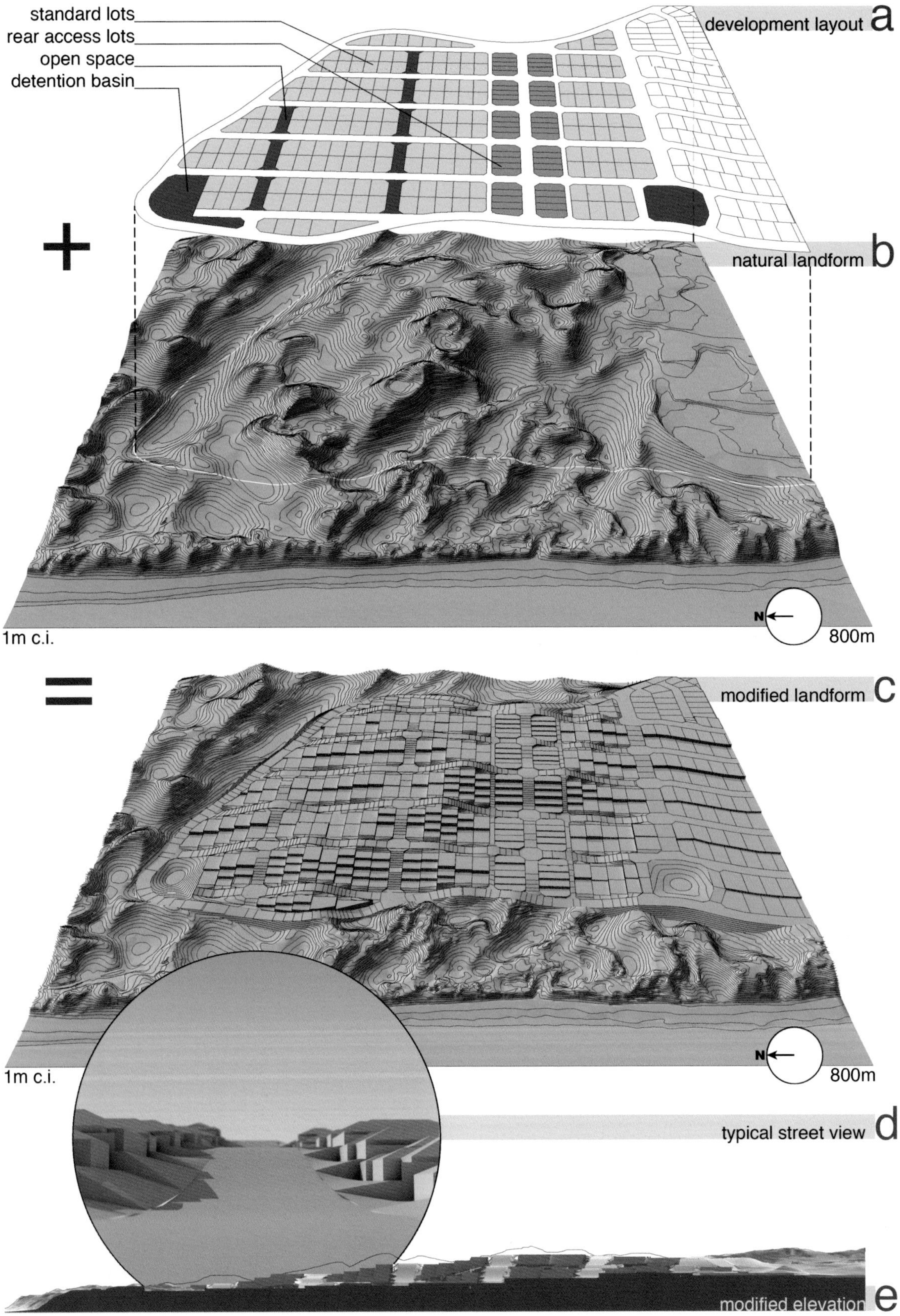

6-15
Grid-iron design scenario utilizing split-level development parcels. Perth, Australia, 2014. [Karl Kullmann]

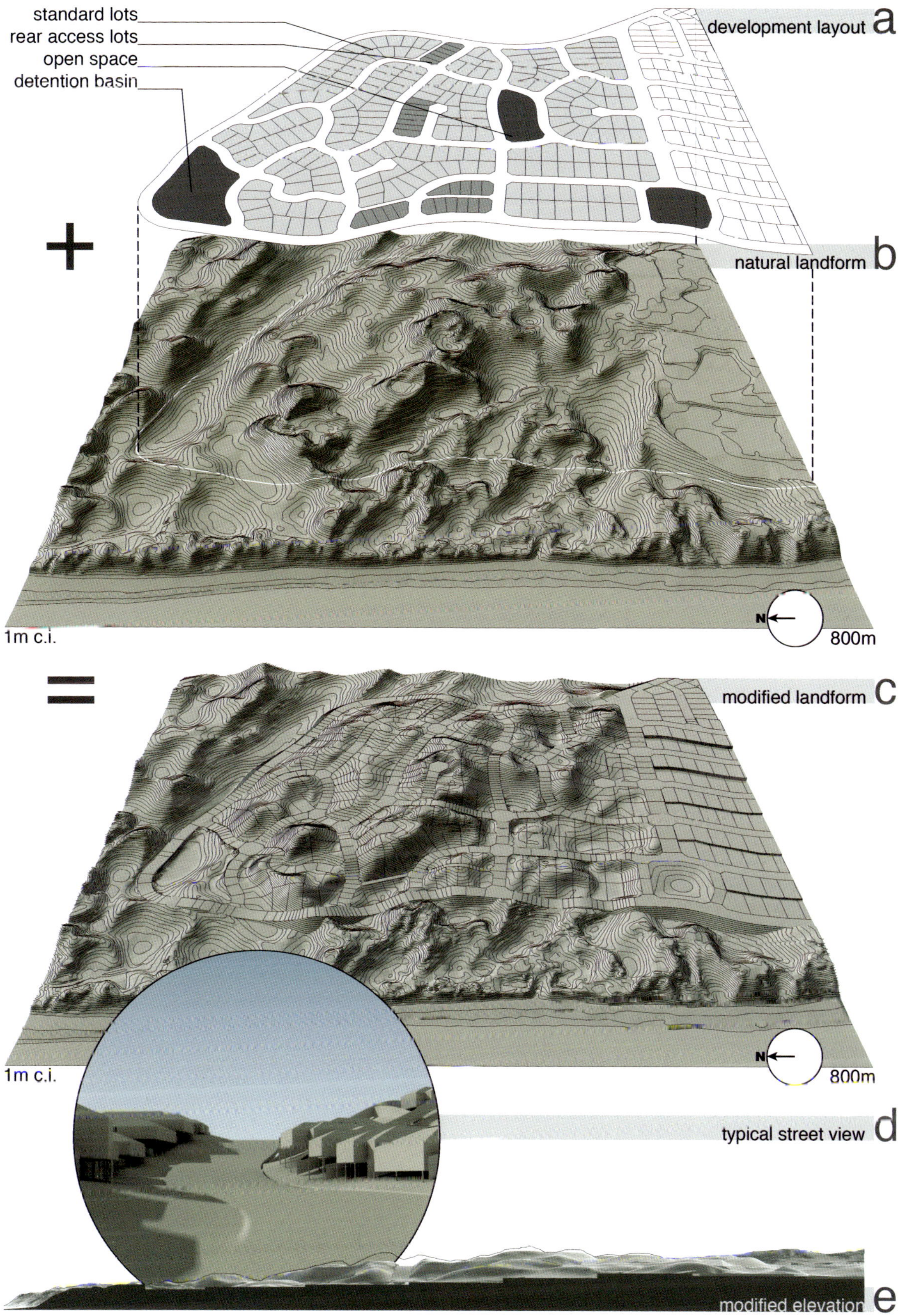

6-16
Swale design scenario with dwellings elevated on columns. Perth, Australia, 2014. [Karl Kullmann]

7. TEN TOPOGRAPHIC ACTS

MARC TREIB

7-1
Gunnar Asplund
and Sigurd Lewerentz.
Woodland Cemetery.
Enskede, Sweden, 1915–40.
[Maj Wetterstrand]

7-2
Emperor Gomizono-o et al.
Shugaku-in Imperial Villa.
Kyoto, Japan, 1660s–.
The Chitose bridge seen
from across the pond.

All photos by Marc Treib,
unless otherwise credited.

Broken Circle, Spiral Hill

Emmen, Netherlands
1971
Robert Smithson

7-3
Robert Smithson.
Broken Circle / Spiral Hill.
Emmen, Netherlands, 1971.
Broken Circle.

7-4
Robert Smithson.
Broken Circle / Spiral Hill.
Emmen, Netherlands, 1971.
Spiral Hill, highly overgrown.

The practice of "cut and fill" transforms topography by removing soil from a rise to fill a depression or level a slope. Ideally, by balancing extraction and deposit all soil remains on-site. In 1971, on the grounds of a sand and gravel quarry in the eastern Netherlands, artist Robert Smithson employed this practice to create an earthwork using only materials found on-site.

Believing that sufficient land had already been despoiled by construction and habitation, and with a predilection for interacting with disturbed terrain, Smithson rejected the offer of a park site for his participation in the 1970 Sonsbeek sculpture exhibition. Instead, Smithson chose a functioning quarry with a residual pond at its heart. His work would comprise two elements: one engaging the water on the quarry's northern shore, the second piled on the bank adjacent to it [7-3].

From a small peninsula that jutted into the pond, Smithson removed sand and gravel to isolate a spit of land shaped as the arc of a circle. From the bank, he dug a narrow canal with a corresponding curve. The resulting circular figure interlocked land and water in a positive/negative arrangement incorporating the opposition of forces represented by the yin/yang of Chinese philosophy. A rare erratic boulder, the product of the terminal moraine by which much of the Netherlands has been shaped, was appropriated as the center of Smithson's circle.

Smithson used the sand and gravel from excavating *Broken Circle*, augmented by the topsoil needed for vegetal growth, to shape *Spiral Hill* on the adjacent shore. The hill's tapering profile and path recall the spiral forms of the minaret of the ninth-century Mosque of al-Moutawakel in Samarra, Iraq, as well as the Tower of Babel, famously depicted in paintings by Pieter Bruegel the Elder [7-4].

The pairing of solid and void, not to mention water and land, confirms the broad range and power of forms that may result from even a basic reworking of topography, with materials neither imported nor removed from the site.

Shugaku-in Imperial Villa

Kyoto, Japan
1660s–
Emperor Gomizuno-o
and artisans

Walking along the road to the upper garden of this grand imperial landscape, the progression of views of the rice fields seen through the pine trees flickers past almost in the manner of a zoetrope: To the left of the road stands a giant wall of vegetation that at first view appears native to the hillside [7-5]. In fact, the hedges disguise a major earthwork: a gigantic dam constructed to retain the water of the ornamental pond at the heart of the villa's upper garden. Well-constructed, the dam has endured for over three and a half centuries, requiring only periodic repair. The use of "hide and reveal," a dramatic sequencing of views and features, heightens the effect of reaching the upper terrace, where a grand panorama of the garden and northern Kyoto is revealed [7-6].

The stepped hedges stabilize the soil while camouflaging the fabricated origins of the hillside dam; configured in stages, their forms diminish the sensed enormity of the venture. The mature trees that punctuate the lines of the hedges trace the passage of the seasons. In autumn, the maples are radiant with warm, almost flaming colors, and perhaps at this time the garden offers its most stunning effect. But the vegetation is also beautiful in other times of year, when wearing wearing only varying shades of green. The garden at the Shugaku-in Imperial Villa is spectacular in many ways, but few of them would have been possible without the sizable modification of the existing hillside topography.

7-5
Emperor Gomizono-o et al.
Shugaku-in Imperial Villa.
Kyoto, Japan, 1660s.
Stepped hedges conceal
the downhill face of the
earthen dam.

7-6
Emperor Gomizono-o et al.
Shugaku-in Imperial Villa.
The climax of the hide-
and-reveal sequence:
a panoramic view
over northern Kyoto.

Domaine de Dampierre

Dampierre-en-Yvelines, France
circa 1680s
André Le Nôtre (attributed)

In the early 1570s, Androuet de Cerceau published the château and grounds of Dampierre in his *Les plus excellents bastiments de France*, a landscape whose small river had been transformed into an imposing *pièce d'eau* by damming and reshaping its banks. A moat surrounds the château and its attached garden on all four sides, accompanied by a garden of much larger dimensions neatly divided into squares, each different in figure and planting. Extending to the southwest, withheld by a large dam that spans the valley, is a formally shaped lake that serves as both ornament and recreation ground.

Some credit André Le Nôtre with the complete reworking of the old terrain around 1683 to better accompany a new, more modern château designed by Jules Hardouin-Mansart. The existing structures, garden, and terrain provided the framework for the new plan, although Mansart's much larger château straddled the north bank of the lower zone, today left dry [7-7]. In turn, Le Nôtre's gardens extended southward across the valley, rising with the terrain on the opposite bank—an audacious reorientation of the historical plan and gardens [7-8, 7-9]. Although the historical gardens, still surrounded by channels of water, retain their shape, the richness of their original plantings has disappeared. The lake has been further regularized, and probably extended, to assume the form of a more purely shaped dog bone.

There is little doubt that realizing the first and subsequent designs of the Domaine de Dampierre involved significant efforts to move earth that redirected and reshaped water. The resulting terrain of solid and liquid both acknowledged and confronted the natural contours, while demanding the expenditure of enormous resources both human and technical. Lacking extensive vegetation, the domaine one encounters today grants the revised topography heightened prominence and even greater lucidity.

(opposite) **7-7**
André Le Nôtre.
Domaine de Dampierre.
Dampierre-en-Yvelines, France,
ca. 1683.
[Google Earth]

7-8
André Le Nôtre.
Domaine de Dampierre.
The dam creating the canal.

7-9
André Le Nôtre.
Domaine de Dampierre.
Landform across the valley seen
from beside the château.

Woodland Cemetery [Skogskyrkogården]

Enskede, Sweden
1915–40
Gunnar Asplund and
Sigurd Lewerentz

7-10
Gunnar Asplund and Sigurd Lewerentz. Woodland Cemetery. Enskede, Sweden, 1915–40. The memorial knoll viewed through the columns of the portico.

7-11
Gunnar Asplund and Sigurd Lewerentz. Woodland Cemetery. The retention pond with the memorial knoll beyond.

The design that won the 1915 competition to extend the South Stockholm Cemetery was dominated by a forest of trees that blanketed the site. From this continuous green canopy, clearings were cut to serve as the sites for the clusters of graves and the principal chapels. The land was neither pristine nor agricultural. Although originally formed as a terminal moraine, decades of gravel mining had significantly modified the primal contours. The winning competition entry by architects Gunnar Asplund and Sigurd Lewerentz positioned the main chapel on the site's highest point and graced it with a small plaza that in plan recalled the Piazza San Marco in Venice. While basically positive, the jury expressed its reservations concerning vehicular movement through the cemetery and the potential monotony resulting from a continuous cover of leaf and needle. Rethinking was necessary.

In revising their scheme, Lewerentz and Asplund first reworked the ground plane to better support the choreography of movement and spatial progressions, deftly employing compression and release as their primary tool [see 7-1]. Entering the cemetery grounds from the street, mourners and visitors traverse a semicircular exedra, then squeeze through a narrow space bounded on both sides by granite walls. Beyond these walls, the space dramatically opens into a great void that joins meadow and memorial knoll with the sky and clouds above. The modeling of the terrain is masterful, with the meadow flowing softly from the processional path at its northern edge to the memorial knoll to the south. From within the garden for urn burials, the view over the wall is unimpeded visually and psychologically bonded to the greater cemetery landscape [see 1-11].

The memorial knoll occupies the site originally assigned to the main chapel [7-10]. Viewed from the summit of the knoll, the line of three chapels reads as an architectonic retaining wall that halts the incursion of the pine forest into the meadow. At its foot lies a small pond that collects rainwater, snow melt, and seepage that varies in size with the weather and the time of year [7-11]. Its surface reflects the sky and knoll and doubles their presence. While many other features of the cemetery landscape are worthy of note—the extensive forest and the quality of the architecture, among them—at its base, literally and figuratively, is the ground in or on which the cemetery's ceremonies and practices are enacted.

Parc Jean Verlhac

Villeneuve-de-Grenoble,
France
1973
Michel Corajoud

7-12
Michel Corajoud.
Parc Jean Verlhac.
Grenoble, France, 1973.
Spaces defined by
earth and trees.

7-13
Michel Corajoud.
Parc Jean Verlhac.
Pond and aquatic features.

A year after successfully hosting the Winter Olympics in 1964, the city of Grenoble embarked on a project to construct 2,000 units of much-needed housing. Two years later, landscape architect Michel Corajoud and architects Henri Ciriani and Borjo Huidobro were commissioned to design the 50-acre park to accompany the new housing. Rubble from the site and from excavating the foundations of the buildings yielded a considerable volume of spoil, materials Corajoud wisely and economically sculpted a landscape of rises, hills, vegetation, and water.

The forms of this new, earthen landscape are hardly mere bumps in the terrain. Quite the contrary, they stand as geometricized hills, most of them circular in plan and graded into shallow hemispheres that at their summits reach thirty feet in height [7-12]. From their proximity, the hills coalesce as a landscape of regularized landforms whose total composition transcends the sum of its parts. Where the slope is too extreme, wooden stairs lead to the crests of the hills. Plantations of trees and shrubs complement the earth forms—vegetation always plays more than one role. Trees provide shade and spatial variation throughout the site, amplified by judiciously distributed shrubs of various heights. Shrubs and trees cover some hills to enhance their profile and discourage damage by foot traffic. In concert with the hills, designed woodlands veil,or at least soften, the presence of the mammoth apartment blocks—and set the park off as an independent terrain. Occupying the zones between the hills and the play areas, water parterres further enhance an already topographically rich environment [7-13].

The Parc Jean Verlhac is a prime example of transforming a seeming liability—tons of excavation spoil—into an asset, used positively and creatively to shape a new land simply by digging and piling in the right places, to shape the appropriate forms.

South Pointe Park

Miami Beach, Florida
2009
Hargreaves Associates

7-14
Hargreaves Associates (now HargreavesJones). South Pointe Park. Miami Beach, Florida, 2011. The promenade along Government Cut.

7-15
Hargreaves Associates. South Pointe Park. The path along the crest of the earth form.

7-16
Hargreaves Associates. South Pointe Park. [Google Earth]

The island city of Miami Beach is itself a topographic construction, made habitable by filling and elevating a barrier island on Biscayne Bay off the coast of Miami. With considerable fanfare, Carl G. Fisher and his partners developed the property in the early years of the twentieth century, converting a quagmire of sand and mangroves into a tropical resort whose hotel construction in the Art Deco style continued even through the years of the Depression. Troops trained or stationed in South Florida during World War II added to its population, which was given a further boost when Miami Beach again became a tourist destination in the immediate postwar years. In contrast to the glamorous hotels that lined Collins Avenue, South Beach remained more modest in its architecture and the net worth of its population. But with its renewed appeal to celebrities and tourists late in the twentieth century came the consequent rise in land values, which, in turn, led to increased density, taller buildings, and extensive redevelopment. To serve that enlarged population as well as those attracted by the park's open space and facilities, Hargreaves Associates (today HargreavesJones) reworked South Pointe Park.

Although there are many worthy aspects to the design—including dune restoration and water sequestration—the primary physical features of the 11-acre park are a relentlessly straight promenade at the tip of the island along Government Cut and a serpentine berm that recalls both the celebrated *Serpent Mound* in Ohio [see 1-11] and the bowed form of Robert Smithson's 1973 *Amarillo Ramp* in Texas [7-14, 7-15]. The mound begins in the west at grade and rises as it snakes toward the Atlantic Ocean. As it twists toward the east, the winding earth form embraces a children's play area and service building, then tapers and descends to meet grade near the dune restoration at the oceanfront [7-16].

Piling and grading order the park's features and many of its activity zones. A paved walkway traverses the length of the berm, grass-covered on both sides, along its crest. From its summit views of the park and its surroundings enfold the bay, the ocean, and Government Cut—depending on the direction of one's walk. South Pointe's serpentine mound demonstrates the ability of a simple form to at once structure and define space, while orchestrating movement and views by day—and even by night.

Weyerhaeuser Headquarters

Tacoma, Washington
1972
SWA / Peter Walker, landscape architects;
Edward Bassett, Skidmore, Owings & Merrill, architects

To secure level terrain from an existing slope is among the most commonly demanded topographic acts. Leveling can be accomplished through obliteration—flat ground created by displacing the mass of the hill—or through terracing. Terraces are most frequently created using cut and fill: taking soil from a higher part of the slope and depositing it below. The net result of this plus and minus operation totals zero: flat land. The site of the Weyerhaeuser forest products headquarters outside Tacoma, Washington, is a valley. Working with Edward "Chuck" Bassett of Skidmore, Owings & Merrill, landscape architects SWA, with Peter Walker as lead, conceived the building as a bar set perpendicular to the axis of the valley almost in the manner of an architectonic dam. East of the building, a new lake serves primarily ornamental purposes; to the west, the land was kept dry and planted with wild-flowers and grasses.

Rather than banishing to some remote spot the parking spaces required by those working in the building, or completely leveling the hillside, the slope was graded into parking terraces positioned at both the northern and southern ends of the building. The figure of the resulting site plan is roughly a Z in form. To avoid the need for major retaining walls, the terrace edges were graded to the soil's angle of repose, thereafter stabilized by blankets of ivy [7-17, 7-18].

Two rows of plane trees line each of the terraces and define walkways that gather employees and bring them to the building [see 7-17]. In addition to strengthening the boundary of each terrace, these allées create leafy filters through which to view the landscape, both proximate and distant. At the base of the trees along the walkway, additional patches of ivy join tree and ground, and support the rhythm created by those coming and going. The cumulative effect is arguably the most pleasant and attractive arrival, parking, and departure experience of any workplace, anywhere.

7-17
SWA / Peter Walker, landscape architects. Weyerhaeuser Headquarters. Tacoma, Washington, 1971. A path at the foot of the parking leads to the entrance. Parking terrace.

7-18
SWA / Peter Walker, landscape architects. Weyerhaeuser Headquarters. To avoid building retaining walls, the earth was banked at its angle of repose and planted with ground cover.

Moerenuma Park

Sapporo, Japan
1988–2015
Isamu Noguchi,
conception;
Shoji Sadao,
Jun'ichiro Kawamura
and Architects 5,
realization

Several months before his death in 1988, Isamu Noguchi received the commission to design a new park in Sapporo, the prefectural capital of Japan's northern island of Hokkaido. Offered his choice of three possible sites, Noguchi opted for a landfill on the northeastern corner of the city on which some conversion activities were already underway. In his remaining time he made numerous studies and achieved a design he regarded as definitive. For seventeen years thereafter, Jun'ichiro Kawamura of Architects 5 in Tokyo, Shoji Sadao at the Noguchi Garden Museum in Long Island City, and the Sapporo parks department guided the completion of Noguchi's original vision as best they could under the constraints imposed by the site and the budget. Fortunately, the terrain resulting from decades of dumping was primarily nontoxic; these deposits were augmented by clean fill fortuitously gathered from excavations for Sapporo's new subway system then under construction.

The design brief called for creating a mountain, fittingly named Moere Mountain [7-19]. In conceiving the park Noguchi revisited several designs from his past, mixing them with new features, resulting in new terrain. Here, he was finally to realize, in modified form, his *Play Mountain*, first proposed in 1933. Originally destined for an unspecified site in New York City, the design was now realized on a suburban landfill at a scale far greater than initially conceived. A slope on the rear side of the hill accommodates those wishing to reach the summit but who are unable or unwilling to mount the granite steps on its primary face. The amphitheater was modeled as a huge sheet of earth, inclined for concerts and other events with large audiences. *Tetra Mound*, a hemispherical dome covered with grass and capped by a colossal steel tripod, welcomes visitors who enter the park from the north [7-20]. In all, Moerenuma Park probably hosts the world's largest collection of recreational earth forms that may also qualify as sculpture.

Elevations in the landscape such as those at Moerenuma face the chronic problems of erosion and dissipation. Yet despite the harsh northern winters, the steepness of some slopes, and the popularity of the park, these giant earth forms in Sapporo have endured and even thrived. The lesson accompanying this happy ending seems to be that any wasteland can be made useful and durable, and if done really right, even joyful.

7-19
Isamu Noguchi, conception; Shoji Sadao, Jun'ichiro Kawamura, and Architects 5, realization. Moerenuma Park. Sapporo, Japan, 2017. Moere Mountain seen from Play Mountain.

7-20
Isamu Noguchi. Moerenuma Park. *Tetra Mound*

Natura Garden, Parque Bicentenario

Azcapotzalco,
Mexico City, Mexico
2011
Mario Schjetnan /
Grupo de Diseño
Urbanos

7-21
Mario Schjetnan / Grupo de Diseño Urbano. Bicentennial Park. Mexico City, Mexico, 2011. New soil, piled to the appropriate depth, blankets the concrete cap.

7-22
Mario Schjetnan / Grupo de Diseño Urbano. Bicentennial Park. Today the mature trees obscure the presence of the soil brought to the site to ensure their growth.

Vacated in 1990, the land of the former Pemex oil refinery in Mexico City was so polluted that in some areas it was impossible to ameliorate the soil or bury it beneath a layer of clean fill. The only remaining solution was to cap the polluted land with a massive concrete slab three feet thick. In conceiving the program for the sports fields, stadium, greenhouses, and sample *chinampa*—all part of the proposed 136-acre park—landscape architect Mario Schjetnan argued that a botanical garden showcasing Mexico's rich palette of flora would be vital for truly commemorating the nation's bicentennial. This botanical zone would also include an arboretum displaying representative species of trees from all parts of the country [7-21].

Although the concrete cap offered a literal tabula rasa for the new design, it did nothing to support the growth of trees, especially large trees. Different species required different volumes of earth imported to the site and subsequently graded as a landscape whose depths and contours had been determined by the needs of the individual families of tree. This variation in the required depth and volume resulted in a softly undulating landscape strictly determined by botanical necessity [7-22]. Today the mature trees appropriately obscure the contours—after all, they are the reason for the garden—diminishing the presence of the topography that plays a decisive role in supporting their existence. But Mario Schjetnan's solution to a functional problem far surpassed mere necessity; need only instigated and provided the basis for this new landscape shaped by both reason and poetry.

Paseo del Mar Punta Pite

Zaballar, Chile
2005
Teresa Moller

7-23
Teresa Moller.
Paseo del Mar.
Punta Pite, Chile, 2010.
Stairs can challenge.

7-24
Teresa Moller.
Paseo del Mar.
Punta Pite, Chile, 2010.
The strength of geometry imposed on, and embedded within, the rocks.

7-25
Teresa Moller.
Paseo del Mar.
Punta Pite, Chile, 2010.
Of the landscape yet . . .

7-26
Teresa Moller.
Paseo del Mar.
Terrain guides design.

Punta Pite lies some 90 miles northwest of Santiago on a rocky Pacific coast in a private residential enclave. The shoreline is granite, rough-hewn, shaped by waves and tides, and virtually impassable to all but the most courageous and able. The project for this oceanside rambla grew from the need to make the coast accessible. A small creek leading from the hilltop to the sea has been left as a linear greenway, with bridges of heavy timber installed where needed to navigate the slope or cross the creek. It stands in stark contrast to the raw shoreline into and upon which the new land bridge of stone has been superimposed.

Movement is supported by the new walk, designed and supervised by landscape architect Teresa Moller, who worked on the project for almost two years, and who ultimately built her own house on a slope nearby. Here, the coastline was neither deformed nor destroyed; here, topography dictated the design [7-23]. If there was ever a lucid dialogue between landform and design intervention, it is found here on the coast of Chile.

In a complete inversion of the normal design process, drawings were made only after construction. Replacing work on paper or screen, every few weeks the Moller team used tape and chalk to mark out the next segment of the path to be realized. Some forty stone craftsman—the project helped renew the craft in the region—executed the design by turning uneven surfaces into smooth planes, adding steps where needed for passage; straight in sections, twisting in others [7-24, 7-25]. No rocks were removed, no surfaces demolished. Rocks may still interrupt the finished path or direct movement into an angled or abrupt turn [7-26]. The play of constructed geometry against natural forms creates a new language, a pidgin design language requiring the participation of both speakers. Here, 1+1 equals at least 5.

Despite the beauty of the intervention, the path remains a physical challenge, lacking handrails and all the other devices normally required to support and ease our movement. Yes, the path is elitist, restrictive, and perhaps discriminatory. But for those who are able and willing, the experience of traversing its kilometer-long path rewards the effort. Here, design bows to terrain, accepts it, and addresses what already exists on-site, completing—rather than competing—with the landscape in a masterful way.

8. MOVING THE EARTH, STIRRING THE SOUL

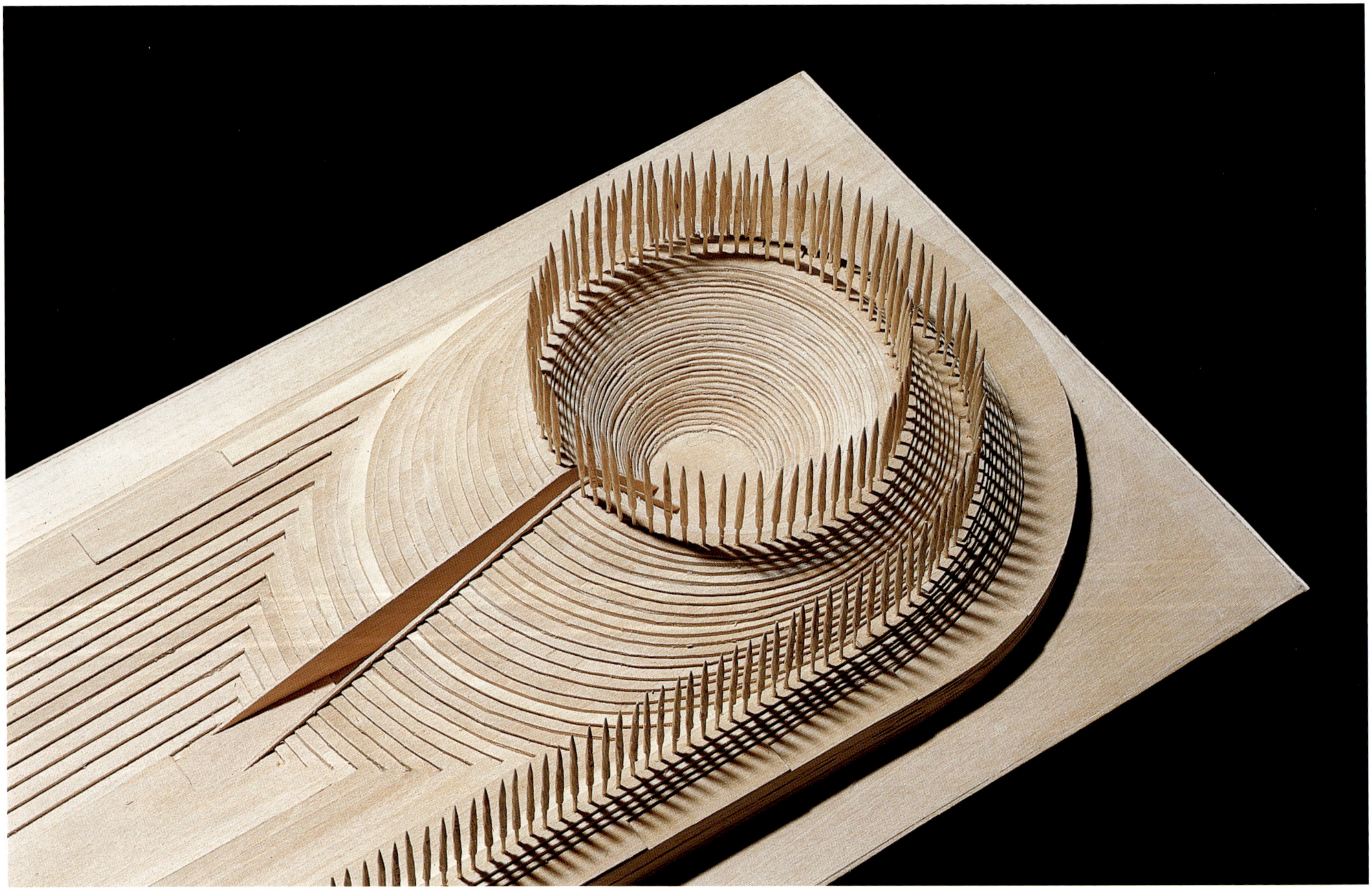

DAVID MEYER

Precedents

The landscapes I've found the most meaningful and compelling are those that have resulted from a consequential and beautiful modeling of the earth [8-1]. In the work of Meyer Studio, topography has either served as a starting point or as the central element of our designs. From sites spanning eras and cultures, we have found many inspiring precedents, learning from the way in which humans have shaped the earth beneath them for varied purposes. A primary reason for such topographic modification has been survival. To provide sufficient water in one of the most arid places in the world, the Nazca civilization of Peru constructed an extensive system of underground aqueducts that used spiraling holes to store, distribute, and regulate the volume and temperature of the water. The Incas who followed them terraced the hillsides to extract arable land from the steep slopes upon which they lived and farmed. Modifications to the land to supply water and maximize food production continue to this day, of course. In Asia, for example, hills and mountains are still terraced to maximize land for the wet cultivation of rice [8-2].

Beyond sustaining life, we have reshaped the earth for the commemoration and glorification of those possessing power and wealth. The largest and most impressive mounds in most kingdoms have been the interment sites of royalty, their mass and heights symbolizing the importance of the throne. The artful manipulation of the land to acknowledge the significance of individuals was practiced throughout the world, at times in stunning ways. In their burial grounds, the Nordic Vikings arranged stones and built earthen mounds resembling their beloved ships, to ensure safe passage into and in the afterlife [8-3]. And in the American Midwest, native cultures fashioned large landforms as effigies of animals, perhaps as acts of devotion, perhaps as attempts to make symbols legible to their ancestors above. One particularly powerful landform is Serpent Mound in southern Ohio, believed to date to ca. 1000 CE [see 1-10]. In its

8-1
David Meyer.
After Maximus.
Rome, Italy, 2000.
Basswood model.
[David Meyer]

sinuous form, the mound evokes a snake with its head pointing to the setting sun on the summer solstice. Its proximity to a four-mile-wide meteor crater has led some to believe that it may speak to an astronomical event, replacing the void created by the impact with an elevated form.

Reshaping topography also addresses the need to defend life and limb. Examples of defensive topography are found throughout the world, some constructed at truly impressive scale, for example, fortifications in Elvas, Portugal, and Lucca, Italy, where terrain once shaped to fend off enemies has been transformed into handsome civic spaces. Though the making of these places may have responded to functional demands, I find each of them to possess an inherent and profound beauty as well as inspiration.

Utility and Aesthetics

As the technology for moving land evolved, architecture and garden design followed suit. The mythical Hanging Gardens of Babylon may represent the historical turning point at which cultivating landscapes purely for pleasure became the primary goal, as opposed to landscapes farmed for food production or shaped for defense. Monumental gardens created during the Italian Renaissance, such as the Villa d'Este in Tivoli, required a major effort to reshape the sloping terrain to address symbolic desires or functional demands. Cutting into hillsides and digging trenches were necessary for securing sufficient water for the garden's obligatory ponds and elaborate fountains. The goal: to stir body, mind, and even the soul. The designer of the Villa Lante gardens in Bagnaia, Italy, crafted storylike aquatic features and used gravity to power the cascades that fed Cardinal Gambara's water table and cooled his wine. Not to be outdone by their predecessors, the makers of formal French gardens in the seventeenth century reformed the land at grand scale, harnessing nature to express the power of the monarch. At Vaux-le-Vicomte, André Le Nôtre mastered the expression of flatness despite the substantial changes of grade across the land, an impressive space that came at enormous monetary and human costs.

In arid climates, courtyards and gardens were designed to collect and move the vital commodity of water. We tend to believe that our current concern with conserving water is a modern priority, but designing the land to preserve water has always been with us. In the Courtyard of the Oranges

8-2
Terraced rice fields. Dak Ya, Vietnam, 2018. [Thanhhoa Tran, Pexels]

8-3
Lindholm Høje Viking Burials. Aalborg, Denmark, Tenth century. [Marc Treib]

in Seville, irrigating runnels sliced through the paving of the patio, itself slightly crowned to shed water and divert it into these narrow channels to nurture the grid of precious orange trees. We see that across the world, both historically and today, water conservation has been executed efficiently by carefully modifying the contour of the land.

While function may instigate modifications to topography, form as an aesthetic pursuit in and of itself also provides motivation. Starting in the later twentieth century, a group of artists began to consciously sculpt the earth to convey their ideas about nature and humanity's place within it. Works such as Robert Smithson's *Spiral Jetty* (1970) pursued a heightened awareness of the environment with a sculpture of piled basalt rocks that toggles between evident and invisible, depending on the water level of Utah's Great Salt Lake [see 1-20]. This periodic appearance and disappearance invites us to contemplate our presence as well as our impermanence on the land. Michael Heizer's *Compression Line* (1968/2016) at Glenstone, an art museum in Potomac, Maryland, uses the earth's pressure to reshape the initial void while beckoning the viewer to consider the passage of time and human vulnerability [8-4]. James Turrell's installations at Roden Crater near Flagstaff, Arizona, have transformed a massive volcanic formation into an artwork that facilitates the contemplation of light and sky, and connects visitors to natural phenomena—art at the grandest scale. In contrast, changes in topography revealed by Richard Long's solitary walks result from his chosen paths rather than a specific intention to create form.

Landscape architect Peter Walker has been inspired by minimalist artists like Donald Judd, Carl Andre, and Agnes Martin, and has treated the ground plane as his canvas to great effect. To achieve his artistic vision, Walker often required his topographic canvas to appear perfectly flat [8-5]. The resulting plane may appear level, but geometrically planned landscapes such as these may in fact be the most difficult to execute with grace. Unlike working with paint on canvas, landscape architects must always modulate the flow of water and the dynamism of all the processes that affect the form of the land.

8-4
Michael Heizer.
Compression Line,
1968/2016.
Glenstone Museum,
Potomac, Maryland.
[Marc Treib]

8-5
Peter Walker & Partners.
McConnell Foundation.
Redding, California, 1995.
[Marc Treib]

8-6
David Meyer.
After Maximus.
Rome, Italy, 2000.
Etching and graphite
on watercolor paper.
[David Meyer]

Conceptual Forms

On a sabbatical at the American Academy in Rome, a residency that nurtured my artistic language and fueled my passion for the monument and the memorial, I was surrounded by the work of Italian masters. Topography became the pillar of my studies. During my stay, I was taken by the way in which the imperial tombs of Rome were sited and how topography had been fundamental to the design of so many of the city's monuments. Set on an axis with the Pantheon, for example, the Tomb of Augustus was the first structure seen when entering the city by boat on the Tiber. The Circus Maximus, today in ruins, was the site of public spectacles, including lion fights and the executions of the innocent.

To counter the memorialization of emperors, I reconceived the Circus Maximus as an anti-imperial memorial—a reimagining of the space to recognize those who had suffered and died there. With *After Maximus* (2000), I set out to capture the essence of loss and hope by sculpting the earth into monumental forms and dramatic spaces to evoke the magnitude of the human drama that had once played out there [8-6; see also 8-1]. With the ruins of Domitian's palace looming above, *After Maximus* had to address the scale of ancient Roman landmarks. The design was configured so that visitors would enter through an earthen slot and pass into a shadowy, confined space, then be drawn onward into an expansive, light-filled bowl crowned with a ring of Italian cypresses.

At Meyer Studio, shaping the ground plane has been critical to all our designs; the ground provides the armature for much of the design that follows. *Limelight* (2002) was a temporary installation at the National Memorial Arboretum in Alrewas, Staffordshire, England, a landscape celebrating what the British refer to as a "champion tree": a designation reserved for the nation's largest representative of that species. The design sought to honor the tree, a Sycamore maple (*Acer pseudoplatanus*), with an earthen "medallion" [8-7, 8-8]. Reaching a height of almost fifteen feet, the grassy crescent framed the champion tree, setting it apart from the rest of the grove and creating an intimate theater that invited visitors to settle in and contemplate the messages offered by the champion.

8-7
Meyer Silberberg Land Architects. *Limelight*. National Memorial Arboretum, Staffordshire, England, 2002. [David Meyer]

8-8
Meyer Silberberg Land Architects. *Limelight*. National Memorial Arboretum. [David Meyer]

The view of the Golden Gate Bridge and San Francisco Bay from the Battery East Overlook is dramatic and constantly changing. On a site where a eucalyptus grove once stood, the National Park Service—the agency that

8-9
Meyer Silberberg Land Architects. Battery East Vista. San Francisco, California, 2016. [Justin Casey]

8-10
Meyer Studio Land Architects. Upper Crescent Vessel, Heartwood. Omaha, Nebraska, 2021. [William Hess]

manages the site—sought to develop an area for viewing all the park's features, including the hillside batteries built in the late 1800s. The challenges for the landscape architects were to accommodate the thousands of tourists who visit the site by car or on foot, as well as the 6,000 bicyclists who stream through the space daily. To fulfill this ambitious program, we first leveled a good portion of the hillside to make the viewing area fully accessible and to provide ample ground for parking. As the existing slope exceeded five percent, most of the site required extensive fill to reduce the slope to less than the required two percent in all directions. Other slopes were mined for the fill necessary to elevate the principal viewing area. To remove them from view, the bike lanes were relocated below this zone [8-9]. A gracious arc of stadium seats now affords unfettered views of all the site's features and beyond, while separating the pedestrian lookout from the busy bike lanes. To help visitors identify the other historical forts, batteries, and sites that rim the bay—including, in the distance, the iconic Angel Island—we designed viewing scopes to be installed along the rim of the plaza. The idea for this visual device was borrowed from the church of Santa Maria del Priorato in Rome, where through a keyhole in a gate outside the church, a perfect view of the Vatican rewards the visitor's effort.

A Major Shaping of Topography

Currently taking shape in Omaha, Nebraska, Heartwood is both a corporate landscape and a public park [8-10]. It is also the largest expanse of land to date modeled by our office. As I was born and raised in Iowa, this vast Midwestern landscape has always spoken to me and has contributed significantly to the development of my aesthetic preferences. In his paintings, Grant Wood captured the essence of that agrarian landscape: rolling terrain overlaid with geometric patterns [8-11]. Whether the land is barren and frozen in January's

8-11
Grant Wood
Spring Turning.
1936.
[Reynolda House Museum of American Art; Wikicommons]

gray light or teeming with the force of life that is summer in Nebraska, the landscape and its expression of nature is always apparent and deeply felt.

Context/Program

Now surrounded by suburban sprawl, the 500-acre Heartwood site was once a part of Boys Town, the beloved institution founded by Father Flanagan to care for orphan youths. Applied Underwriters, the current owner of the land, has been developing the site as an anchor for their corporate campus as well as a neighborhood filled with amenities serving its staff and the general public alike. The land lies within a watershed recently ravaged by storms and floods of unprecedented force, a weather pattern that is sadly becoming the norm for the region. As a result of these storms, the Omaha community has suffered more than a billion dollars in damages over the past two years. Many farms have been shuttered, and families have lost their homes. Reshaping and rethinking the watershed for flood control was an essential aspect of the site's development, which included the 40-acre headquarters for Applied Underwriters, a 20-acre central park, and a pedestrian promenade. Framed by housing and retail development, the promenade will link the park to the Greenways, a preserve of 115 acres of native prairie and forest. Its adjacency was fortuitous, as the Greenways provided the necessary land on which to store 170 acre-feet of stormwater necessary for protection against flooding [8-12].

At the time our studio interviewed for the project, civil engineers had already planned and built a series of unremarkable ponds on the site's boundaries. The ponds were designed to be functional but they didn't really function, as the region's recent storms had quickly eroded the ponds or filled them with silt. Encouraged by Applied Underwriters to exceed normal expectations, Meyer Studio offered a vision for the site based on a hyper-efficient hydraulic infrastructure conceived as art from the start. The backbone of the system is a series of sculpted vessels shaped to collect rain and surface water [8-13, 8-14, 8-15]. Twelve in number and monumental in scale, they grant Heartwood a distinctive character. Constructed of earth and dry-stacked native limestone, the design of the vessels was refined with the help of basswood models, built at a scale of one inch = thirty feet. Each vessel's shape speaks to its context. Because space at the north end of the Greenway was limited, the large, linear vessel that

8-12
Meyer Studio
Land Architects.
Upper Crescent Vessel
Heartwood.
Omaha, Nebraska, 2020–.
[MSLA]

8-13
Meyer Studio
Land Architects.
Cosmic Bowl, Heartwood.
Omaha, Nebraska, 2021.
Basswood model.
[MSLA]

8-14
Meyer Studio
Land Architects.
Folly Park, Heartwood.
Digital rendering.
[MSLA]

8-15
Meyer Studio
Land Architects.
Axial and Radial Vessels,
Heartwood.
Digital rendering.
[MSLA]

8-16
Meyer Studio
Land Architects.
Cosmic Bowl and
Folly Park, Heartwood.
Omaha, Nebraska, 2021.
Etching.
[MSLA]

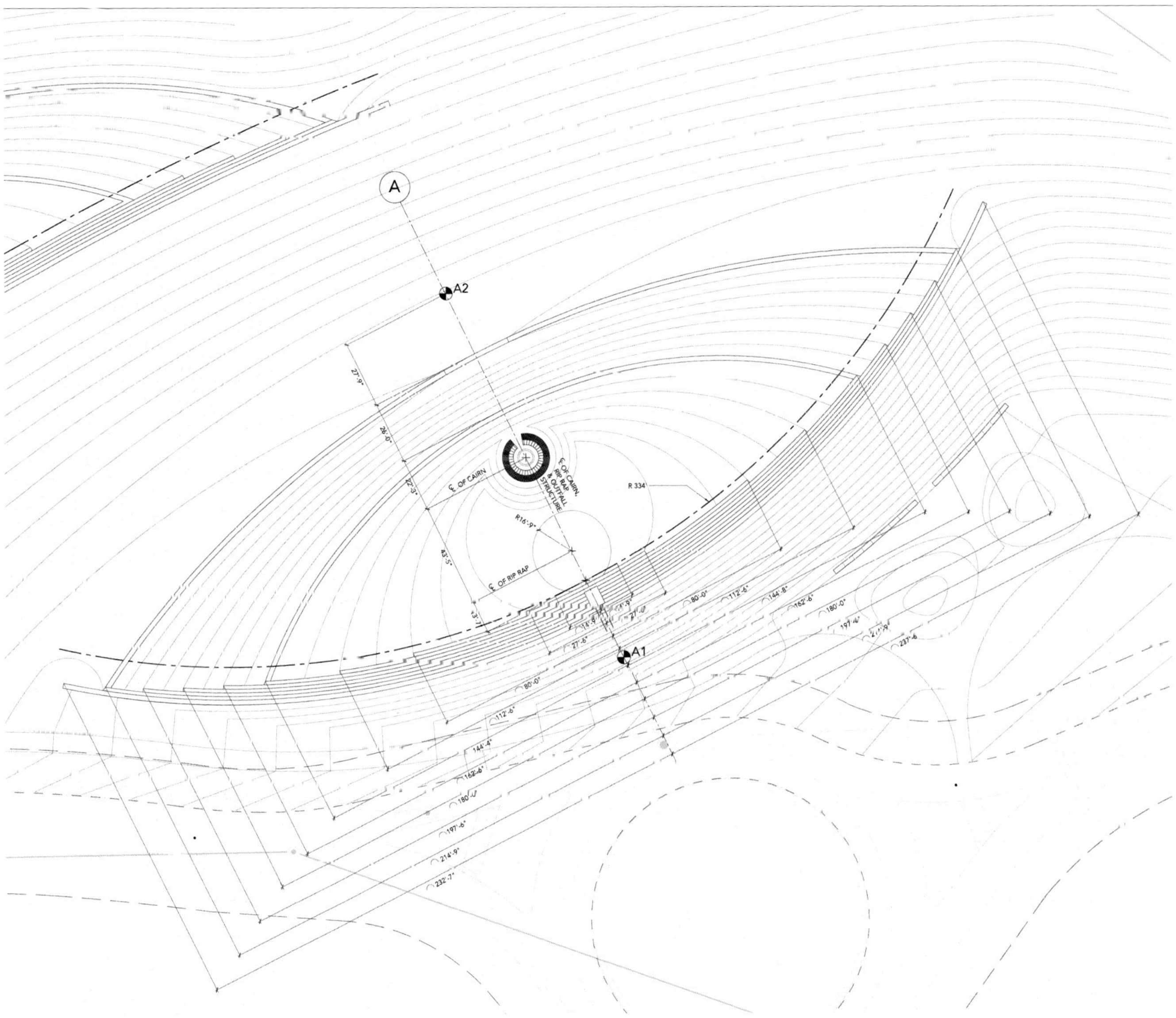

8-17
Meyer Studio
Land Architects.
Crescent Vessels,
Heartwood.
Construction drawing.
[MSLA]

narrows at its terminus is dedicated to the collection of stormwater. To reinforce the lines of its form, we framed it with an allée of Kindred Spirit Oaks (*Quercus x warei* 'Nadler') set on axis with a lone cottonwood tree.

Elsewhere, greater acreage of land allowed other vessels to assume their own character, thus providing more nuance to the park experience. Serpentine trails move across the land, weaving their way through the wooded areas surrounding the vessels. The footprint of the iconic Cosmic Bowl, the largest vessel, evokes the historical pothole prairies of Nebraska [8-16]. As a formal foil for the surrounding prairie and woodlands, a circle of trees rims the edges of the Bowl and provides a horizon. Collectively, the maximum storage capacity of the vessels is 55 million gallons, their scale resulting in sizable clearings in the wooded landscape [8-17]. Whether marshy, filled with water, or dry, the vessels and their surroundings serve as poetic revelations of the land. As the seasons change the vessels serve different purposes, which range from wading in summer to ice-skating in winter. Studded within the clearings are amenities such as council rings, firepits, small amphitheaters, and stone cairns that offer shelter while also serving as follies.

To add further definition and add amenity to the dramatic landforms, over 10,000 trees will be planted throughout the project. Stylized orchards will honor the agrarian history of the site and give a nod to Arbor Day, which originated in Nebraska. Trees removed to create the clearings for each vessel will find new homes throughout the park; as they decay, they will serve as memorial totems and habitat for native woodpeckers, nuthatches, and chickadees.

A few words about our process. Our initial ideas come to life using pencil, paper, and intuition [8-18]. Topographic sketch studies are then scanned and developed in AutoCAD, thereafter submitted to collaborative review and a round or more of red-line corrections [8-19]. This process is repeated several times to refine the composition. Once the design is finalized, a set of meticulous construction drawings is produced to guide earth movement and construction [see 8-17]. I find these drawings beautiful in their own right. Today, the connection between the construction drawings and those in the field can be remarkably seamless because drawings transmitted via GPS (Global Positioning System) directly guide the army of scrapers and compactors operating on the site. Because of this close correlation between design and execution, it's critical that our contours are carefully determined, precise, and beautiful. A rigorous approach to designing and communicating the contours is essential for quality earth movement.

Construction of the first vessel, which is nearly 500 feet across and sixteen feet deep, began in 2020 [see 8-10]. Grading the land was only one part of the task, however. We also needed to consider how water would enter and leave the vessels, and how we could dramatize those dynamic processes. As a control mechanism, each vessel has an overflow catch basin that allows water to drain slowly during and after storms. Over time—perhaps fifteen years, perhaps a hundred years—nature will leave its mark on the stone and record the passage of time. Here, the design and materials render the invisible visible, chronicling the history of the site, sparking interest among visitors, and providing pleasure for the people and other creatures who will walk and play there.

Most of Nebraska's original ecosystems have been transformed by centuries of agriculture. Rich topsoil has been eroded, and only a small fraction of the native landscape remains. Our design for Heartwood is intended to be restorative: to rebuild ecologies and to revitalize soil, water, vegetation, and the wildlife that depends on them. Today, those actions are more essential than ever before. Thankfully, most of these practices—some dating back to Frederick Law Olmsted Sr.—have become widely adopted by the profession. But Meyer Studio's mission extends beyond addressing functional necessities and the righteous making of habitat. We are pursuing what we regard as an ecological art form throughout the site. In monumental and intimate ways, we attempt to fuse art with sound environmental practices. Discussing these places—built or imagined, ancient or new—has probably just confirmed things many practitioners already know: that there is beauty in utility and, when done well, utility in beauty. And that for landscape architects, the most essential and most exciting medium is the earth beneath us.

(following pages)

8-18
Meyer Studio Land Architects. Greenway Vessels, Heartwood. Omaha, Nebraska, 2020–. Concept sketch. [MSLA]

8-19
Meyer Studio Land Architects. Greenway Vessels. Heartwood. Site plan with edits and comments. [MSLA]

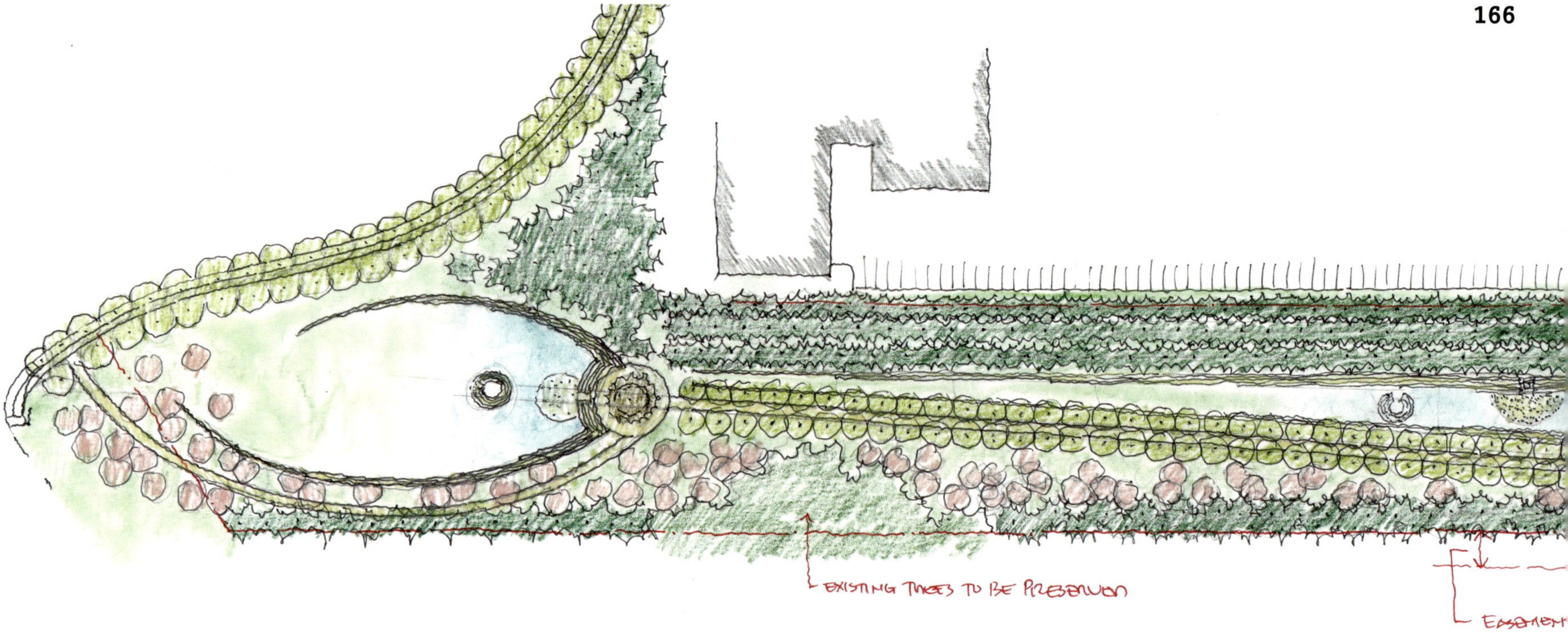
EXISTING TREES TO BE PRESERVED

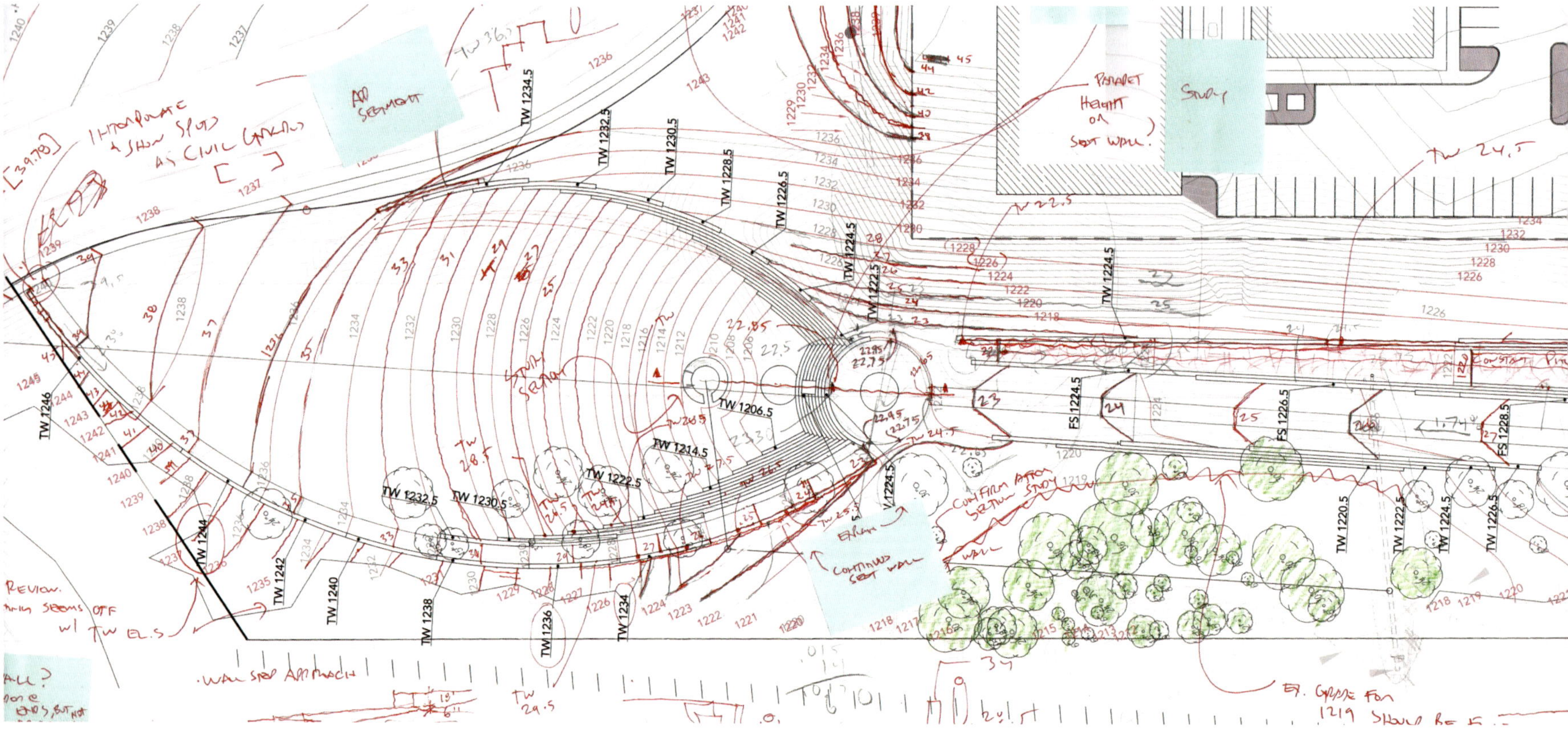
TW 1234.5
TW 1232.5
TW 1230.5
TW 1228.5
TW 1226.5
TW 1224.5
TW 1222.5
TW 1206.5
TW 1214.5
TW 1222.5
TW 1232.5
TW 1230.5
TW 1246
TW 1244
TW 1242
TW 1240
TW 1238
TW 1236
TW 1234
FS 1224.5
FS 1226.5
FS 1228.5
TW 1220.5
TW 1222.5
TW 1224.5
TW 1226.5
V 1224.5
STUDY

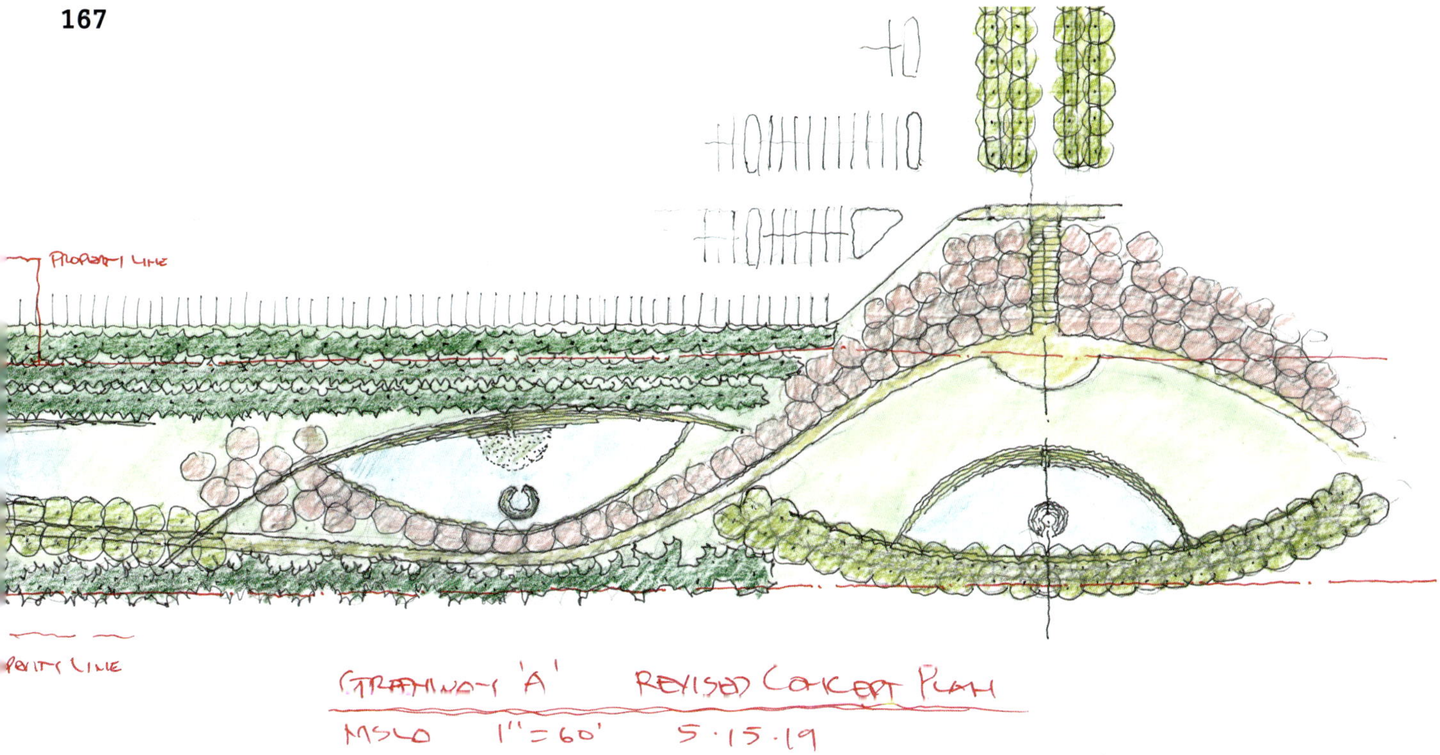
PROPERTY LINE
STREAMWAY 'A' REVISED CONCEPT PLAN
MSLO 1"=60' 5.15.19

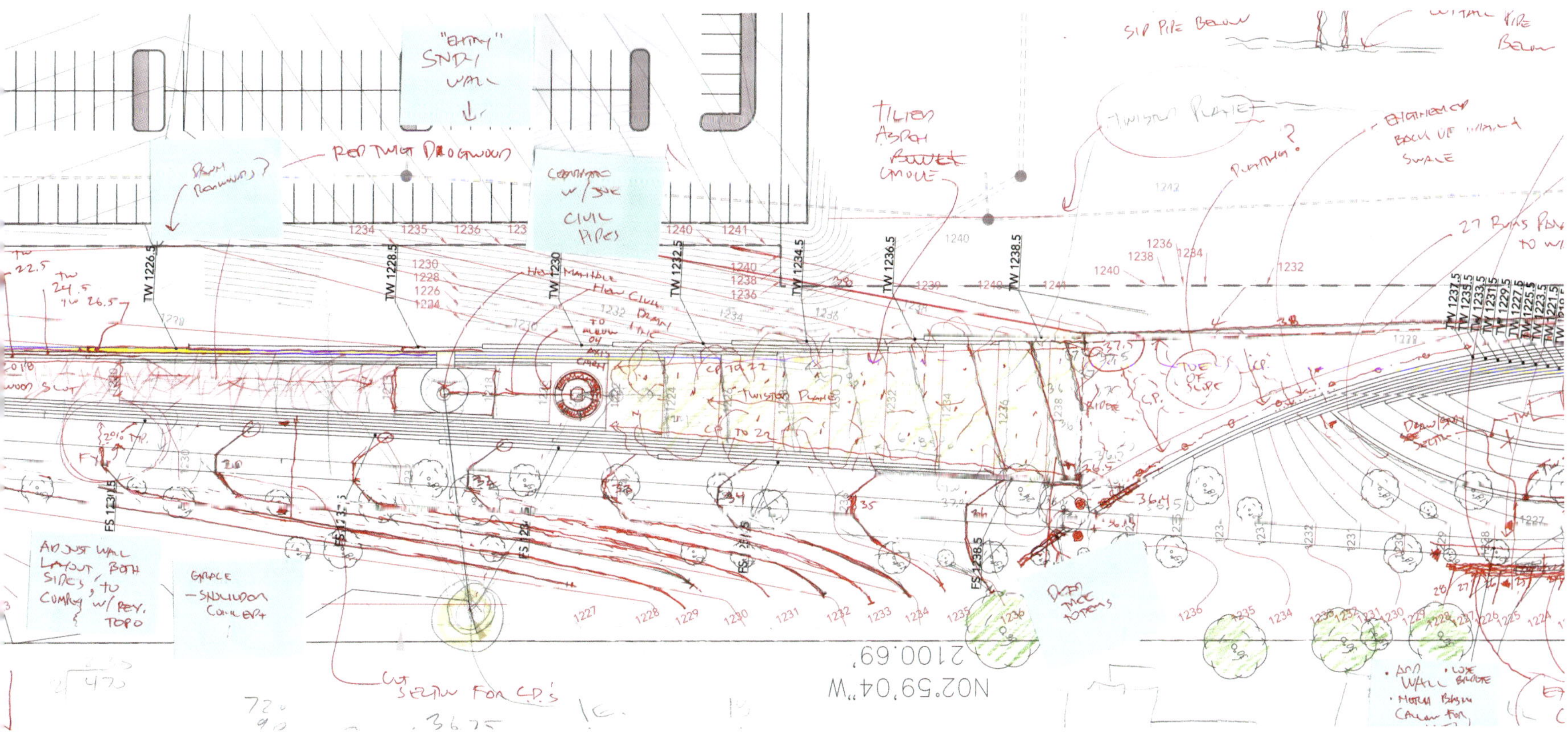
RED TWIG DOGWOOD
NO2°59'04"W
2100.69'

9. TRASH TOPOGRAPHY: SHAPING POSTINDUSTRIAL LAND

ELISSA ROSENBERG

Form and Formlessness

In the 1950s, long before apocalyptic views of emptiness and picturesque urban decay filled photography collections and popular magazines such as *Time* and *Life*, photographers Bernd and Hilla Becher began their systematic documentation of Germany's industrial architecture [9-1].[1] The abstract quality of the Bechers' images aestheticized these abandoned water towers, blast furnaces, gas tanks, mineheads, and grain elevators; they were shot frontally in black and white, stripped of their contexts, and generally organized in a grid. The Bechers referred to them as "anonymous sculptures."[2] By transforming these derelict structures into objects of beauty and granting them architectural value, the Bechers' photographs made an important contribution to a nascent industrial aesthetic.

Around the same time the Bechers were recording abandoned mining sites, artist Robert Smithson was exploring the postindustrial landscape. "My own experience," he wrote, "is that the best sites for 'earth art' are sites that have been disrupted by industry, reckless urbanization or nature's own devastation."[3] In 1967, he published his celebrated essay "The Monuments of Passaic" in *Artforum*, a tribute to the industrial remnants of Smithson's hometown in New Jersey.[4] Using a cheap Instamatic camera, he extolled the banal decaying "monuments" of the contemporary American city: the steel bridge, the "fountain monument" of sewage-outfall pipes, parking lots, and a suburban sandbox [9-2].

A year later Smithson joined the Bechers on a "field trip" to Oberhausen, one of the largest industrial complexes in the Ruhr district, not far from Düsseldorf, where Smithson was to have his first solo exhibition. Smithson's snapshots from that visit stand in stark contrast to the Bechers' analytic and even elegiac photographs. While the Bechers were preoccupied with the subtle formal aspects of the industrial structures, Smithson was drawn to the formlessness and disintegration of the surrounding landscape: the wasted ground, the mounds of slag, the marks left by tires. Terrain, he held, was a constantly changing, physical material, subject to what he called "chance and change in the material order of nature."[5]

9-1
Bernd Becher and Hilla Becher. *Pitheads*, 1974. [© Estate of Bernd Becher & Hilla Becher, Tate Collection]

With the shift from a production economy to a service-oriented consumer economy, the abandoned sites of industry and disused infrastructure have become the new ground of our public realm. Parks built on the sites of empty blast furnaces; abandoned quarries; or decommissioned rails and railyards, landfills, and ports have generated a renewed fascination with industrial sites. Much has been written about the current "ruin craze," which has sparked a voyeuristic interest in industrial heritage in ghost towns and waste sites, from Fukushima to Detroit.[6] Ruins have become aestheticized and stripped of social context as sites for "ruin tourism," destinations that today attract outsiders with no stake or interest in the city—a trend derisively termed "ruin porn."[7] A new postindustrial aesthetic has come into focus, largely as viewed through the photographer's lens.[8] Many of the images of urban decay that feed this aesthetic draw upon romantic notions of inevitability, showing images of empty lots reverting to fields or trees sprouting in abandoned buildings [9-3]. Nature seems to be reclaiming the city as a powerful yet external force that exists beyond human life and history.

The conversion of these sites to public use has required landscape architects to think and work in new ways, transforming landscape-architectural practice as well as its theories.[9] To what extent do recent designs play to prevailing landscape conventions, such as the picturesque or the sublime, or even ruin porn—and how do they challenge them? Geographer Matthew Gandy has argued that "urban wastelands unsettle the familiar terrain of cultural landscapes, designed spaces, and the organizational logic of modernity."[10] In response to these conditions an alternate aesthetic is emerging from recent postindustrial landscape projects marked by their engagement with terrain. Rather than focusing on the Romantic imagery of ruin, the key element in the remediation of these sites is the earth itself: disturbed, eroded, toxic soils; or oozing trash. In his 1973 essay "Frederick Law Olmsted and the Dialectical Landscape," Smithson underscored the primacy of the earth: "a consciousness of mud and realms of sedimentation is necessary in order to understand the landscape as it exists."[11] He and other land artists working on reclamation sites in the 1960s and 1970s used earth as a sculptural medium to express a range of themes that ranged from disruption, devastation, and entropy (Smithson), to earth as "a thing in itself" used to support living systems (Helen and Newton Harrison).[12]

9-2
Robert Smithson.
The Pumping Derrick.
"The Monuments of Passaic,"
Artforum (December 1967).
[Robert Smithson;
© Holt/Smithson Foundation
/ VAGA at Artists Rights
Society (ARS), NY]

9-3
Andrew Moore.
Birches Growing in Decayed Books.
Detroit Public Library Book Depository, 2010.
[© Andrew Moore, from *Detroit Disassembled*]

A set of themes has emerged from contemporary work on deindustrialized sites that highlights the fundamental role of topography and landform in shaping an aesthetic of regeneration. For the most part, this material runs counter to ideas of the picturesque that photographic traditions have reinforced through evocative images of ruin. These landscapes derive, instead, from the more process-oriented traditions of land art and ecology that stress the sculptural and cross-sectional aspects of landform, and the materiality of soil, sediment, and dredge within the context of larger ecological and hydrological systems. Ariel Sharon Park, the site of a former sanitary landfill currently under construction on the outskirts of Tel Aviv, Israel, serves as a case study of the urban role of landform in a remediated postindustrial landscape.

Earthworks

Smithson's influence can be seen in two parks in California designed by Hargreaves Associates converted from landfills, where earth was used to evoke a sense of flux. In both projects, large-scale, abstract earthworks highlighted the qualities of the site and the natural processes that drive the changing characteristics of the rubble and trash of which the parks were built. Occupying 18 acres on San Francisco Bay, Candlestick Point Cultural Park (1993) was designed in collaboration with architect Mark Mack and artist Doug Hollis [9-4]. The park immersed the visitor in the ephemeral and sensory qualities of the site: its industrial character, windswept and open, filled with the smell and the wide-open views of the bay.[13] Besides Hollis's *Windgate* entrance, which amplified the sounds of the strong afternoon winds, the main feature of the park was a large-scale earthwork: a grassy plane that sloped toward the water. Rubble-filled gabion walls edged the central lawn to form long channels that allowed the bay to flow in and out of the park with the tides. The crispness of the grass plane presented a counterpoint to the openness and roughness beyond its edges—the detritus that filled the channels, the successional vegetation, and the sweeping views of the bay. With minimal means, the design of the ground plane seemed to gather up and intensify the experience of the site.[14]

Byxbee Park (1990–91), a former sanitary landfill in East Palo Alto, California, was a collaboration by Hargreaves Associates and artists

9-4
Hargreaves Associates. Candlestick Point Park. San Francisco, California, ca. 1987. [HargreavesJones]

9-5
Hargreaves Associates. Byxbee Park. East Palo Alto, California, 1992. [Marc Treib]

Peter Richards and Michael Oppenheimer [9-5]. Since the landfill cap precluded the planting of trees, landform became the primary spatial medium: the plastic sculpting of the topography itself created a rolling landscape of biomorphic hillocks planted with shaggy, native grasses.[15] This and Candlestick Point Cultural Park utilized abstract, minimalist landforms against which to register the open-ended, indeterminate qualities of the environment, highlighting the dynamic qualities of the natural processes acting on the site.[16]

Landform as Strata and Surfaces

A different approach can be seen in Latz + Partner's landmark Landschaftspark Duisburg-Nord (1990–2002), located in Germany's Ruhr Valley on the grounds of the former Thyssen-Meiderich ironworks. As part of the International Building Exhibition (IBA), the goal of the project was to use ecological restoration and cultural and economic renewal to revitalize the deindustrialized region along the Emscher River. "Destruction has to be protected so that it isn't destroyed again by recultivation," wrote Peter Latz.[17] Their intention was not to "heal" the landscape in the sense of restoring it to some prior ideal state, but rather to accept the existing conditions of disturbance while converting them to new uses and creating new meanings. While most critics have analyzed the park through the lens of the sublime, as inspired by the monumental industrial ruins that dominate the site, the project is better understood through the redesign of its landscape.[18] Landform plays an important role in structuring the remediated landscape, although not in a sculptural or object-oriented sense. The earth was not sculpted into bizarre or extraordinary forms, but instead was used to describe the ordinary landscape of production. The design of the park was based upon an analytic, almost archaeological approach that sought to investigate how the industrial landscape was made, how its various components functioned, and what impact production had on the shape of the land [9-6].

The park is designed as a series of autonomous sequences, or "layers," linked at specific points. There is no unitary composition or unfolding narrative as one moves through the park, but a synchronic experience of vertically stacked systems. Landform offers up clues to the systems that once operated on-site, whether by tracing the patterns of the former railroad through its embankments and tunnels, or those of the canal system typical of the region.

9-6
Latz + Partner. Landschaftspark Duisburg-Nord. Duisburg, Germany, 1989–. [Michael Latz]

The composition of the park is thus expressed in stratigraphic terms. Each linear system—the promenade, the Bahnpark (or Rail Park), and the canal—slices through the park like a datum, defining and "explaining" the section and making it legible. Latz referred to this design approach as an expression of the syntax of the landscape, stressing structure over spectacle: "the design process is the search for a new syntax of information layers."[19] It is the landscape's structure, not its imagery—however seductive or sublime—that establishes a sense of place and offers a record of the site's history.[20]

The ground plane can also act as an expressive layer or surface. At the Louvre-Lens Museum Park, France, designed by Mosbach Paysagistes on a former coal-mining site (2012), the surface of the ground is designed to evoke the history of disturbance [9-7].[21] Mosbach has described the ground as a "skin" or a "recording surface" on which memories of the site are inscribed.[22] Some of these are actual historical traces, such as former haulage lines that are cut into the lawn [9-8]. Others are more graphic renderings of disturbance as a general condition, like the blistered surface of the paved areas around the museum—perforated, pocked, and cut away to create strange, evocative forms through which the soil seems to bubble up, allowing new ruderal vegetation to take hold [9-9].

Constructed Ecologies: Microtopography, Dredge, Sediment

Topography has played a critical role in the design of postindustrial landscapes, not only as an expressive medium but also as the means to create new, self-organizing systems to guide the formation of wetlands and rivers, or the creation of new habitats.[23] The 57-acre La Tancada Lagoon Park Eco-Museum (2011) in the intertidal Ebro River delta, Spain, designed by Estudi Martí Franch (EMF), provides a poetic example of a microtopographic approach for creating new habitat and protecting rare plants and birds on a significant flyway [9-10]. The project established a bird sanctuary on the site of fishponds that had been developed in a former salt field. The landscape architects transformed the ponds by subtly regrading them to produce differing slopes, water depths, salt concentration, and flood regimes [9-11]. The minimal yet systematic sectional manipulation of the pools created four distinct conditions that simulate the habitats of Mediterranean salt steppes, mudflats, scrub, and coastal lagoons [9-12].

9-7
Mosbach Paysagistes. Louvre-Lens Museum Park. Lens, France, 2012. Site plan. [© Catherine Mosbach]

9-8
Mosbach Paysagistes. Louvre-Lens Museum Park. Site plan. [© Mosbach Paysagistes -Sanaa]

9-9
Mosbach Paysagistes. Louvre-Lens Museum Park. Path through the dry meadow. [© Catherine Mosbach]

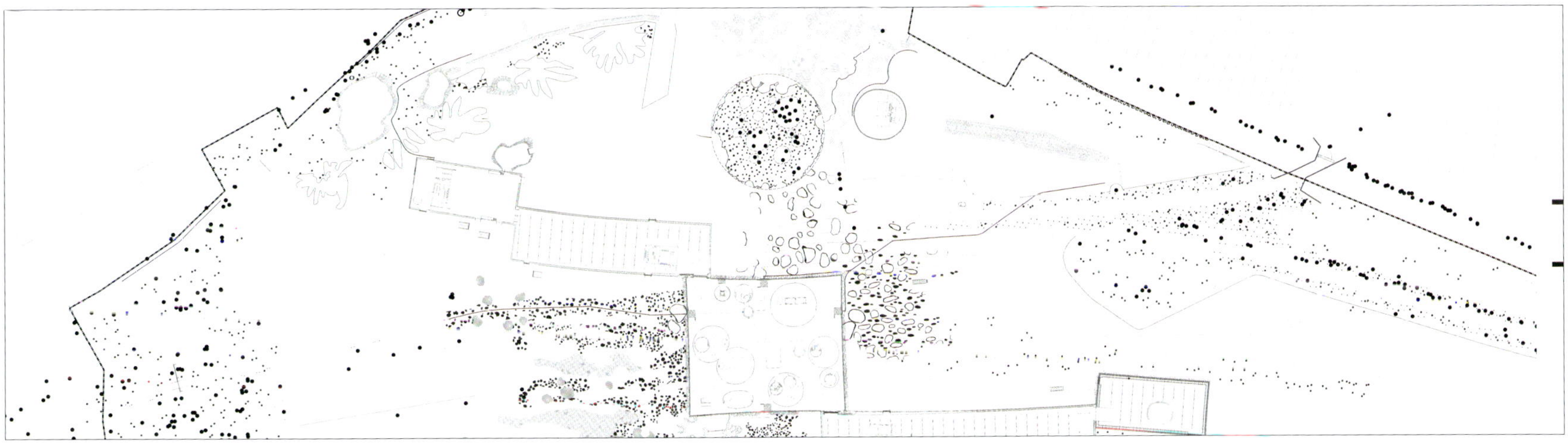

(opposite) **9-10**
Estudi Martí Franch.
La Tancada Salt Fields.
Delta de l'Ebre, Tarragon,
Spain, 2012.
Micro-grading altered
the dike sections to
diversify the land-water
ecotone and create
four distinct habitats.
[EMF]

(left) **9-11**
Estudi Martí Franch.
La Tancada Salt Fields.
Micro grading created
four distinct habitats:
Mediterranean
salt steppes,
Mediterranean scrubs,
mudflats and sandflats,
and coastal lagoons.
[EMF]

(below) **9-12**
Estudi Martí Franch.
La Tancada Salt Fields.
Sections showing
process over time.
[EMF]

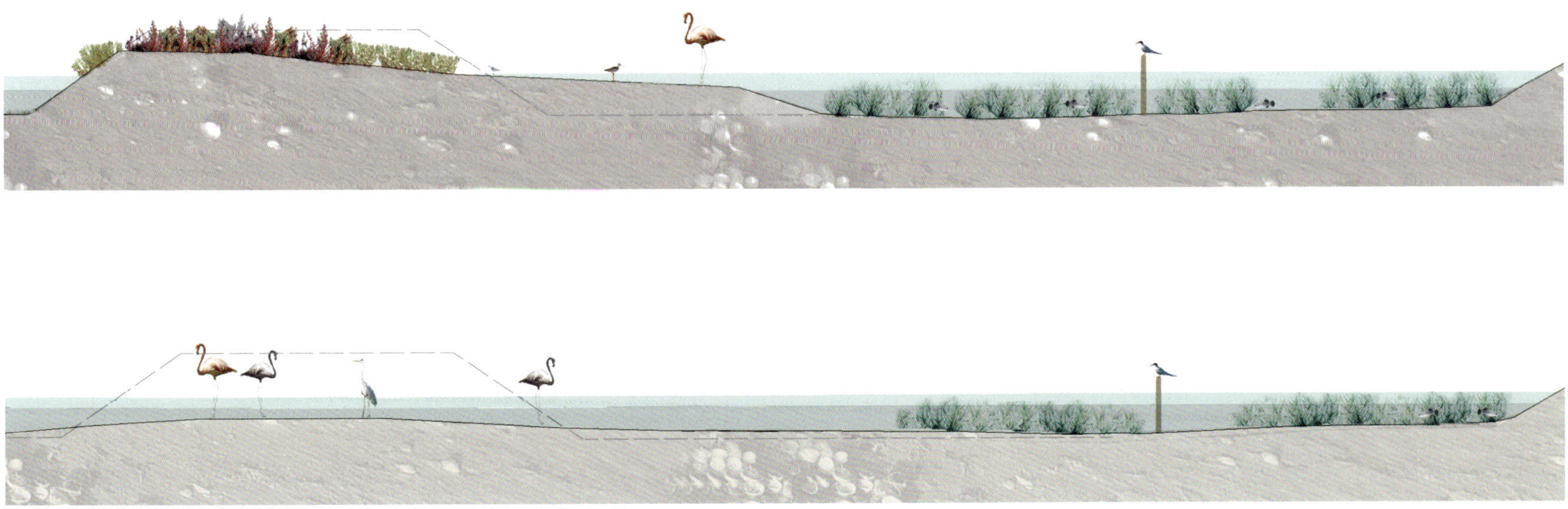

Ariel Sharon Park: "Hinterland Urbanism"[24]

In 2004, Latz + Partner won the international competition for the design of the metropolitan park located at the southern entrance to Tel Aviv, now known as Ariel Sharon Park. The park includes Hiriya, a monumental mountain of trash, as well as the surrounding floodplains of the Ayalon and the Shapirim Rivers. Bounded by South Tel Aviv's low-income neighborhoods, two highways, and a mix of open lands, the converted landfill park has a strategic urban role to play in reorganizing the city's fragmented, discontinuous edge and expanding the meaning, uses, and imagery of the metropolitan park [9-13].

When it closed in 1998, Hiriya was the largest sanitary landfill in the Middle East, reaching a height of almost 200 feet and sprawling over some 110 acres. It was in operation for almost fifty years. By 1997, 3,200 tons of domestic waste were being dumped daily.[25] Residents had complained about odors from the landfill for years, and its environmental hazards were well-known. These included groundwater contamination and methane emissions, as well as the dangers to airplanes taking off and landing in the nearby international airport caused by the thousands of seagulls and other birds attracted to the decomposing garbage. The landfill was finally closed after its partial collapse into the adjacent Ayalon River. Today, it functions as a transfer station for domestic waste, which is subsequently trucked to a larger landfill in the Negev desert.

The public park on and around the landfill would need to address two engineering challenges: first, stabilizing the heap of decomposing organic waste; and second, designing a new floodplain to surround Hiriya and divert or store floodwater from the city of Tel Aviv. An elaborate flood-retention landscape was proposed for the valley by creating a braided channel in the existing stream along with a new bypass channel. The excavated material and recycled building waste were used to shore up the landfill and create new landforms to spatially define the park.

Latz sought to preserve Hiriya's highly imageable topography. A plateau with almost vertical slopes, the mountain of trash had become a Tel Aviv icon, an ambivalent landmark that marked the entrance to the city. Rather than moderating its steep slopes, a circular earthen terrace was installed around Hiriya's base to stabilize it and maintain its distinct silhouette.

9-13
Hiraya Landfill.
Tel Aviv, Israel.
Aerial view of the site
before the construction
of Ariel Sharon Park.
[Beracha Foundation]

ברוכים הבאים
לפארק אריאל שרון

Designed in collaboration with landscape architects Moria-Sekely, the first phase of the park opened in 2014. It was structured around two contrasting topographic experiences. First is the dramatic urban panorama of Tel Aviv that unfolds at the summit. Paths slice through the trash as a procession to a "belvedere" at the summit from which to view the city skyline [9-14]. A large, open deck offers space for kite flying, skateboarding, or simply experiencing the spatial grandeur of this heap of trash. The dry-stone retaining walls along the paths are composed of recycled building-demolition waste that allow adjustment as the organic soils continue to settle. One is keenly aware of the strangeness of the ground; there is no terra firma here [9-15]. The second experience is that of enclosure and retreat. Within a depression at the center of the plateau, one enters an intensely planted, sunken, green "oasis." A painterly composition of tropical and semitropical plants surrounds a pool fed by harvested rainwater stored in two underground reservoirs. A visitor center and café occupy a surviving concrete platform that once supported large machinery. This hidden, lush, secret garden is implanted in the center of the hill of garbage; the contrast is stark and unsettling [9-16].

The second phase of work, designed by Latz + Partner with landscape architects Braudo Maoz, is currently under construction and will expand the park into the surrounding 2,000 acres of the floodplains of the Ayalon and the Shapirim Rivers. The section of the Ayalon River that flows through Tel Aviv was channelized when the Ayalon Highway and railway lines were constructed, and current plans to add a fourth railway line have made the park's flood-control function an urgent priority. The current expansion of the park is funded as a public overlay to what is essentially a large scale drainage project [9-17].[26]

Both recreational and infrastructural, this hybrid landscape features plantings and open spaces created on the sculpted topography of a reshaped valley. Crisp, angular landforms have been constructed using the earth excavated on-site; regular rows of plantings highlight the geometry of the oversized landforms that reflect the infrastructural scale of the park. Their regularity highlights the engineered origins of the space while also alluding to the vestiges of the agricultural landscape that surround part of the site [9-18].

Ariel Sharon Park is an operational or infrastructural landscape situated on an urban margin. It serves as an intermediary between the

9-14
Latz + Partner and Moria-Sekely. Ariel Sharon Park. Tel Aviv, Israel, 2016. Belvedere with views of the Tel Aviv skyline. [Latz + Partner]

9-15
Latz + Partner and Moria-Sekely. Ariel Sharon Park. Retaining walls using recycled materials. [Amir Lotan]

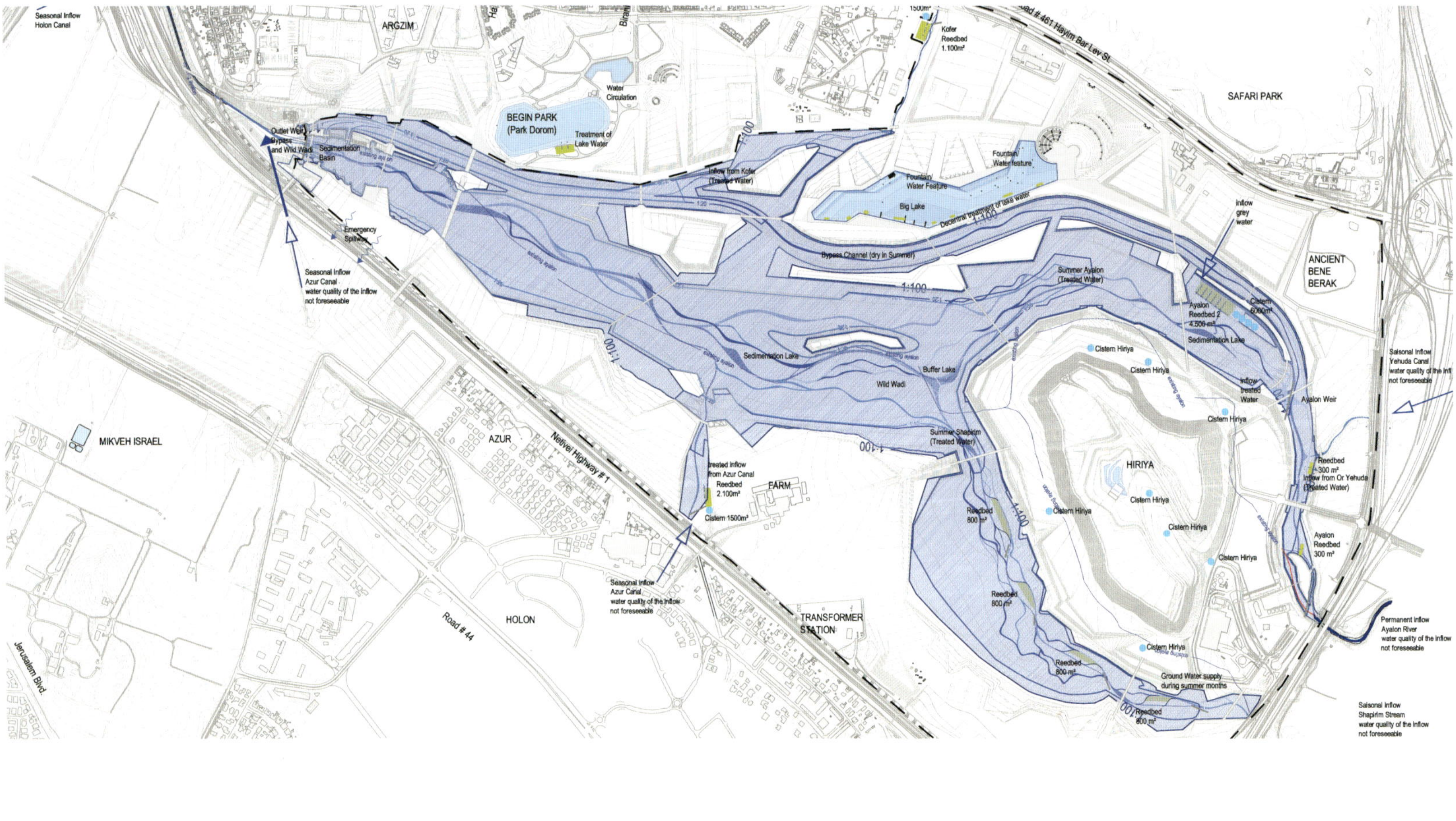
Seasonal Inflow
Holon Canal
ARGZIM
Water
Circulation
BEGIN PARK
(Park Dorom)
Treatment of
Lake Water
Outlet Weir
Bypass
and Wild Wadi
Sedimentation
Basin
Emergency
Spillway
Seasonal Inflow
Azur Canal
water quality of the inflow
not foreseeable
1500m³
Kofer
Reedbed
1.100m²
Road # 461 Hayim Bar Lev St
SAFARI PARK
Inflow from Kofer
(Treated Water)
Fountain/
Water feature
Fountain/
Water Feature
Big Lake
Decentral treatment of lake water
1:100
Bypass Channel (dry in Summer)
Summer Ayalon
(Treated Water)
inflow
grey
water
ANCIENT
BENE
BERAK
Ayalon
Reedbed 2
4.500 m²
Cistern
6000m³
Sedimentation Lake
Sedimentation Lake
Buffer Lake
Wild Wadi
Cistern Hiriya
Inflow
treated
Water
Ayalon Weir
Salsonal Inflow
Yehuda Canal
water quality of the infl
not foreseeable
MIKVEH ISRAEL
AZUR
Netivei Highway # 1
Summer Shapirim
(Treated Water)
treated Inflow
from Azur Canal
Reedbed
2.100m²
Cistern 1500m³
FARM
HIRIYA
Reedbed
800 m²
Reedbed
300 m²
Inflow from Or Yehuda
(Treated Water)
Ayalon
Reedbed
300 m²
Seasonal Inflow
Azur Canal
water quality of the inflow
not foreseeable
Road # 44
HOLON
TRANSFORMER
STATION
Permanent Inflow
Ayalon River
water quality of the inflow
not foreseeable
Ground Water supply
during summer months
Jerusalem Blvd.
Salsonal Inflow
Shapirim Stream
water quality of the inflow
not foreseeable

disconnected, fragmented city edge and the surrounding agricultural landscape, using a vocabulary of landform, vegetation, and water at a large infrastructural scale. The forceful presence of the trash mound and the expansive dimensions of the floodplain, with its strange, angled landforms and their regular grids of trees, preserve the tension and ambivalence at the heart of this park. As Latz wrote, "It must be possible to be able to understand this formation as a mountain of rubbish for as long as possible."[27] The park's spatial language prevents the converted landfill from being naturalized in a newly planted green landscape. In this way, the park also challenges the divide between the city and its hinterland, or its "non-city" uses. The site continues to function as an operational landscape that supports the metabolic flows of the city, but instead of storing the urban waste flowing out of Tel Aviv, the site is now used to store the water flowing into it. These functions are no longer out of sight, concealed inside a "black box."[28] On the contrary, flood management is integrated within a broader vision that reframes the operational landscape as a living setting for recreation as well as habitat creation, giving new urban meaning and form to the hinterland.

The landscape projects discussed here argue against a view of nature as a healing, regenerative force external to culture and history. Their engagement with topography suggests a different relationship to time. Rather than naturalizing the effects of deindustrialization, they highlight the temporality of the landscape and its perpetual transformation. These landscapes stress the complexity of human engagement with nature, an engagement that can be at once destructive and regenerative. The acceptance of disturbance and flux replaces popular romantic imagery of renewal with an ethos of experimentation, here associated with the material, tectonic qualities of the ground. Regeneration is not inevitable, as the images of overgrown Detroit might suggest. It is a profoundly human act.

9-16
Latz + Partner and Moria Sekely. Ariel Sharon Park. Tel Aviv, Israel, 2016. The Oasis. [Latz + Partner]

9-17
Latz + Partner and Braudo Maoz. Ariel Sharon Park. Water-system plan, c. 2015. [Latz + Partner, Braudo Maoz]

9-18
Latz + Partner and Moria Sekely. Ariel Sharon Park. Tel Aviv, Israel, 2016. Planting rows on berms. [Amir Lotan]

Notes

1 See, for example, the images of abandoned Detroit in the work of Yves Marchand and Romain Meffre, *The Ruins of Detroit* (Göttingen: Steidl Verlag, 2010), and Andrew Moore, *Detroit Disassembled* (Akron, OH: Damiani; Akron Art Museum, 2010).

2 Their first collection was entitled *Anonyme Skulpturen: Eine Typologie technischer Bauten* (Anonymous Sculptures: A Typology of Technical Buildings) (Düsseldorf: Art-Press Verlag, Wittenborn, 1970).

3 Robert Smithson, "Frederick Law Olmsted and the Dialectical Landscape" (1973), reprinted in *Robert Smithson: The Collected Writings*, ed. Jack Flam (Berkeley: University of California Press, 1996), p. 165.

4 Robert Smithson, "A Tour of the Monuments of Passaic, New Jersey" (1967), reprinted in Flam, ed., *Robert Smithson: Collected Writings*, pp. 68–74.

5 Smithson, "Frederick Law Olmsted and the Dialectical Landscape," p. 159.

6 See Andreas Huyssen, "Nostalgia for Ruins," *Grey Room 23* (Spring 2006): p. 7.

7 Thomas Morton coined this term in "Something, Something, Something, Detroit: Lazy Journalists Love Pictures of Abandoned Stuff," *Vice* (August 2009). http://www.vice.com/read/something-something-something-detroit-994-v10n8.

8 For example, by bringing previously hidden views of wild, urban nature into wide circulation, Joel Sternfeld's revelatory images of the High Line in Lower Manhattan helped make the case for saving the abandoned structure; http://www.thehighline.org.

9 See Ross McLean, *Transformative Ground: A Field Guide to the Postindustrial Landscape* (Abingdon: Routledge, 2020).

10 Matthew Gandy, "Marginalia: Aesthetics, Ecology, and Urban Wastelands," *Annals of the Association of American Geographers 103*, no. 6 (2013): p. 1,311.

11 Smithson, "Frederick Law Olmsted," p. 170.

12 For works of reclamation by earth artists, see *Robert Morris's Johnson Pit #30* (1979), Kings County, Washington [1-22]; Smithson's *Broken Circle/Spiral Hill* (1971), near Emmen, Netherlands [7-3, 7-4]; and the Harrsons' *Spoils Pile Reclamation Project* (1977–78), discussed in Lesley Ryan, "Art + Ecology: Land Reclamation Works of Artists Robert Smithson, Robert Morris, and Helen Mayer Harrison and Newton Harrison," *Environmental Philosophy*, Special Issue: Environmental Aesthetics and Ecological Restoration 4, nos. 1–2 (Spring/Fall 2007): pp. 95–116.

13 Today, almost nothing of the original design remains.

14 The emphasis on landform was reinforced by the design process itself. Hollis noted that design work was largely done on-site or with his collaborators, using a six-by-six-foot sandbox rather than drawings. See Smithsonian Archives of American Art, *Oral history interview with Douglas W. Hollis*, 20–24 May 2010; https://www.aaa.si.edu/download_pdf_transcript/ajax?record_id=edanmdm-AAAD-CD_oh_290227.

15 After decades of subsidence due to decomposition and consolidation of the organic waste and the compaction and dewatering of the underlying bay muds, in 2012–13 the City of Palo Alto undertook major changes to the original design, including leveling most of the hillocks. See Sonja Dümpelmann, "Byxbee Park," Palo Alto, California, *SAH Archipedia;* http://sah-archipedia.org/buildings/CA-01-043-8014.

16 George Hargreaves has written about the impact Smithson's art had on his own work. John Beardsley, "Entropy and the New Landscapes," in *Hargreaves: Landscape Works, Process Architecture 128* (Tokyo: Process Architecture, 1996), pp. 14–25; and Elizabeth Meyer, "The Post-Earth Day Conundrum: Translating Environmental Values into Landscape Design," in *Environmentalism in Landscape Architecture*, ed. Michel Conan (Washington, DC: Dumbarton Oaks, 2000), pp. 187–244.

17 Peter Beard, "Peter Latz, Poet of Pollution," *Blueprint 130* (1996): p. 35.

18 See Elissa Rosenberg, "Gardens, Landscape, Nature: Duisburg Nord, Germany," in *The Hand and the Soul: Aesthetics and Ethics in Architecture and Art*, ed. Sanda Iliescu (Charlottesville: University of Virginia Press, 2009), pp. 210–30.

19 See Peter Latz, "Design is Experimental Invention," in *Creating Knowledge: Innovation Strategies for Designing Urban Landscapes*, ed. Hille von Seggern, Julia Werner and Lucia Grosse Bächle (Berlin, Boston: JOVIS Verlag GmbH, 2015), pp. 240–56.

20 See Udo Weilacher, *Between Landscape Architecture and Land Art* (Basel: Birkhäuser, 1996).

21 For a discussion of the idea of surfaces in landscape design, see Mary Pat McGuire, "Is Landscape Surface?" *Journal of Landscape Architecture*, (1, 2020): pp. 18–31.

22 http://landezine.com/index.php/2016/09/museum-park-louvre-lens-by-mosbach-paysagistes/.

23 See also the microtopography grading techniques used to create new wetland habitats at Tommy Thompson Park, on a former fill site at Leslie Avenue Spit, Toronto. Walter Kehm, *Accidental Wilderness: The Origins and Ecology of Toronto's Tommy Thompson Park* (Toronto: University of Toronto Press, 2020). For examples of grading and fluvial morphology, see SUPERPOSITIONS' experimental techniques used to reestablish a river corridor on the River Aire, Switzerland. Mathias Kondolf, "The Aire's Free Space: A Geomorphic Perspective," in *Aire*, ed. SUPERPOSITIONS (Zurich: Park Books, 2018), pp. 169–244. See also chapters 12 and 13 in this volume.

24 Neil Brenner and Nikos Katsikis coined this term in "Operational Landscapes: Hinterlands of the Capitalocene," *Architectural Digest* 90, (January/February 2020): pp. 22–31.

25 Udo Weilacher, *The Syntax of Landscape* (Basel: Birkhäuser, 2008).

26 Author's interview with Aliza Braudo, Principal, Braudo Maoz, Tel Aviv, Israel, 4 February 2020.

27 Weilacher, *Syntax of Landscape*, p. 155.

28 See Brenner and Katsikis, "Operational Landscapes," p. 27.

10. TOPOGRAPHY AS EXPRESSIVE FORM

ANA KUČAN

Every human act is expressive in itself: expressive of our understanding of the world, an attitude toward nature, a political view, the state of the art, or just a current mood. In this respect, my title is somewhat tautological and raises various philosophical questions that I must admit I am incapable of answering. In landscape design, we shape the land for at least three, often intertwined reasons: utility, aesthetics, and meaning. With water and trees, topography is one of the three basic mediums by which we construct space and create appropriate, expressive, and at times powerful forms [10-1]. These result from either topographical transformations or interventions into topography. Occasionally, we also shape entirely new topography. We respond to the land and face the challenges and possibilities it offers as a means of expression.

The question "What is the essence of landscape architecture?" is basic to everyone in the field as well as those who reflect upon it. This is a question extremely difficult to answer because, as Ian Thompson argues, landscape architecture encompasses many types, values, and approaches involving a network of overlapping but discontinuous similarities.[1] In addition, the range of scales in which landscape architects undertake their research and practice is extremely broad. However, landscape architects must work with specific materials and processes that result in specific formal expressions that in time inevitably prosper or decline beyond their control. This understanding produces a specific formal language regardless of the project's scale.

Over the centuries, landscape architects have created and developed various means of expression. Without these expressive means, asserts Slovenian landscape architect and professor Dušan Ogrin, landscape architects would be unable to imbue landscapes with symbolic meanings that have endured throughout the history of civilization.[2] Ogrin's claim is based on empirical studies and supported by landscapes from historical periods and cultures around the world. Symbolic transformation, Ogrin further argues, is a process based

10-1
Studio AKKA;
Studio abiro, STVAR.
Nordic Ski Centre Planica.
Rateče, Slovenia, 2015.
Panorama of the ski terrain.
[Miran Kambič]

on abstractions inherent and fundamental, and therefore indispensable, to any landscape design.[3]

In *Philosophy in a New Key*, Susan K. Langer elaborates on neo-Kantian philosopher Ernst Cassirer's notion of man as an *animal symbolicum*—a symbol-making or symbolizing animal—by asserting that the creation of symbols is at once a basic need and a fundamental human capacity.[4] Symbolization is thus *differentia specifica*: the most advanced human intellectual faculty, an ability developed even prior to the acquisition of language. This leads us to the most primal, and perhaps most meaningful, ancient architectural gestures for the expressive shaping of the land: the burial mound and the absolutely flat rectangular clearing in the woods.[5] As symbolic interventions into nature, both forms were created to transcend the world along an *axis mundi*, requiring an order or shape distinct from those already in existence. Through formal abstraction, the distinction of these shapes from surroundings—at times a pragmatic reality—heightened their expressive power.[6]

Of the symbolic forms of the constructed landscape, the burial mound was probably the earliest. All over the world, numerous surviving examples of these artificial landforms support this assumption. The expressive power of the mound, paired with the materials of its construction, produced a highly generalized form used repeatedly in landscape design for religious as well as secular purposes.

Throughout history, the functional, aesthetic, and meaningful manipulation of topography—the shaping of the land—has resulted in fascinating landscapes around the world, functionally in agricultural and industrial production, and symbolically and aesthetically in garden and park design. Science and technology have increased the possibilities for manipulating the existing terrain, extending and hastening processes long present in human history to unprecedented proportions. Several examples drawn from the history of landscape architecture will illustrate this point.

Versailles

Among all their other achievements, the spectacular gardens and park at Versailles represent a masterful manipulation of landform. To achieve André Le Nôtre's desired effect, the land was leveled, terraced, or modeled in an impressive manner. Here, reflecting pools rotated the *axis mundi* from vertical to horizontal, triumphing over nature to manifest the ambitions of earthly power [10-2]. In its gardens the measure of rational form has tamed the preexisting landscape, with geometry employed to master chaos as an act of political propaganda and an arrogant display of power and wealth. These were largely made possible by an elegantly graded topography along the garden's main axis that descends smoothly toward infinity. In this most magnificent, illusionistic space, a topographic height differential of some 30 meters has been rendered nearly invisible. Attaining the desired impression of grandeur and dynamic balance required the shifting of enormous quantities of soil. Although Le Nôtre followed the natural slope, he redesigned and transformed it to a significant degree. By means of excessive optical shortenings (anamorphosis or metric distension), the elements aligned along the main axis appear of equal width. In addition, the lengthening of the vistas to create the illusion of ever-extending space involved the careful study of all features in section and the making of the necessary adjustments.

As Slovenian philosopher Mladen Dolar writes in *Geometry and Enigma*, a text that accompanied the photography exhibition *L'espace infini*, and published by the University of Ljubljana in 2017:

> *Le Nôtre was a master of perspective and illusion. In the midst of transparent orderliness he constantly offers traps for our gaze; in the midst of the expected he presents us with the unexpected. In Versailles illusion lives and reigns; yet not simply as a misleading delusion of the real world, but as something which has a power according to which the real world begins to show itself as illusory and derealized.*[7]

Le Nôtre's vistas were planned to be experienced through movement. To achieve the desired effect, distances and levels were carefully coordinated. To determine the heights and shapes of the earthworks, he established a sequence of visually aligned points along the path and calculated the distances and desired views.[8] The visual and haptic experience gained along the main axis thus gradually unfolds through passage. At Versailles, through the manipulation of the ground plane, Le Nôtre rendered topography an expression of power.

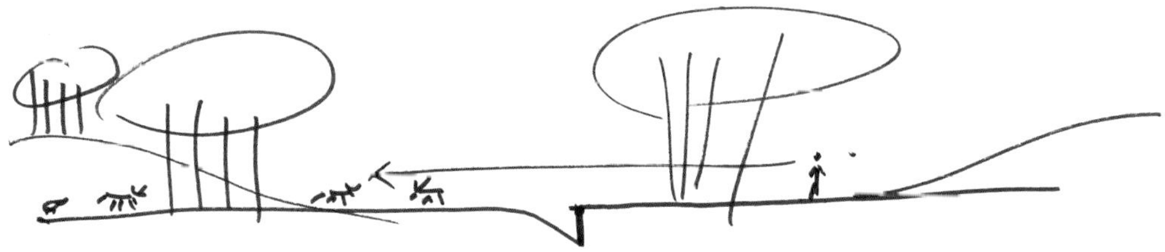

The English Landscape Garden

The landscape garden developed in eighteenth-century England introduced to landscape design a new idea of space by emphatically eradicating and supplanting the spatial configurations of the former era. A changing political order demanded its new spatial representation. Undulating terrain populated with irregularly placed clumps of trees superseded the axis and the unhindered view—a completely novel and dynamic concept of space that symbolized a government more liberal than the autocracy established in France during the prior century [10-3].

This newly emergent compositional freedom featured curvature: the "line of beauty" championed by artist William Hogarth.[9] Although supposedly following lines found in nature, the serpentine curve was nonetheless a purified, geometricized ideal. Applied in plan and section to guide the design and construction of the undulating land, it was used to shape the open meadow or the clustering of trees. Irregular geometry also generated new forms like the "ha-ha," or sunken fence, one of many expressions of this profound shift in the construction of space.[10] So that one's gaze from the manor would travel unimpeded across the lawn and then continue over the park and pastures, all intervening obstacles had to be removed—most of all, walls and fences. Yet some form of barrier was needed to prevent the sheep from intruding upon the lawn adjacent to the manor. By excavating a ditch with a sloping bottom supported by a stone wall—a feature with probable origins in military fortifications—the view could continue uninterrupted, while also keeping the animals at bay [10-4]. In the centuries that followed, the freely undulating topography and the open lawn were adopted in the designs of public parks around the world, likely reinforced by the appeal of an aesthetic that required limited maintenance, unlike the formal landscape it succeeded. And as a parable of human freedom, the naturalistic landscape provided space in which people could freely move and gather as they wished.

10-2
André Le Nôtre.
Park of Versailles.
France, 1668–89.
The perception of space and distance is enhanced by the precise modeling of land.
[Ana Kučan]

10-3
Lancelot "Capability" Brown.
Petworth.
West Sussex, England, 1753–65.
The undulating ground and irregularly placed clumps of trees.
[Danijel Mohorič]

(above) **10-4**
Ha-ha, or sunken fence.
[Ana Kučan]

Topography as Commemoration

In the aftermath of World War II, many of the arts questioned the nature and existence of a truly modern experience. Was it possible to truly create after the Holocaust, and if so, in what way? What might serve as an appropriate language for monuments and memorials in the postwar era? Finding an appropriate

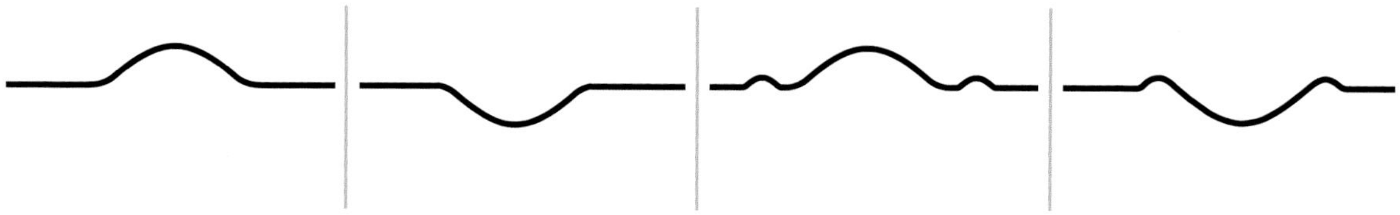

expression for commemorating the victims of war and oppression through the vehicle of landscape design was not an easy task. Perhaps this is why architects and landscape architects often returned to primal forms of expression—the tumulus, for example—to retrieve a symbol identified and understood universally across cultures, space, and time.

Yugoslavia's large scale monuments to antifascism, national-liberation, and class struggles after World War II engaged their sites in complex ways. In type, they range from monuments to victory to memorials for the victims of extermination. Topography has played a vital role in their design, especially in the memorials designed by architect Bogdan Bogdanović. While in most cases Bogdanović has taken advantage of the existing topography, for the Jasenovac memorial park, situated on the site of a former extermination camp, he chose to create a new landscape [10-5]. Built in 1966, the resulting memorial is quiet and contemplative, a calm yet powerful site of mourning and remembrance that surrounds a monument formed in the shape of a flower [10-6]. While recalling burials of the past, Bogdanović's subversive design revisited the traditional tumulus form, using negative spaces to undermine the solidity of some mounds while configuring others as a ring [10-7, 10-8].[11] The tumuli are positioned rather loosely on the land, their locations determined by the sites of the former barracks. Collectively they symbolize the missing graves in a manner decidedly absent from historical precedents.

Due to political-ideological issues impossible to resolve at the time of construction, the mounds do not mark the locations of the graves of those murdered in the camp; these lie on the opposite side of the river. But the way in which Bogdanović has shaped this wind-beaten terrain highlights the presence of the horizontal plane as a possible path to a final tranquility. At the same time, the tumuli instill in us a sense of unease and discomfort by pitting the freedom suggested by unbounded space against human vulnerability, employing both actual and metaphorical exposure. At the Jasenovac memorial Bogdanovic retrieved universal forms and spatial relations to prompt reflection and introspection, and created a space that yields a poetics of solitude. Its power derives from its undefined and incomplete quality, an openness that reveals the fragmentary nature of our lives.

10-5
Bogdan Bogdanović. Jasenovac Memorial. Jasenovac, Croatia (Yugoslavia), 1966. The landscape of mounds. [Ana Kučan].

10-6
Bogdan Bogdanović. Jasenovac Memorial. Aerial view of the monument area showing the positions of the mounds; shadows reveal the forms of the ring mounds. [Google Earth]

10-7
Bogdan Bogdanović. Jasenovac Memorial. Alternation of positive and void. [Ana Kučan]

10-8
Bogdan Bogdanović. Jasenovac Memorial. Ring mound with a void at its center. [Ana Kučan]

Google

Although landscape architecture has oriented its recent efforts toward solving the increasingly overwhelming environmental challenges, the assumption that issues of form and aesthetics are less significant is misguided; the divide between sustainability and aesthetic issues is false.[12] In addition to solving the environmental problems that confront us, we need designed landscapes that are intriguing and mysterious—landscapes that can provoke albeit not always comfort.

Buitenshot Park and MAX IV Laboratory Landscape

Designed by H+N+S Landscape Architects in collaboration with a multidisciplinary project team, Buitenshot Park is a recreational landscape outside Amsterdam primarily intended to reduce ground noise from Schiphol Airport [10-9]. Almost as soon as the airport's fifth runway opened for operation in 2003, residents living in the area began to complain about the increased level of ground noise: the low-frequency sound generated by aircraft during takeoff. Using innovative technology to effectively reduce noise pollution, the park's design is nonetheless highly aesthetic. Technical calculations suggested using a series of longitudinal mounds triangular in section, positioned in colliding geometries. These forms effectively deflect ground sound while creating a landscape of corridors, ruled by repetition and enriched by sudden shifts in perspective. The shaped land is thus fully operational, and while instigated by functional need, it is intriguing and beautiful.

Snøhetta's 19-hectare park in Lund, Sweden, was designed as a functional landscape for the high-performance synchrotron radiation laboratory MAX IV. The landscape design addressed a set of parameters that supported the performance of the laboratory's research. Testing led by researchers and engineers revealed that traffic on the neighboring highway was causing ground vibrations that could influence the results of experiments made inside the buildings. Study revealed that on flatter land, ground vibrations represented a greater risk to experimentation. This knowledge, Snøhetta explains, prompted the creation of a constellation of mounds configured in a bold pattern, which also serve to manage water runoff on the site [10-10].

Both parks are witty and powerful materializations of scientific findings, translated into extremely attractive and functional landscapes. The appearance, precision, and repetition of their earth forms express society's ever-growing acquisition of knowledge and at times, even an interest in beauty.

10-9
H+N+S Landscape Architects. Buitenshot Park. Amsterdam, Netherlands, 2013. [Your Captain Luchtfotografie]

Studio AKKA: Four Projects

Although Studio AKKA has not yet had the opportunity to design a project completely dependent on landform, topographic issues have played a prominent role in almost all our work. We see topography as one of our primary mediums and aspire to use it expressively, regardless of scale and task. Four typologically diverse projects in Slovenia represent various approaches to the topography, each using the potential of the site in its own way and shaping the land in its own manner.

Bled: Levels and Enhancements

The renovation of the grounds of the White Mansion at Bled involved no reshaping of the land; on the contrary, the design appropriated the existing topography to enhance the character of this exquisite setting [10-11]. The neo-Renaissance villa is situated on a lake whose shoreline is mostly covered with forest and in places steeply sloped. The paths and scattered remnants of masonry provoke memories of features formerly existing on the site. A walk through the forest reveals a sequence of magnificent views of the lake, the island at its center, and a castle framed by the dark verticals of the trees. The features of the forest—a hut and stone water-management structures—stimulate significant emotional responses. The redesign conserved and enhanced the existing qualities of the site by uncovering certain old structures and adding new ones, utilizing the topography to strengthen the views outward and to facilitate the use of the forest without diminishing the calm of its wilderness [10-12].

Kranj: Vertical Interventions

Set on the rim of Kokra Canyon, the medieval town of Kranj long ago turned its back to the river and the crumbling canyon walls around it. Despite this seeming rejection of the natural topography, the canyon was, and remains, a subject with a strong symbolic, almost mythical charge. The competition brief for its redesign featured an inherent contradiction by calling for a connection between the historically divided town and nature. In addition, no intervention that would disturb the natural state of the canyon was permitted. Together, these two constraints rendered the task almost impossible. Taking the competition guidelines literally, in our design we sought to reveal the underlying contradictions.

We reworked the areas where the town and canyon meet, where the edge of one is the edge of the other [10-13]. Developed using segments

10 10
Snøhetta.
MAX IV Laboratory landscape.
Lund, Sweden, 2016.
Aerial view.
[Mikal Schlosser, ABML4]

10-11
Studio AKKA.
Grounds of the
White Mansion.
Bled, Slovenia, 2010.
Topography enhanced
by leveling.
[Peter Koštrun]

10-12
Studio AKKA.
Grounds of the
White Mansion.
The sway of
topography capped
by a narrow platform
directing the view.
[Peter Koštrun]

of the historical retaining walls, the vertical landscape reveals and enhances the natural topography of the river canyon; functionally, it connects the town to the canyon but makes no attempt to enter it [10-14]. The connection we proposed was to function as a divide as well as a suture by preserving the traditional dichotomy between city and canyon. The two entities meet in active superimposition: the vertical landscape allows the canyon to be visible from the town, while the town floats above it and warrants enthusiastic admiration.

Sports Park Stožice: Extractions and Fillings

Stožice was planned as a sports park combining into a coherent whole a football stadium, a sports hall, an underground shopping mall, and a park. As "urban generators," these functions were to be intertwined as an interactive social space that would facilitate events of varied types. The park was planned as Ljubljana's new, primary recreation space by converting to new uses thirteen hectares of a former gravel pit. The hybrid structure preserved the flatness of the surrounding suburban agricultural landscape while relating the dome of the sports hall and the roof of the stadium with the primary landscape features, among them a remnant of the ancient riparian forest and an allée of mature trees that extends along the southern edge of the area [10-15]. An extensive plane of grass became the central element of the scheme, extending into the more elaborated edges of the plaza and integrating the sports park's features both visually and functionally. Crucial for the layout of the park were the buildings over which it is built, structures that periodically penetrate the park's surface. All the design decisions addressed constraints imposed by a landscape built on structure.

10-13
Studio AKKA.
The Floating City.
Kranj, Slovenia, 2010.
Model.
Connecting city and canyon, while keeping the identities of both distinct.
[Studio AKKA]

10-14
Studio AKKA.
The Floating City.
Proposed vertical landscape; view over the canyon.
[Studio AKKA]

The park's main role was to harmonize the functions of the three principal structures beneath and above it—stadium, sports hall, and shopping center—while also using the new topography to transition gradually into the adjacent agricultural plots. An important goal was to restore the area's original flatness. The thick, constructed "slab," a concrete plane built over the former pit, was pierced with features to support the operations taking place beneath the park. This network of vents, skylights, and staircases enables elements of the park to descend to the floor levels of the shopping center. Only two public buildings rise above the upper riparian terrace once formed by the dynamics of the Sava River [10-16]. In the early stages of design, we ambitiously envisioned the park to

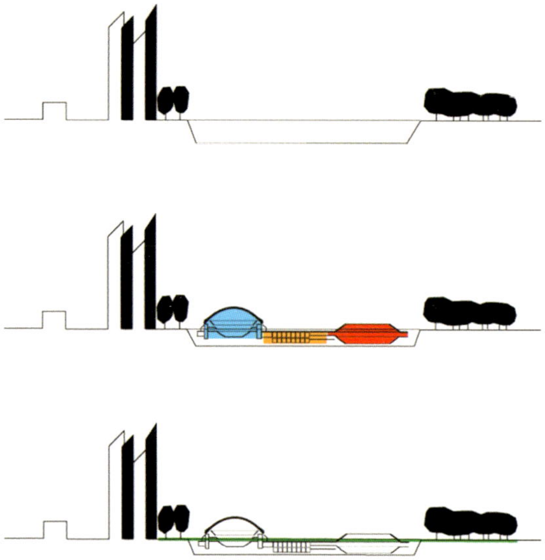

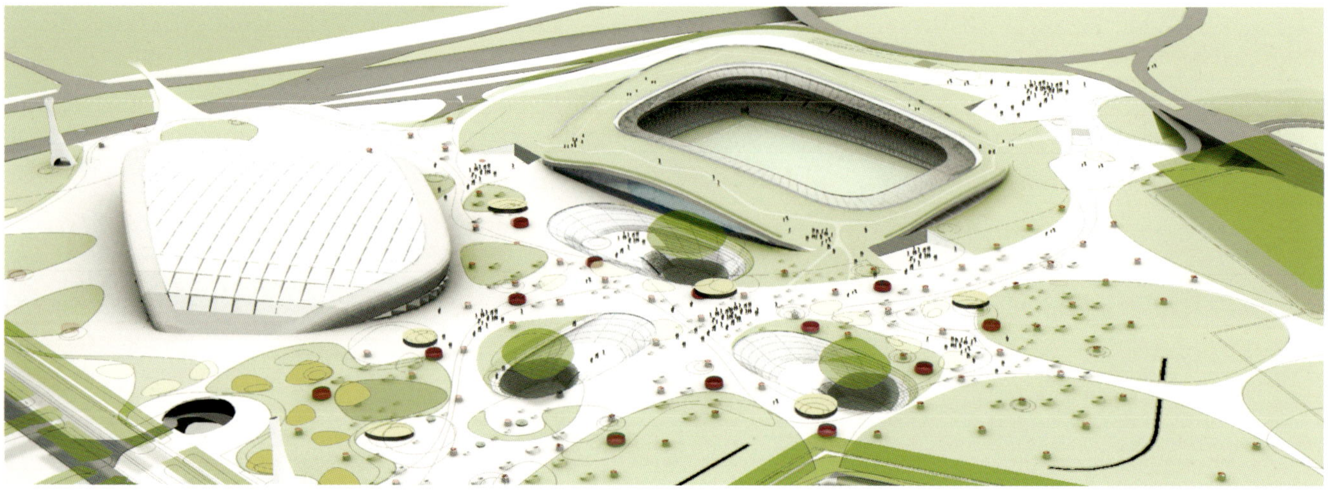

(opposite top) **10-15**
Sadar+Vuga, architects; Studio AKKA. Sports Park Stožice. Ljubljana, Slovenia, 2011. The schematic presentation of the new topography: rims of the formal gravel pit, the filling (new buildings), and the unifying concrete slab covering the pit and connecting it to the various levels. [Studio AKKA]

(opposite center) **10-16**
Sadar+Vuga, architects; Studio AKKA. Sports Park Stožice. Aerial view, complex that filled a former gravel pit. [Studio AKKA]

(opposite bottom) **10-17**
Sadar+Vuga, architects; Studio AKKA. Sports Park Stožice. The undulating landform in the roundabout. The shape is maintained below the level of the original alluvial terrace formerly quarried for gravel. [Studio AKKA]

(right) **10-18**
Studio AKKA, Studio abiro, STVAR. Nordic Ski Centre Planica. Rateče, Slovenia, 2015. Site plan determining the new topography of the valley. [Studio AKKA]

climb onto the roof of the stadium—the land falls some six meters from one end to the other—to enable visitors to mount an otherwise flat landscape and enjoy views over the area. Because the municipality could not find a private partner to assist in the development of the project, the construction of the shopping center was halted in 2011, and the park was left unfinished. In our design we aspired to express the character of the alluvial plain and the history of the site connected with its exploitation. The interruption of construction left both our aspiration and its construction incomplete [10-17].

Planica: Shaping the Land

Our largest project to date involved the transformation of an alpine landscape for the Nordic Centre Planica in Rateče, where our respect for the beauty of the valley guided the reconfiguration of the topography to serve sports and spectacle. Planica has hosted international ski-jumping competitions since the early 1930s, and over the years gradually became known as the venue for the World Cup Sky Flying Finals. From many years of use, the ski jumps at Planica had deteriorated and were in need of renovation and modernization. In 2009, the decision was made not only to renovate the facilities but also to transform the site into the far larger Nordic Ski Centre. The driving concept for the design addressed the profound relationship among the natural setting, the ski jumps, and the other structures on-site [10-18; see also 10-1]. The precise design of the topography; the systematic selection and reduction of materials; and the bold shapes and clear, geometric forms of the architecture of the ski jumps all contrast, yet resonate, with the existing silhouette of the mountains and the calm of the spruce-and-beech forest that covers its slopes. Working on many levels and to profit from various formal relations, the design plays solid against void, stiff against pliable, resistant against ephemeral, cold against warm, and monumental against intimate. Seasonal changes enhance the contrast between the sharp profile of the mountains and its accompanying topography, and the forms of the concrete structures. In times of colorful abundance—late summer and autumn—the buildings visually play only a supporting role.

10-19
Studio AKKA; Studio abiro; STVAR. Nordic Ski Centre Planica. Rateče, Slovenia, 2015. The altered valley serves as a tribune for the Nordic ski stadium. [Studio AKKA]

Planica stands at the foot of the largest nature conservation area, and forms one of the most exciting entrances to Triglav National Park [10-19]. In deference to the magnificent natural setting and because Planica is already symbolically charged, our design was restrained. The alpine setting of this structured sports ritual is unique and recognizable. Every aspect of the design precisely addresses the technical and organizational requirements of a large sports facility that shapes the character of the new space. In contrast to the natural dynamics of the surrounding mountain landscape, it offers an organized, functional, and technically precise counterpoint, perfected through the logic of engineering. The ski jumps that fan across the landscape apply a new order to the topography that unites all the elements into a nonhierarchical whole [see 10-1, 10-17]. This allowed the topography to emerge as the principal material by which to better use the bottom of the valley, which must accommodate large-scale events requiring extensive infrastructure and demanding logistics. The rest of the design followed. When more than 30,000 people come to this fragile valley, the shaped land gives way to the demands of sports. On the everyday level, when a handful of young ski jumpers or Nordic skiers come to train in solitude, the simplicity and robustness of the new landform retreats in favor of the monumentality of the mountains. To achieve this balance all the service buildings, such as the visitor center, were pushed to the edges of the valley to maintain the long vistas from the valley to the surrounding slopes.

In my view, as our society has become more and more pragmatic, governed by money, insensitive, and disenchanted, the quest for the expressive, even poetic aspects of landscape architecture has become a subversive act. And one that is much needed.

Notes

1 Ian Thompson, "Essence-less Landscape Architecture and Its Extended Family," *Harvard Design Magazine* (Spring/Summer 2013), p. 27.

2 Dušan Ogrin, "Symbolism in Landscape Artefact / Symboliek van artefacten in het landschap," in *The Landscape of Symbols / Landschap van symbolen*, ed. Klaas Kerkstra and Meto Vroom (Wageningen: Uitgeverij Blauwdruk, 2003), pp. 64–99.

3 Ogrin, "Symbolism in Landscape Artefact."

4 Ogrin, "Symbolism in Landscape Artefact."

5 The rectangular clearing at Shinto shrines–*yuniwa* in Japanese–is among the first topographic planes constructed for nonutilitarian (nonagricultural) purposes.

6 The gesture of clearing and leveling is very similar to Ingold's description of the initial stages of agriculture: "What agriculture achieves through the practical operations of ground clearance and preparation is the separation of the land from its embodiment in the landscape." Tim Ingold, *The Appropriation of Nature: Essays on Human Ecology and Social Relations* (Manchester: Manchester University Press, 1986), p. 154.

7 http://landezine.com/index php/2017/10/ana-kucan-versailles-lespace-infini/; trans. Miroslav Griško. First published in Slovenian as Mladen Dolar, "Geometrija in uganka / La géométrie et l'énigme," in *Struktura neskoncnosti / L'espace infini*, artzinc, Biotechnical Faculty, University of Ljubljana, Ljubljana, 2017.

8 Visualized as part of a short presentation on the work of Le Nôtre on the Versailles official website: https://youtu.be/-RnjYn-pWWU?t=272.

9 English painter and social critic William Hogart (1697–1764) defined the natural curve as the formal imperative in his treatise *The Analysis of Beauty*. William Hogarth (1753; repr., New York: Cosimo Classics, 2009). As a child of the rococo, Hogarth defined the principles of beauty and grace as represented by the serpentine line, which attracted the viewer's attention and evoked liveliness and movement. *The Analysis of Beauty* formed the intellectual centerpiece of what the historian Ernst Gombrich described as Hogarth's "grim campaign against the fashionable taste." Ernst Gombrich, *The Story of Art* (New York: Phaidon Press, 1995), p. 519.

10 For further discussion on the emphatic rejection of the perpendicularity associated with the *ancien régime*, see Christian Cay Lorenz Hirschfeld, *Theorie der Gartenkunst* (1785; repr., Berlin: Union Verlag, 1990).

11 My assertion is based on the concept of "counter-memory and counter-monuments," embodied in the negtive form of Horst Hoheisel's 1985 Aschrott Fountain in the center of Kassel, Germany. Counter-monuments condemn images representing the Holocaust as an unimaginable and sacred event. See Kristine Nielsen, "Monumental Attack: The Visual Tools of the German Counter Monument in Two Works by Jochen Gerz and Esther Shalev-Gerz, and Horst Hoheisel," *Images* 9 (2016): pp. 122–39, James E. Young, "The Counter-Monument: Memory Against Itself in Germany Today," *Critical Inquiry* 2 (1992): pp. 267–96.

12 See Elisabeth K. Meyer, "Sustaining Beauty: The Performance of Appearance," *Journal of Landscape Architecture* 3 (2008): pp. 6–23.

11. THE WASHINGTON MONUMENT TOPOGRAPHICALLY CONSIDERED

KATHLEEN JOHN-ALDER

Conceived in 1783, repeatedly designed and topographically manipulated, yet never quite finished, the Washington Monument stands as a testament to heroic action and design persistence. Dedicated to the memory of the first president of the United States and the political and geographic struggles that gave birth to a nation, the Monument is also the most prominent, and abstract, structure on the National Mall. Ten times higher than it is wide, the striking silhouette towers above the surrounding skyline, austere and majestic [11-1].

As a reminder of the legendary sacrifices and enlightened idealism of the world of 1776, the Monument intentionally proffers what the cultural critic J. B. Jackson calls an incentive to imitate the "virtues, glory, honor, and heroic deeds of those whose efforts shaped our national consciousness and made our lives today possible." Traditional monuments of this sort, he further claims, are "an echo of the remote past" made "present and actual," and they "exist to put people in mind of some obligation that they have incurred: a great public figure, a great public event, a great public declaration which the group had pledged itself to honor."[1] The Monument, in this sense, projects to the nation and the world aspirations related to the highest ideals of the United States. And yet, upon close inspection, imperfections emerge. It is easy, for instance, to discern a color difference in the stone—it is lighter at the bottom and darker at the top—a residue of construction, which, due to insufficient funding, soil stability, and issues with the foundation, occurred in distinct phases associated with several commemorative moments.

11-1
Washington National Monument looking toward the Capitol. *Senate Park Commission Report*. Washington, DC, ca. 1902. [Detroit Publishing Company]

The fact that the land surrounding the Monument remains unfinished even though, like the Monument, it has been the focus of multiple design and construction efforts, also suggests the virtues and deeds this edifice commemorates are more politically fraught and less idealistically pure than the white marble obelisk makes them appear to be. Originally the end point of the National Mall, as the federal city grew and dredge spoils filled the banks of the Potomac, the Monument became, literally, stuck in the middle—the physical manifestation of an awkward nexus of economics, politics, and bureaucratic decision-making. Consequently, the history of this landscape is, as these circumstances suggest, the story of a certain type of democratic topography in the making, composed of incremental changes and additions as the ground transitioned from a muddy riverbank to the stately hill it is today.

To capture this landscape drama and its intriguing mix of design initiatives, economic constraints, and political equivocations, this essay presents a collection of topographic tableaux for consideration. Separated by a series of actions and nonactions, these scenes are not just about, or not only about, the object described: the Washington Monument and its grounds. Instead, they track over two centuries of efforts to shape the lay of the land and design a particular vision for what the country could and should be.

The Washington National Monument Society

In the summer of 1783, several months before the Treaty of Paris officially recognized the independence of the United States, the Continental Congress resolved to build an equestrian statue of George Washington in gratitude for his service to the country during the Revolutionary War. Pressing financial concerns at that time, however, prevented its implementation. Nearly fifty years later, the centennial of Washington's birth in 1832 revived interest in the monument, which could now be built in the city bearing his name. Congress debated the issue without arriving at a definitive conclusion.[2]

Angered by Congress's failure to appropriate monies for a monument in honor of the first president, prominent citizens, led by the Chief Justice of the Supreme Court, formed the Washington National Monument Society and began to solicit private funds for the project. To stimulate interest in their endeavors, the Society sponsored a design competition and invited American artists and architects to submit ideas that "harmoniously blend durability, simplicity, and grandeur." In 1836, it selected a proposal by Robert Mills.[3]

Inspired by ancient Egypt and the Greek and Roman revival architecture popular at the time, Mills's design for the Washington Monument consisted of a circular colonnade, 250 feet in diameter and 100 feet high, with a 500-foot obelisk rising from its center. Doric columns, interspersed with statues of Revolutionary War heroes and signers of the Declaration of Independence, supported the roof. A statue of Washington in a horse-drawn chariot stood guard over the entrance portico, and a star at the top of the obelisk symbolized his glorious presence [11-2].[4]

The site for this eclectic edifice—the intersection of the east-west axis of the Capitol and the north-south axis of the President's House (the White House)—corresponded to the location of an equestrian statue of Washington established in Pierre Charles L'Enfant's 1791 plan for the federal city [11-3]. In addition to noting that Washington had examined and approved the L'Enfant scheme, the Society justified their decision to locate the Monument on a small rise near a riverbank thus: it "presents a beautiful view of the Potomac; it is so elevated that the Monument will be seen from all parts of the city and the surrounding country, and being a public reservation, it is safe from any obstruction of view. It is so near the river that materials for constructing the Monument can be conveyed to it from the river at but little expense" [11-4].[5]

Since no funds had to be allocated, Congress acted and transferred ownership of the land to the Society, and work on the Monument began in 1849 under the supervision of Mills. To support the weight of the proposed structure—the riverbank site consisted of unconsolidated sand and clay—the foundation was relocated 351.6 feet east and 123 feet west of the intersecting axes. This action enabled construction but also negated L'Enfant's carefully considered placement of the statue in relation to topography, axial views, and important buildings.[6]

Funding remained an issue, and all monies were dedicated to the construction of the obelisk. Nevertheless, despite ongoing efforts, funds were exhausted by 1854, and the work halted. The foundation was complete but only 152 feet of the obelisk—less than a third—had been built.[7] The unfinished structure stood abandoned in a muddy field, surrounded by wooden shacks. Upon the outbreak of the Civil War, it lingered in this incomplete and nearly ruinous state for more than twenty years [11-5].

The Army Corps of Engineers

A Congressional resolution initiated in 1876 to honor the centennial of the Declaration of Independence enabled work on the Monument to resume. The resolution specified $200,000 for construction providing the following stipulations were met: the Society had to cede the land and the Monument back to the federal government, and relinquish control to the Army Corps of Engineers, which would certify that the foundations could support the Monument's full height and weight.[8]

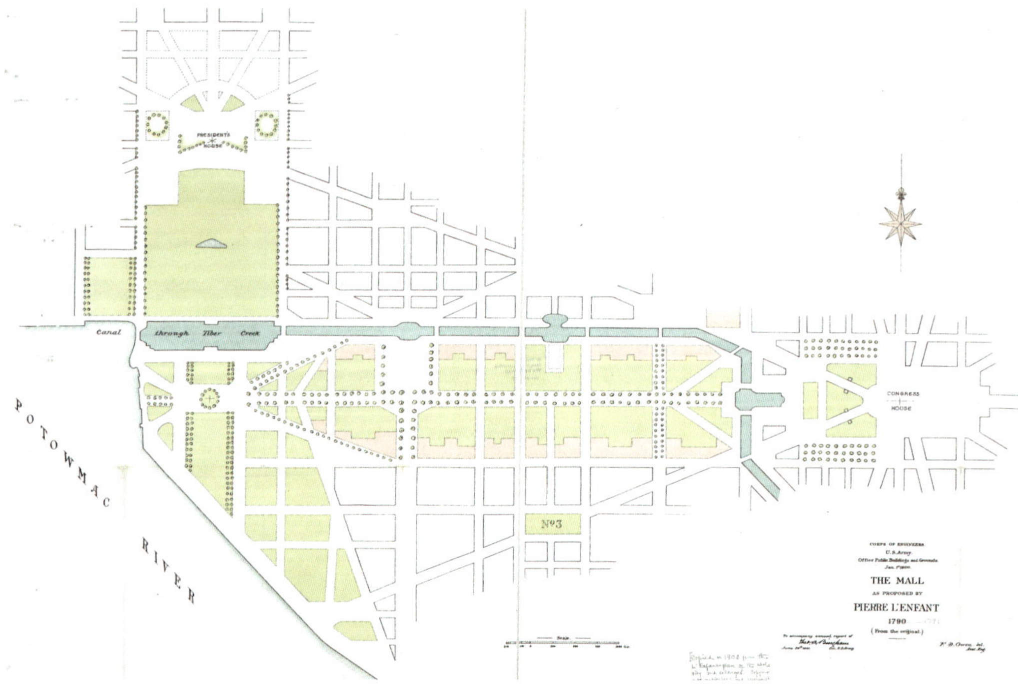

11-2
Robert Mills.
Washington National Monument.
Washington, DC, 1846.
Lithograph after the Mills original.
[Library of Congress]

11-3
Pierre L'Enfant.
National Mall.
Washington, DC, 1791.
Site plan.
The Mall as a tree-lined avenue with the equestrian statue of George Washington at the intersection of the axis of the Capitol and the President's House.
[Library of Congress]

11-4
Currier and Ives.
Bird's-eye View of Washington, DC, Illustrating the Relationship of the Washington National Monument to the Capitol, White House, Potomac River, and Babcock Lake, ca. 1880.
[Library of Congress]

To fulfill the Congressional mandate, the Corps of Engineers appointed Thomas Lincoln Casey to oversee construction. Casey's overriding concern was the strength of the foundation and the stability of the obelisk. A subsequent examination determined that the foundation's rough-hewn stone did not provide adequate support given the soil conditions. To address the situation, Casey constructed a concrete footing underneath the existing foundation. Concrete buttresses carved into the stone distributed the weight of the obelisk to the new footing. The excavation and underpinning for the project was a delicate task, done in stages. Work began in 1879 and lasted one year. To provide additional support and conceal the concrete, the foundation was covered with the excavated stone and soil. The resulting embankment extended slightly over 200 feet from the Monument [11-6, 11-7].[9] To further complicate matters, artists and architects seized the opportunity presented by the change in project oversight to propose new designs in keeping with the ornate Victorian aesthetics of the era. Although members of Congress were receptive to the proposals, the Speaker of the House favored the simple obelisk, stating that it reflected the donations of a generation of citizens, and that their contributions should be honored.[10]

As worked neared completion, Casey turned his attention to the grounds and petitioned Congress for funds to place soil around the foundation embankment to create a more natural setting. He also requested filling Babcock Lake, a remnant canal basin on the north side of the site. Casey believed subterranean water flow to this skating and fishing pond would undermine the new foundation and cause settlement. Congress initially balked at the price but eventually agreed the stability of the Monument merited the cost. In 1888, the grounds opened to the public [11-8].[11]

The Senate Park Commission

The year 1900 marked the centennial of Congress's move to Washington, DC. To commemorate this event, prominent designers, at the urging of the American Institute of Architects (AIA), developed schemes for a boulevard situated in the center of the National Mall. Proponents of the scheme argued that it embodied the intent of the L'Enfant plan, which showed an avenue in this location.[12] Moreover, the dredging of the river and the creation of the Potomac Flats had extended the Mall, and it was generally felt that a landscaped boulevard lined by important buildings would beautify the new land.

11-5
Mathew Brady. Washington National Monument. Washington, DC, ca. 1860. The incomplete obelisk. [Library of Congress]

11-6
Army Corps of Engineers. Washington National Monument. Excavation of the foundation. Washington, DC, 15 December 1879. [Library of Congress]

11-7
Washington National Monument and completed embankment. Washington, DC, 15 December 1879. [Historic American Buildings Survey, Library of Congress]

Senator James MacMillan, Chairman of the Senate Committee on the District of Columbia, became the political champion of the centennial project, and through deft political maneuvering established a Park Commission to devise a plan "commensurate with the dignity and the resources of the American nation."[13] MacMillan proposed that architect Daniel Burnham and landscape architect Frederick Law Olmsted Jr. carry out the study. Burnham proposed the addition of architect Charles McKim and sculptor Augustus Saint-Gaudens.[14] To initiate the work, Burnham, Olmsted, McKim, and Charles Moore, the Clerk of the District Committee, traveled to Europe to visit L'Enfant's sources of inspiration and discover design elements that would provide pleasure from "generation to generation."[15] The team determined that "simplicity, directness and subordination of ornament to structural issues should prevail," and that this should be achieved through "tree-crowned terraces" where "the configuration of land permitted."[16] Olmsted had already articulated these principles in remarks to the AIA annual conference held in Washington, DC, in 1900, when he observed, "simplicity is required when the scale of a formal landscape is large." Olmsted also argued against the central boulevard and instead proposed four carriage lanes lined with trees.[17]

In 1902, MacMillan delivered the *Report of the Park Commission* to the Senate. This lavishly illustrated document depicted the Mall as a symmetrical, "kite-shaped figure bisected from east to west by the axis of the Capitol and from north to south by the White House axis."[18] The east–west axis, as Olmsted later observed, is "slanted sufficiently from a right angle from the face of the Capitol to make it center on the Monument," thus resolving the awkward geometry that arose when the decision was made to relocate the Monument foundation to higher and drier ground.[19] A central panel of lawn, rows of trees, and an overlook terrace enhanced the new alignment of topography and views:

> *The bordering columns of elms march to the Monument grounds, climb the slope, and, spreading themselves to the right and left on extended terraces, form a great body of green, strengthening the broad platform from which the obelisk rises in majestic serenity. The groves on the terraces become places of rest, from which one gets views of the busy city; of the Capitol, crowning the heights at the end of the broad vista; of sunny stretches of river at the foot of the Virginia hills.*[20]

11-8
Harris & Ewing. Crowds gathering on the "natural" hill created by Thomas Lincoln Casey and the Army Corps of Engineers. Washington, DC, ca. 1909. [Library of Congress]

11-9
Senate Park Commission. Washington National Monument terrace and garden. Washington, DC, 1902. Aerial perspective. [National Geographic Society Library and Archives]

Marble stairs, the width of the Mall, descended from the terrace to a garden, where a circular fountain, positioned at the intersection of the axes, captured a reflection of the obelisk [11-9]. These design considerations granted the Monument the same sense of grandeur whether seen up close or from a distance. Accordingly, the report stated, the Monument, no longer "a bare obelisk missing its base," stands resplendent on its lofty pediment "as one of the most beautiful human creations. Indeed, it is at once so great and so simple that it almost seems to be a work of nature."[21]

Most of the Park Commission recommendations for the Mall were realized, except for the grounds of the Washington Monument, which remained unfinished. The proposed terrace was too tall and heavy, and the proposed garden was too low and close to the foundation. Both alterations to the topography would have toppled the obelisk.

National Security

In April of 1995, a rental truck containing a powerful bomb exploded in front of the Alfred P. Murrah Federal Building in Oklahoma City, resulting in numerous fatalities. Following the incident, security increased in federal facilities, including physical barriers such as fences, planters, benches, bollards, and walls designed to stop an explosive-filled vehicle traveling fifty miles per hour.[22]

Subsequent action by Congress led to the installation of bollards around the Capitol, but once again the Washington Monument and its grounds were ignored: that is, until the 9/11 terrorist attacks on the World Trade Center and the Pentagon provided added urgency. In response, John Parsons of the National Park Service orchestrated a program for security upgrades that would beautify the landscape and restore the Monument grounds to their intended cultural status. Funds channeled through a design-build addition to the World War II Memorial, then under construction, would pay for design and installation.[23]

An invited competition, held in December of 2001, led to the selection of a security-landscape design by Laurie Olin. At the time of the competition, Jersey Barriers—concrete highway medians—formed a loose ring around the Monument plaza and its fifty flags. To reach the obelisk, visitors had to negotiate the barriers and the police cars guarding the cracked and broken plaza [11-10]. Moreover, the soil Casey had placed around the foundation was thoroughly compacted, the lawn was threadbare, and the paths ascending the knoll did not conform to the provisions of the Americans with Disabilities Act (ADA).

Olin's design harmoniously blended security, simplicity, and grandeur. Inspired by the critique of security preparedness mounted by Benjamin Forgey, the architecture critic of the *Washington Post*, the proposed alterations transformed what had become an unsightly "hilltop fort" into a patriotic public landscape with a privileged view.[24] A granite-clad wall at the base of the knoll, 400 feet from the obelisk, deters bomb-laden trucks and provides visitors a place to sit and rest [11-11]. The granite's rusticated surface intentionally evokes the rough-hewn stone of the foundation. Paths, in the form of two intersecting ovals, pass through the wall and gracefully ascend the knoll to a redesigned plaza encircled by flags and marble benches. Eight retractable bollards, two at each wall opening, prevent the passage of unwanted vehicles [11-12, 11-13]. Additional paths follow the outside perimeter of the wall and provide east–west circulation. Precise contouring established a constant elevation for the wall and allowed the oval paths to curve up and around at an incline that accommodates ADA accessibility [11-14]. The broad, gently sloping profile both forms a pediment for the Monument and makes the design appear natural, as if it always existed. And this feat of topographic legerdemain was accomplished—as a dramatic cut-and-fill drawing indicates—by moving less than one foot of soil within 200 feet of the foundation (the width of the Casey embankment): anything greater would have threatened the stability of the obelisk [11-15, 11-16].

History, and the lessons it teaches, matters to Olin, and it is fitting that he infused the design with a romantic spirit: an inspiring view of a monument on a hill, encircled by landscape, with distant views of the sunset and the water. A similar sensibility motivated Andrew Jackson Downing's 1850 design of the Mall and Smithsonian grounds. According to landscape architect Elbert Peets, it is also apparent in the Commission plan, which, despite its references to the civic geometry of L'Enfant, creates an urban setting immersed in the intricate textures of nature.[25] Olin stripped this impulse of superfluous details to make a simple but elegant statement about cultural heritage and the importance of topography and views in the aesthetics of the capital city. A concept sketch by Olin reveals the care taken to create a design in sympathy with the existing topography and previous design efforts [11-17]. Like the Commission plan, trees flow from the Mall and surround the obelisk in a body of green. In this case, however, rather than an ornate garden and terrace, a low wall and grassy knoll ground the composition. Due to insufficient funds, the body of trees never materialized.[26]

11-10
Washington National Monument.
Temporary security measures.
Washington, DC, 2002.
[Kathleen John-Alder]

11-11
Laurie Olin.
Security design.
Washington National Monument, 2002.
Illustrative site plan.
[The Olin Studio]

11-12
Washington National Monument. Washington, DC, 2006. Granite security wall, bollards, and oval paths. [Kathleen John-Alder]

11-13
Washington National Monument plaza looking toward the World War II and Lincoln Memorials. Washington, DC, 2006. [Kathleen John-Alder]

11-14
Laurie Olin. Bench. Constructed with marble from the original quarry that provided material for the obelisk. [Marc Treib]

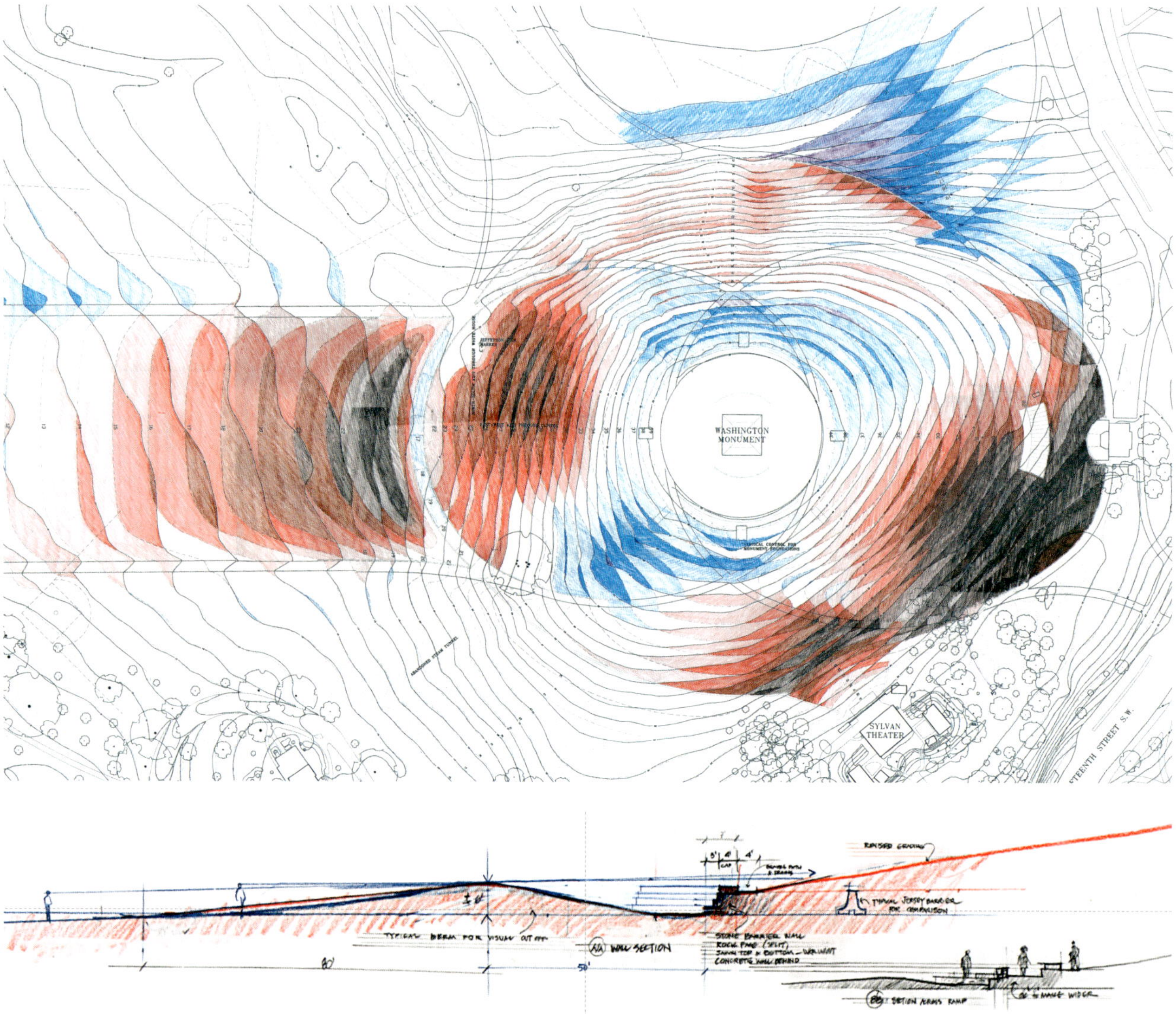

11-15
Washington National Monument. Contouring the knoll. Washington, DC, 2004. [Kathleen John-Alder]

11-16
Laurie Olin and Project Design Team. Washington National Monument. Washington, DC, 2002. Security-design cut-and-fill grading plan. *(above)*: Within 200 feet of the obelisk less than one foot of soil was disturbed; *(below)*: Cross section through the security wall, showing the care taken to screen it from the Lincoln Memorial. [The Olin Studio]

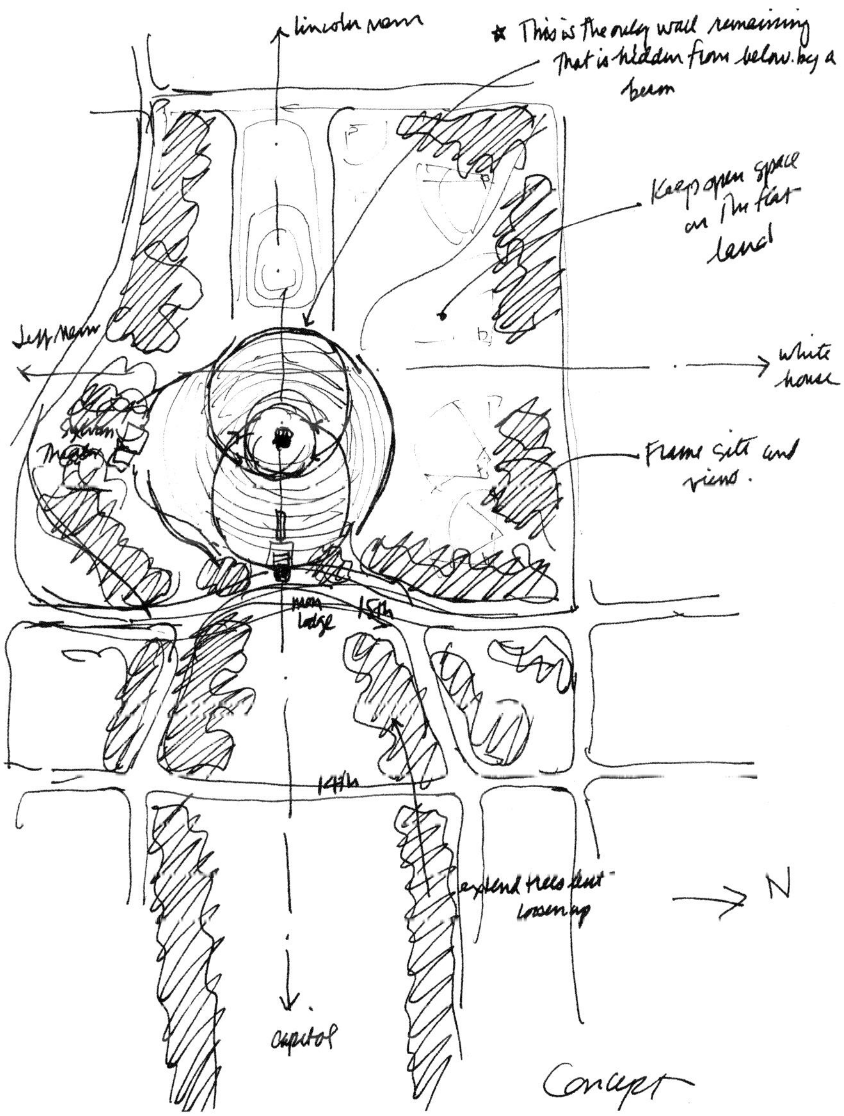

11-17
Laurie Olin.
Washington National
Monument security design.
Washington, DC, 2001.
Concept sketch.
[The Olin Studio]

11-18
Laurie Olin.
Buscot House and Park.
England.
late eighteenth century.
Sketch of the lawn
and ha-ha, 1995.
[from *Across the Open Field: Essays Drawn from the English Landscape*]

Olin's book *Across the Open Field: Essays Drawn from the English Landscape* provided further inspiration for the design. This text documents the English countryside and its vernacular traditions, including the use of the "ha-ha" wall to keep livestock away from the mansion house while also retaining uninterrupted views of the landscape [11-18]. In the security design, the wall encircling the Monument is in essence a ha-ha that keeps terrorist trucks away from the obelisk while also retaining an uninterrupted view. To enhance this effect, the lawn facing the Lincoln Memorial was sloped to conceal the security wall from this important vantage point. But, as indicated in the introduction to *Across the Open Field*, Olin intended more than a humorous reference to walls, cows, and security when he called attention to this inspiration:

> *Certainly one of the principal reasons for designers to study the past and to visit the creations of other people, other countries, and other times is to find works that inspire, that can serve as touchstones for their own imagination and efforts. The ambition and optimism (at times amounting to hubris), the sweeping worldview and wit of those who created the parks and gardens, towns and architecture of the seventeenth and eighteenth centuries moved me then and still does . . . Our own period in history, with its tumult and disasters, is sorely in need of such creative and inventive efforts.*[27]

When recently asked to describe the project, Olin, perhaps intentionally, echoed the Park Commission, stating that the design is "all about a return to dignity" that responds to security without limiting movement, speech, freedom, or vision. In combination with the obelisk's "elevated placement on the summit of a hill," these attributes resonate spiritually and symbolically at multiple levels. The walk to the terrace, in his words, is "a rocky climb to salvation," an "ascent to heaven," and a tribute to "Moses on the Mount."[28] For Olin, these things are a gift passed from one generation to the next, and, like his design, this gift is generous, heroic, impeccably crafted, and by no means accidental. And yet, the imagery he evokes does not speak equally to everyone, which raises problematic questions concerning our national heritage and foundational ideals, and the fact that we as a people have never really spoken or thought in a unified voice. How, then, should we consider this landscape? What echoes from the past does it make present and actual, and how does it deliver these messages? Is it an inspirational reminder of our covenants and obligations, or does it speak down to us like Moses on the Mount? In response to this line of questioning, Olin stressed topography and the physical openness of the design: "The paths ascend gracefully, and views keep changing as you go up—changing what is in front of you and what is behind you," allowing you to "leave the city and the world of commerce behind," and to observe your surroundings: the river and the Virginia hills, the other monuments and memorials, the White House and the Capitol, the city and its people.

This elevated prospect embodies objects and truths that expand and diversify the heritage referenced by Olin. But it does not negate the fact that the design inspirations for the Mall and the Monument are steeped in the traditions of the French and English aristocracy—sources that, at least from today's perspective, are not what one would necessarily expect or consider the most appropriate emblems of a pluralistic society. Now, don't get me wrong. This is a masterful design by a talented designer. The elements are perfectly proportioned, the security wall is unobtrusive and provides seating for people to rest and watch summer softball games and Fourth of July fireworks, the circulation is elegant, and the views are awe-inspiring. And all of this is geared toward producing an inclusive landscape while also satisfying security requirements. The design, simply stated, prevents the world of terrorism and bomb threats from dominating our lives and the National Mall. Moreover, by physically embracing both the enlightened formalism of L'Enfant and the romantic informality of Downing, the design somehow manages to merge these aesthetics with the philosophical and political ideals they affirm. To look at the Monument today it is hard, if not impossible, to imagine the piecemeal reality and awkward conjunction of economics, politics, and bureaucracy that led to its making—much of it instigated by the state of the soil [11-19]. But then again, a hallmark of democracy is the desire to have it more than one way.

Final Considerations

If there is a moral to this story—something to consider and a lesson to learn—it is that change is incremental and takes time; appearances are not always what they seem; ideals are quite different from reality and mean different things to different people; topography dramatizes and democratizes; persistence is a virtue. Also true is that the messy, complicated design of the Washington Monument is not only more interesting than the ideals it honors, but also makes it more difficult—as Jackson observed in his discussion of monuments—to create a dreamed-of past that charms us "into a state of innocence," where we can "relive the golden age and be purged of historical guilt."[29]

11-19
Carol M. Highsmith. The Washington National Monument seen from the Reflecting Pool and World War II Memorial. Washington, DC, 2006. [Library of Congress]

Notes

1 J. B. Jackson, *The Necessity for Ruins, and Other Topics* (Amherst, MA: University of Massachusetts Press, 1980), pp. 91–93.

2 George J. Olszewski, *A History of the Washington Monument, 1844–1968* (Washington, DC: United States Department of the Interior, National Park Service, 1971), pp. 1–2.

3 Louis Torres, *The United States Army Corps of Engineers and the Construction of the Washington Monument* (Washington, DC: Office of Administrative Services, 1985), pp. 11–12.

4 Olszewski, *History of the Washington Monument*, p. 18; Frederick L. Harvey, *History of the Washington National Monument and of the Washington National Monument Society* (Washington, DC: Norman T. Elliott, 1902), pp. 6–8.

5 Harvey, *History of the Washington National Monument*, p. 18.

6 "Washington Monument: Written Historical and Descriptive Data," Historic American Building Survey (Washington, DC: National Park Service, 1983), p. 8.

7 Olszewski, *History of the Washington Monument*, p. 10.

8 Olszewski, *History of the Washington Monument*, pp. 16–20.

9 Torres, *United States Army Corps of Engineers*, pp. 42–43, 67–70. Casey corresponded with George Perkins Marsh, the US Ambassador to the Kingdom of Italy, regarding the height, and thus the weight, of the obelisk. Marsh traveled extensively on diplomatic assignments, and during his travels studied Egyptian obelisks. According to Marsh, an obelisk's height should be ten times the width of the base. He also provided dimensions for the pyramidion. See Olszewski, *History of the Washington Monument*, pp. 121–22.

10 Torres, *United States Army Corps of Engineers*, pp. 49–54.

11 Torres, *United States Army Corps of Engineers*, pp. 90–97; 110. Casey also convinced the Society to fund construction of Marble Lodge (Monument Lodge), a small building for public amenities.

12 Charles Moore, ed., *The Improvement of the Park System of the District of Columbia: Report of the Park Commission* (Washington, DC: Government Printing Office, 1902), p. 35; John W. Reps, *Monumental Washington: The Planning and Development of the National City* (Princeton, NJ: Princeton University Press, 1967), pp. 70–93.

13 Moore, *Improvement of the Park System*, p. 8.

14 Moore, *Improvement of the Park System*, pp. 7–29. The team's credentials were unquestionable. Three members, and the father of the fourth, were leading figures in the design and implementation of the World Columbian Exposition of 1893, a neoclassical extravaganza that established the principles of civic design in the United States for decades. Due to ill health, Saint-Gaudens served only as an advisor to the Park Commission. See Thomas S. Hines, "The Imperial Mall: The City Beautiful Movement and the Washington Plan of 1901–1902," in *The Mall in Washington*, 1791–1991, ed. Richard Longstreth (New Haven, CT: Yale University Press, 2002), pp. 79–99.

15 Moore, *Improvement of the Park System*, pp. 15, 26. The itinerary included London, Paris, Versailles, Vaux le-Vicomte, Fontainebleau, Rome, Venice, Vienna, Budapest, and Berlin.

16 Reps, *Monumental Washington*, p. 97.

17 Reps, *Monumental Washington*, pp. 91–97.

18 Moore, *Improvement of the Park System*, p. 36.

19 Frederick Law Olmsted, Jr., *Independent*, 7 August 1902, pp. 1870–77.

20 Moore, *Improvement of the Park System* p. 47.

21 Reps, *Monumental Washington*, pp. 119–20.

22 National Capital Planning Commission, *Designing for Security in the Nation's Capitol* (Washington, DC: National Capitol Planning Commission, 2001).

23 Author's conversation with Laurie Olin, Philadelphia, 30 April 2021; and records of the author, the associate partner for the project. Olin Partnership signed a contract for design-build documents in 2002. Construction began in 2004, and the site reopened in 2005. The initial design included an underground visitor center, which was not approved by the Fine Arts Commission. See "Design Concept (Visitor and Security Improvements) Washington Monument Grounds," NCPC File No. 1303/6152, 7 February 2002; https://www.hsdl.org/?view&did=449135.

24 Benjamin Forgey. "Does Safety Have to Mean Ugly?" *Washington Post*, 5 September 1998; https://www.washingtonpost.com/archive/lifestyle/1998/09/05/does-safe-have-to-mean-ugly/42b92cad-63a3-4266-92e9-6cb12fe973fc/.

25 Elbert Peets, *On the Art of Designing Cities: Selected Essays of Albert Peets* (Cambridge, MA: MIT Press, 1968), pp. 89–92; See also Theresa O'Malley, "'A Public Museum of Trees': Mid-Nineteenth Century Plans for the Mall," in Longstreth, ed., *The Mall in Washington*, pp. 61–76.

26 The Olin sketch appeared in *Landscape Architecture Magazine*. See Vernon Mars, "Invisible Barriers" *Landscape Architecture Magazine* (September 2002): pp. 75–79. The sketch bears a strong resemblance to a 1932 scheme proposed by Frederick Law Olmsted Jr. and Henry Hubbard in honor of the bicentennial of Washington's birth. Aware of the earlier design, Olin removed the cars and parking, strengthened the east-west axis, and appropriated and refined the ovals. See Thomas Jeffers, "The Washington Monument: Various Plans for Improving Its Surroundings," *Landscape Architecture Magazine* (July 1949): pp. 157–63.

27 Laurie Olin, *Across the Open Field: Essays Drawn from the English Landscape* (Philadelphia: University of Pennsylvania Press, 2000), pp. 9–10.

28 Author's conversation with Laurie Olin.

29 Jackson, *Necessity for Ruins*, pp. 100–102.

12. TO ACT OR NOT TO ACT

GEORGES DESCOMBES

In recent years, biomimicry—using models from nature to renew established forms—has become more widely adopted in design practice, including at the territorial scale of landscape architecture. Sand dunes, earth mounds, and wave forms have become commonplace in the search for suitable expressions of an ecological ethos. The products of many of these efforts appear as strange fruits, however: troubling or petrified re-creations of nature—some appropriate but many inappropriate, lazy solutions to the legitimate quest for new ways of addressing the "contour lines" that describe the site through graphic abstraction. Fixed dunes and static waves may suggest natural processes, but often without performing their actual roles when a functioning part of an active landscape. Perhaps more troublesome is the illusion of movement suggested by these static forms—a complete denial of how natural forces truly operate. I find something uncomfortable about using fixed forms to represent dynamic processes; only the plants that complement, or in some cases cover, these topographic features embody the processes that change the landscape, whether seasonally, annually, or over time. A limitless variety of forms can be produced—both in nature and through design—from the development of a relatively small number of sets of basic structures or cells. It is perhaps a paradox that the more narrowly these structures are defined, the greater the variety of shapes that result.

The search for new forms for landscape architecture is far more difficult than in architecture, where, in the majority of cases, the entire work is constructed and new. In contrast, landscapes of larger scale must begin with the environmental conditions that govern the site and will, or should, direct the nature and shaping of the landscape. Topography is one of these constituents and the basis of most landscape designs, topography modeled by the natural forces acting upon it and shaped to best contend with those forces [12-1]. These considerations played a decisive role in the design of the riverbed of the renaturalized River Aire that flows along the outskirts of Geneva and thereafter through the city.

12-1
SUPERPOSITIONS. Renaturalization of the River Aire. Geneva, Switzerland, 2000–2021+. The field of lozenges. [Aerial Works Fabio Chironi, 20 February 2014]

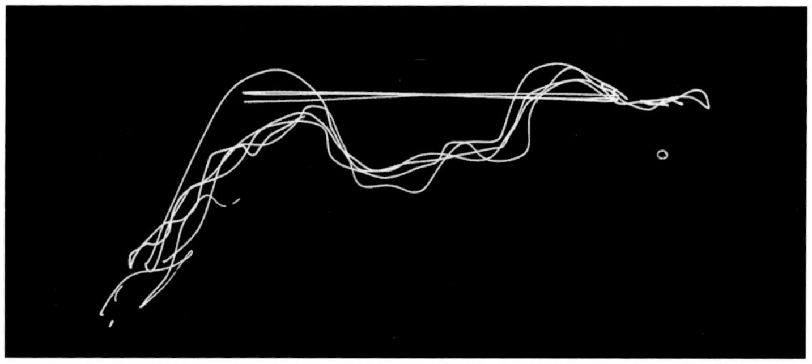

The management of rivers has tended to rely on two basic methods or approaches. The first is that of the hydraulic engineer, who uses numbers and calculations to plan the river in response to the volume and velocity of water. The second is the model frequently adopted by the landscape architect, who, influenced by cultural archetypes, pursues a picturesque landscape characterized by a meandering stream flowing through soft, green banks. While different in philosophy and method, the two approaches tend to produce the same characteristic result: riverbeds of fixed form. In contrast, our design for the Aire questioned these traditional models, ultimately rejecting both of them.

The program for a competition held in 2000 implied the destruction of the existing Aire canal, which had been built in the 1930s primarily for drainage and flood control. The brief called for the removal of the rigorously straight canal and its conversion into a renaturalized river configured to address contemporary problems of inundation, problems that had intensified from decades of construction in the valley. While the designs of our competitors removed all vestiges of the existing waterway, our team valued the canal as a cultural landscape. In our scheme we proposed retaining certain of its features and integrating them with a new River Aire able to manage periods of high water while providing the terrain and facilities for year-round recreation [12-12, 12-3, 12-4, 12-5]. Local plants that would thrive and support animal life were a major element of the design, and thousands of varied species have been planted. Now, after almost two decades of interventions that have consistently been judged successful, we are still designing additional segments of the river and adding to its story.

Our design began with research focused on science and engineering. In our studies we discovered, somewhat by chance, that we could adapt lessons derived from the percolation tests that traced the passage of a liquid through a porous material, in this case soil [12-6]. These findings led to the modification of a "percolation model" as the basis for designing the new riverbed. The principal challenge was to reduce the velocity of water during times of high and rapid flow—primarily from major rains and snowmelt in spring—so that plants could take hold, prosper, absorb, and retard major flooding in the future. This idea positioned topography in the service of botany, and ultimately, hydraulics [12-7, 12-8]. To address this issue, we designed a series of transitory earth forms that would interrupt the flow of water but dissipate and disappear over a relatively short period of time.

12-2
Julian Descombes. Renaturalization of the River Aire. Geneva, Switzerland, 2000–2021+. Concept sketch, ca. 2008. [SUPERPOSITIONS]

12-3
SUPERPOSITIONS. Renaturalization of the River Aire. Site plan including the first four stages. [SUPERPOSITIONS]

12-4
SUPERPOSITIONS. Renaturalization of the River Aire. Geneva, Switzerland, 2000–2021+. In addition to flood management, the revised river supports year-round recreation. [Marc Treib]

12-5
SUPERPOSITIONS. Renaturalization of the River Aire Study model. [SUPERPOSITIONS]

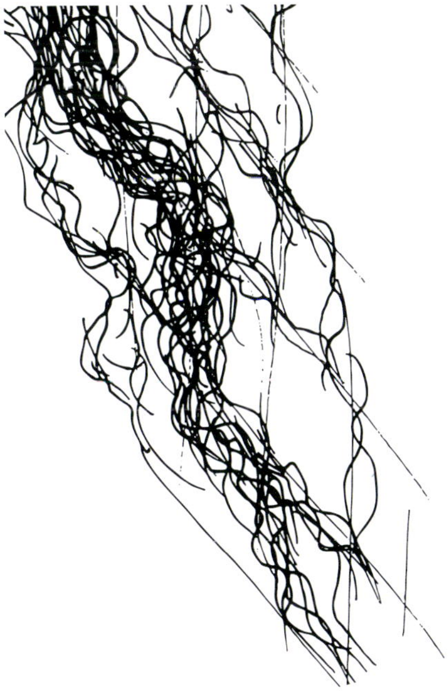

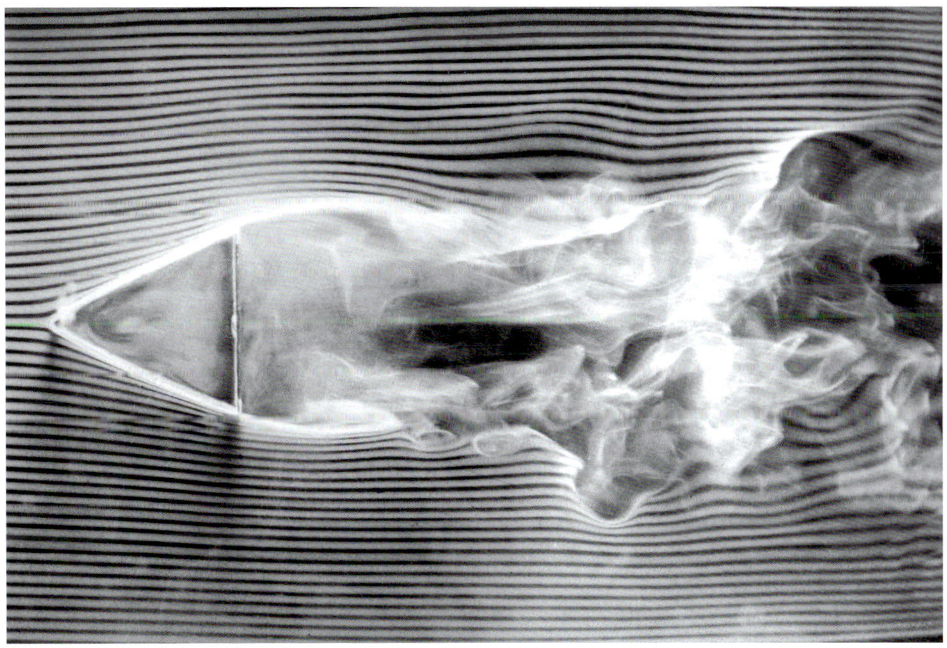

12-6
Georges Descombes.
Sketch studying river flow.
[Georges Descombes]

12-7
SUPERPOSITIONS.
Renaturalization of
the River Aire.
Geneva, Switzerland,
2000–2021+.
Conceptual test using milk
and Swiss chocolate.
[SUPERPOSITIONS]

12-8
Étienne Jules Marey.
Étude aérodynamique-machine à fumée avec obstacle, 1901.
[Wikicommons]

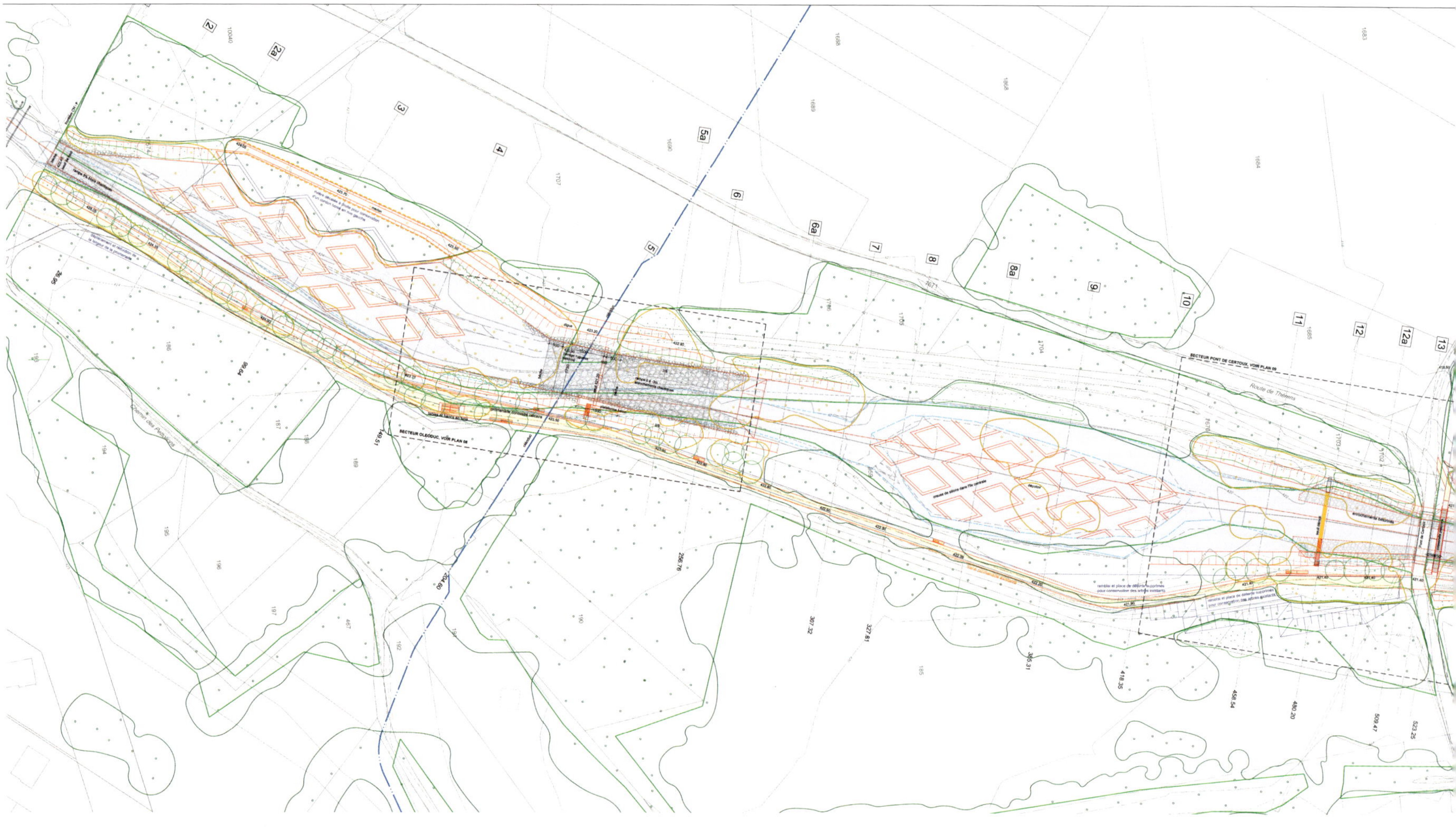
2
2a
3
4
5a
5
6
6a
7
8
8a
9
10
11
12
12a
13

12-9
Tracing water flow around the lozenges. [Georges Descombes]

12-10
SUPERPOSITIONS. Renaturalization of the River Aire. Geneva, Switzerland, 2000–2021+. Engineering plan showing the lozenge field in relation to the surrounding landscape. [SUPERPOSITIONS]

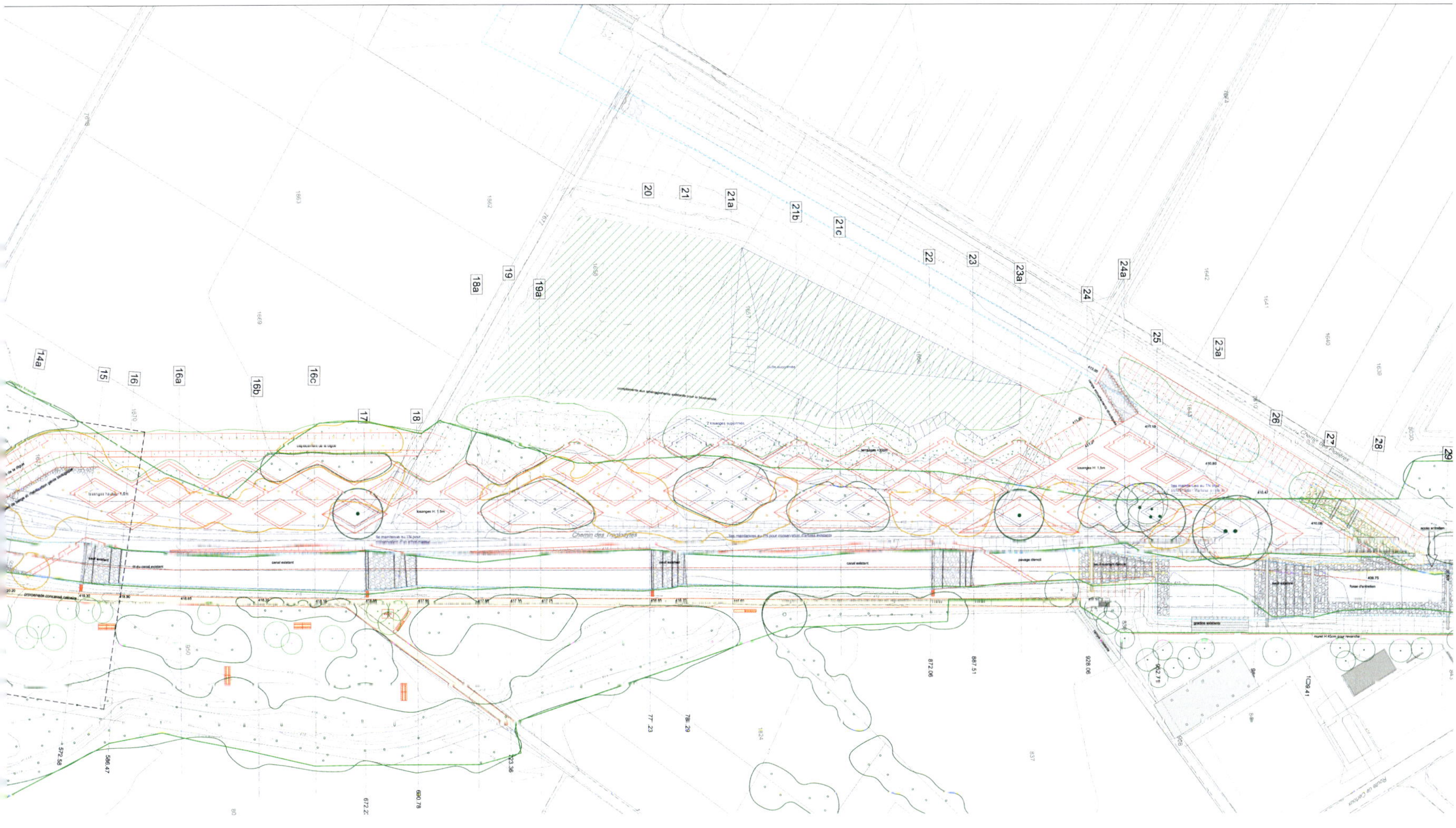

(*opposite*) **12-11**
SUPERPOSITIONS.
Renaturalization of
the River Aire.
Geneva, Switzerland,
2000–2021+.
The completed lozenge field
excavated from the riverbed.
[Aerial Works Fabio Chironi]

12-12
SUPERPOSITIONS.
Renaturalization
of the River Aire.
Excavating the lozenges.
[SUPERPOSITIONS]

12-13
SUPERPOSITIONS.
Renaturalization
of the River Aire.
First stormwater flowing
through the lozenge field.
[SUPERPOSITIONS]

12-14
SUPERPOSITIONS.
Renaturalization
of the River Aire.
Each major surge
modifies the course of
the river and its bed.
[Georges Descombes]

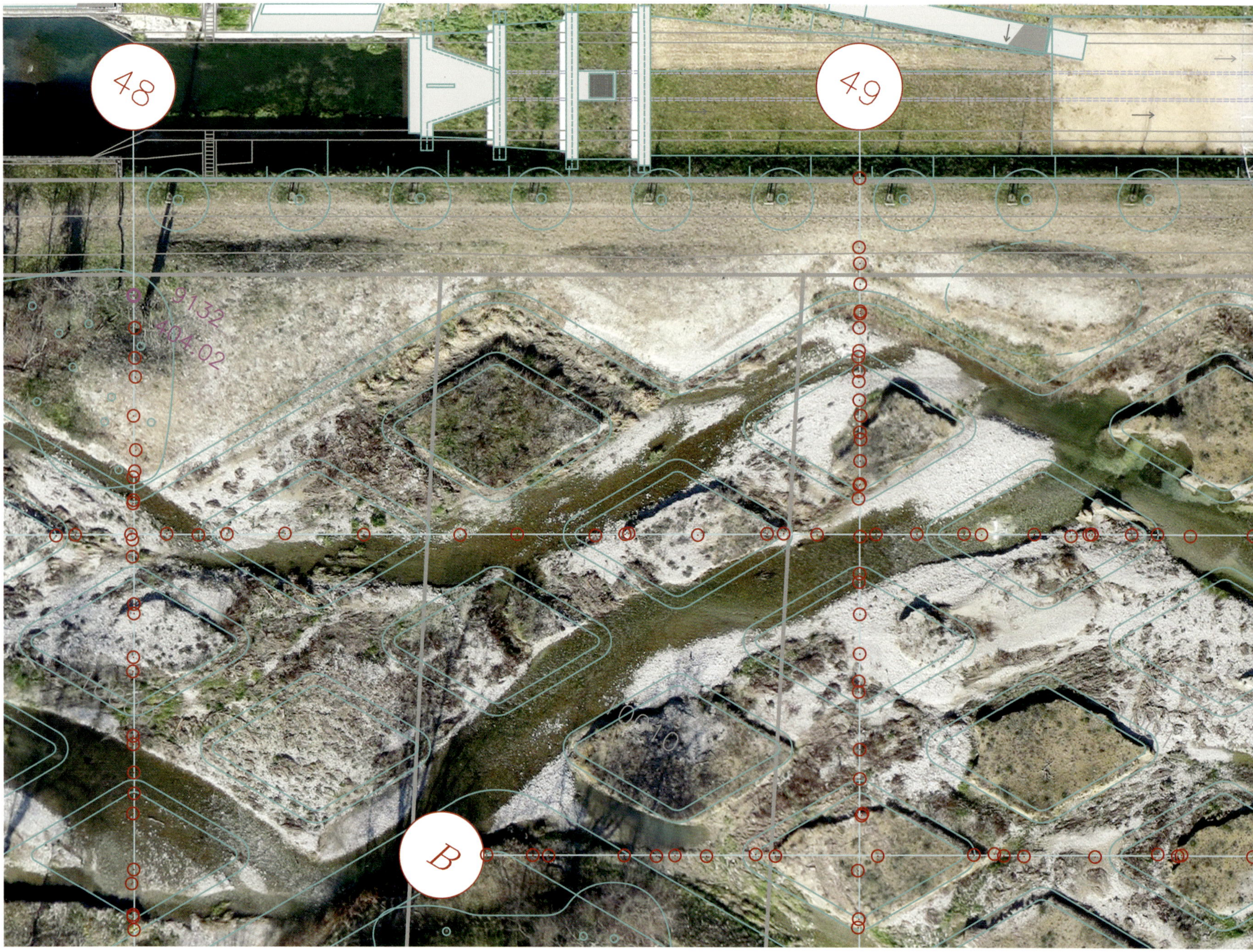
48
49
9132
404.02
B

12-15
SUPERPOSITIONS.
Renaturalization of the River Aire. Geneva, Switzerland, 2000–2021+. Tracking the erosion of the lozenges. [Aerial Works Fabio Chironi]

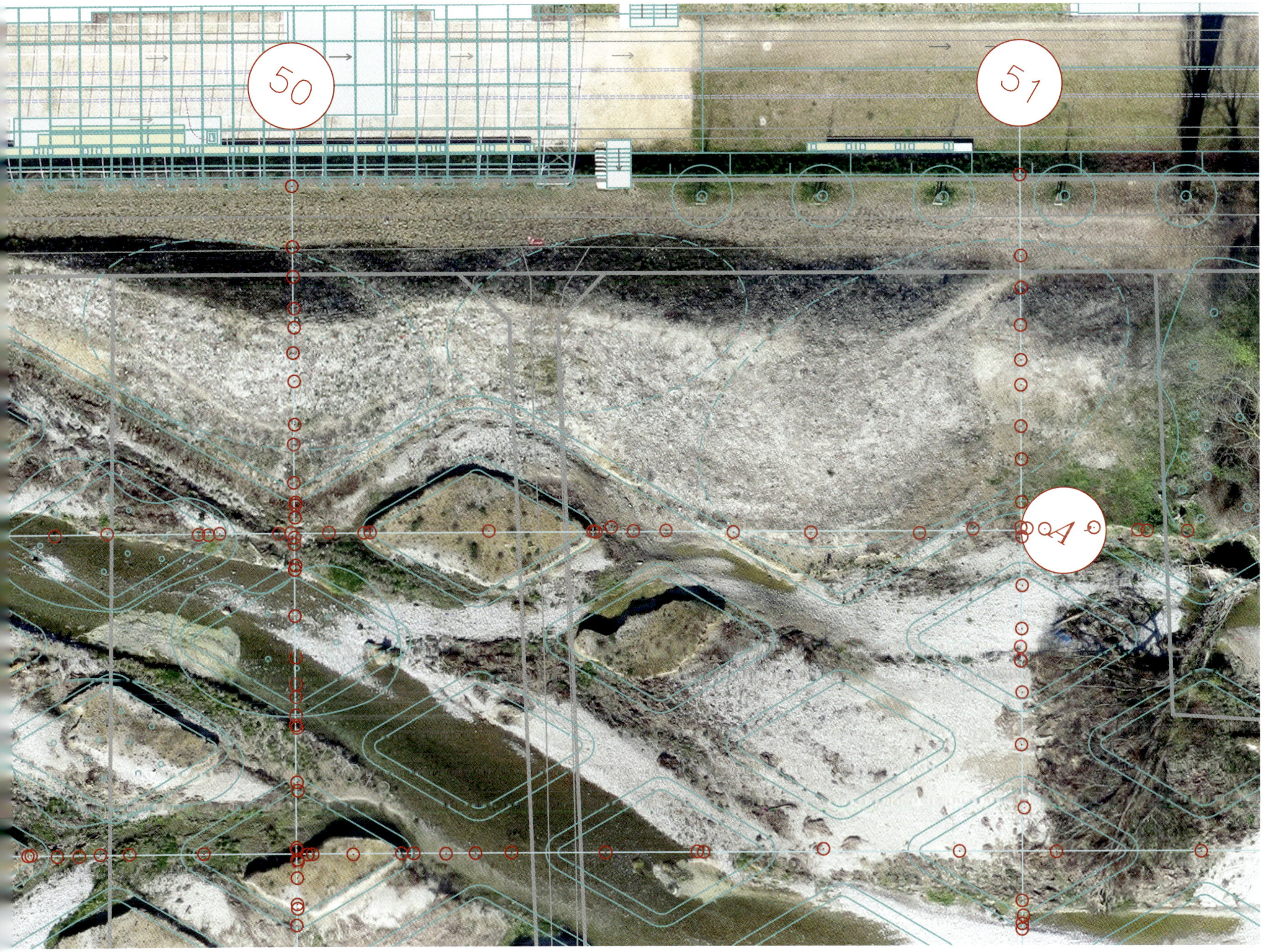

To realize these features, an angled grid was inscribed over the surface of a segment of the land newly given to the river [see 12-1; 12-9, 12-10, 12-11]. Governed by that geometric scheme, ditches were excavated in two directions, leaving the islands formed as diamonds or lozenges [12-12]. Through this intentionally ephemeral topography the river would freely flow, choose its preferred path, and begin a process of erosion that would recontour the riverbed according to its needs. The speed of the new riverbed's morphogenesis was spectacular [12-13, 12-14, 12-15]. The lozenges rapidly eroded, their spoil being washed away downriver, redeposited on the outer edge of a convex curve, or increasing the scouring material from the river's inner curves [12-16]. This process evolved more quickly than we had anticipated. Although the grid was rigidly defined by the generating diagram, the forms and conditions created by erosion and deposition were highly varied. After only two years, the topography of the river's bed, as well as its banks, displayed a morphological diversity that would have been impossible to predict, design, or build. For this reason, I have always regarded the river itself as a member of SUPERPOSITIONS, our team of designers and specialists responsible for the design and realization of the project. In critical locations, dikes were constructed, banks reinforced, and concrete steps and terraces to support recreation installed [12-17, 12-18].

It is somewhat ironic that when people see the images of the lozenges at the time of their construction, they regard them as earthworks, as works of art produced by reshaping the land. Many have thought it a pity, or even a minor crime, that they were intended to disappear, sacrificed to the service of ecological goals. Yet, as noted above, the lozenges were always regarded as provisional—as a means to an end, and not an end in themselves. In this regard, the diagram that shaped the lozenges spoke to the interests of earthwork artists such as Robert Smithson, not in terms of shape however, but to the processes of entropy that leave form to the mercy of natural forces.

To be sure, the lozenges were only one part of the story of incessant upheavals and revisions to construction necessary for achieving broad biodiversity in and around the new River Aire. The phenomena of erosion and deposition that have been modeling the river are similar to those observed in the alluvial plains from which our study profited. Since we began our work, diverse milieux have formed throughout the space given to the riverbed: sand and gravel

12-16
SUPERPOSITIONS. Renaturalization of the River Aire. Geneva, Switzerland, 2000–2021+. The former canal has been retained in places and converted to gardens and other recreational uses, while the river once contained by the canal's banks today pursues its own path within a new course established by the SUPERPOSITIONS design. [Aerial Works Fabio Chironi]

banks, temporary ponds, terraces at different levels, land continually shifting between wet and dry. The successive floods, many of them in spring when snows on the mountains begin to melt, deform these topographic masses or disappear and reappear in a string of constant mutations. There is neither the possibility for a static river nor static forms.

Both annually and over time the riverine topography undergoes severe modifications, among them the formation of seasonal pools that provide refuge for fish during the low water of the dry periods. In these small pockets in the riverbed, topography supports life. The width of the river changes along its course, causing variation in the speed of the current and the differentiated coarseness of the sediments it carries and deposits downstream. Following the Venturi principle, when the river narrows, its velocity increases and scours more rapidly; as it widens, the flow and its effects relax. Velocity is also affected by water depth, however, the reason for digging deep trenches at the bases of the waterfalls that result from a severe drop in the level of the river bottom. These pools collect and hold, but then release the water they have retained, thus modulating the river's flow.

The substrates are highly diverse throughout the length of the river: a mix of sand, gravel, and larger stones. Like these substrates, the palette of plants and their corresponding patterns of succession vary with the rainfall and the atmospheric humidity at different times of year [12-19]. Major tree species such as field oak, Norway maple, silver linden, and elms have thrived, as have many shrubs. In turn, these have attracted countless butterflies, dragonflies, amphibians, reptiles, and small mammals such as foxes, squirrels, and brown hares. Birds such as sparrows, woodpeckers, doves, and warblers also benefit from the intensity of diverse plants. To stimulate the growth of the plants and to limit the influence of invasive plants, the soils were seeded immediately after the earthwork was completed. These procedures were augmented by planting numerous trees and shrubs to reestablish a continuum of vegetation that will shade the river, attract and support wildlife, and provide a more interesting and engaging landscape for recreation [12-20].

12-17
SUPERPOSITIONS. Renaturalization of the River Aire. Geneva, Switzerland, 2000–2021+. A dike/bridge traversing the river provides passage for a pedestrian path on its upper surface. [Marc Treib]

12-18
SUPERPOSITIONS.
Renaturalization of the River Aire.
Geneva, Switzerland, 2000–2021+.
In the bed of the former canal, today a series of gardens, surface water is collected and directed underground through these openings.
[Marc Treib]

12-19
SUPERPOSITIONS.
Renaturalization of the River Aire.
A significant number of plants, both planted and volunteer, line the banks of the river.
[Marc Treib]

Reflection

The innovative technique of using a grid of excavated canals to initiate and accelerate a stream's self-morphogenesis is potentially applicable to other river-restoration projects. Critical is the stream's energy and ability to displace a sufficient load of sediment. But there is also a paradox involved: the more the grid is defined, the more the stream will itself react and establish its new bed. One may view this as a lesson taught by the river: permit the diagram to evolve by allowing the current and sediments to determine their forms to come. By extension, how can we not consider the grid of our cities and the potential diversification of urban forms that may evolve from its initial regularity? Dynamic forms, spatial constructions reworked and rebuilt over time, transformed through moments of growth, eradication, or incorporation. The city as a self-organizing entity. Should we not also consider the two types of impatience: the morphology of cities or rivers too quickly defined and frozen as an inappropriate grimace; and the intolerance resulting in the impeding of fluid interpretations and transformations that occur with the passage of time. Rather, we should consider cities, like rivers, as incomplete forms, unfinished and open to editing and revision over time—that is to say, treat them as living forms.

12-20
SUPERPOSITIONS.
Renaturalization of the River Aire.
At times, visitors to the site participate in managing the river's flow.
[Georges Descombes]

13. RENEWAL AND TOPOPHILIA: TORONTO'S PORT LANDS

LAURA SOLANO

Geology, the combination of natural stresses and processes that shape the surface of the earth; and topography, the visible expression of those forces, are entwined within our personal histories [13-1]. My mother grew up in a tiny town in Colorado at the foot of the Rocky Mountains, and after my parents moved to the flatlands of Washington, DC, she longed for mountainous terrain. For those of us who had never been to Colorado, she would often point to massive cumulonimbus clouds—especially when they reflected light—and say, "That's what the mountains feel like" [13-2]. As a child I thought she was nostalgic for something physical, but in adulthood I came to understand that for my mother the topographic enormity of the Rockies elicited a topophilic response to the place; the mountains drew her closer to her Mexican heritage and all the visual, familial, and cultural experiences that accompanied it.

"Topophilia," a term coined by geographer Yi-Fu Tuan in 1974, describes the affective bond between people and place.[1] It refers to the varied human emotional responses colored by cultural background, gender, race, and historical context that are tied to the physicality, materiality, and spirituality of a place. Topophilia accumulates over time and varies with the scale and type of landscape. Tuan considered that an aesthetic response to topophilia evoked a sudden reaction that in and of itself cannot be long-lasting. For landscape architects, this poses a challenge: how to understand the ways in which the parts and sum of their designs can establish the circumstances for making an enduring connection between people and place. To that end, I am particularly intrigued by the role of topography in achieving that goal.

13-1
Michael Van Valkenburgh Associates [MVVA]. The Port Lands. Toronto, Ontario, 2017–23. The river valley provides access for water recreation. [MVVA, 2018]

Considerations for Topography

Terrain gives the landscape presence. The human experience of that presence is the sum of the topographic parts plus scale, coverage, setting, and the feelings they evoke. Geographers have given various names to landforms—"mountain,"

"hill," "plateau," "plain," "ridge," "valley," "basin," "canyon"—and in design we often use these metaphorically to form spaces that guide movement and induce the conscious and unconscious experiences, both those immediate and those stored in our memory of place. Collectively, these factors enable the felt experience of landscape, what Frederick Law Olmsted Sr. called the "unconscious influence of scenery."[2]

The difficulties of site-specific topographic design are those of scale, measurement, arrangement, contrast, and proximity. Designed landscapes must respond to the existing terrain and what lies beneath it, as well as the topographic and spatial imperatives of program and use, such as parking, recreation, paths, and connections. Although these pragmatic uses may seem topographically ordinary, they are opportunities for spatial poetics in the design of unprogrammed but necessary places to meet, sit, watch, and be. How the "in-between" spaces are graded is just as critical for topophilia because they contribute to the overall appearance and cohesion of the design: the grace or sharpness of transitions, the pace and convenience of movement, the engagement with ephemera, and the references to context.

It is impossible to separate topographic experience and function from natural systems. Topography gives specificity to landscapes through natural processes and supports the reading of landscape as a living medium. Although topography is often perceived as static, in truth it is dynamic, shaped by forces and exerting its own impact. For instance, the accumulation of soil, the formation of plant ecologies, and the foraging and range of animals are all influenced by form, gradient, aspect, materials, and coverage. Water management is a science, but when combined with topographic design it can be psychologically immersive and instructive about natural processes that might otherwise go unnoticed. The landscape is replete with fascinations but the intermittent appearance of water and its activation by terrain gives us pause, letting us temporarily see, hear, feel, and touch it. The ecologies produced by landform and water are a palimpsest of periodic water flow that add and enable richness in design.

The designs of my firm, Michael Van Valkenburgh Associates (MVVA), are known for their shaping of topography. Whether flat or steep—and often using the contrast between the two—topography is central to the appearance, movement, spatiality, quality, look, function of natural systems,

13-2
Cumulonimbus Clouds. "That's what the mountains feel like." [Public domain]

13-3
Michael Van Valkenburgh Associates. Connecticut Water Treatment Plant, 2005. The design is marked by its sculpted landforms. [Steve Turner, 2009]

and use of our landscapes. At the Connecticut Water Treatment Plant, our grading is a microcosm of the surrounding regional watershed, from mountain source to reservoir [13-3]. The result is a rich, humanely scaled terrain that invites people to engage with the land from the perspective of the water that flows through it. Other projects require an "unflattening" of sites leveled by industry or commerce to produce a landscape more interesting and pleasurable to explore. Perhaps my mother's voice exerts an influence when we push topography to better highlight a sense of place.

What is probably not as evident from the user's perspective is that our topographic designs are also propelled by practicality, economics, and sustainability. A guiding principle for our grading is a balance between cut and fill to minimize soil import to or export from the site. This is a best practice for all site design, but excess fill on our projects frequently results from the need to manage excavations from buildings, infrastructure projects, and land remediation. For MVVA, excess soil is usually a positive opportunity for landscape design because it expands the possibilities for spatial and ecological variety.

The Port Lands

While every landscape project has topographic expression, some designs are driven by it. This is the case with MVVA's project for the Port Lands Flood Protection Landform Enabling Infrastructure (the official name for the Port Lands) in Toronto, a 140-acre former industrial site at the confluence of Lake Ontario and the mouth of the Don River [13-4]. The Port Lands will address the obliteration of a key urban river mouth caused by 175 years of unfettered industrial expansion—and depletion—in a major metropolis. During the Industrial Revolution in North America, exploitation of natural resources was an active part of the system that made technical advancements possible. Water transported goods enabled operations, and served as an expedient garbage-disposal system. In mid-nineteenth century thinking, the Don was put to its highest use as a working landscape, dutifully deployed to do its part in creating the future of Toronto. In 1892 the city straightened the river's path and lined it with concrete, cutting its length and capacity by half, while also speeding up its flow [13-5]. Soon after, rainstorms caused flooding on the industrialized banks of the river, an occurrence that continues today.

13-4
The Port Lands. Toronto, Ontario. A 140-acre former industrial site at the confluence of the Don River and Lake Ontario. [City of Toronto Archives]

13-5
The Lower Don River. Toronto, Ontario. The 1886 plan to straighten the Lower Don River, implemented in 1892. [City of Toronto Archives]

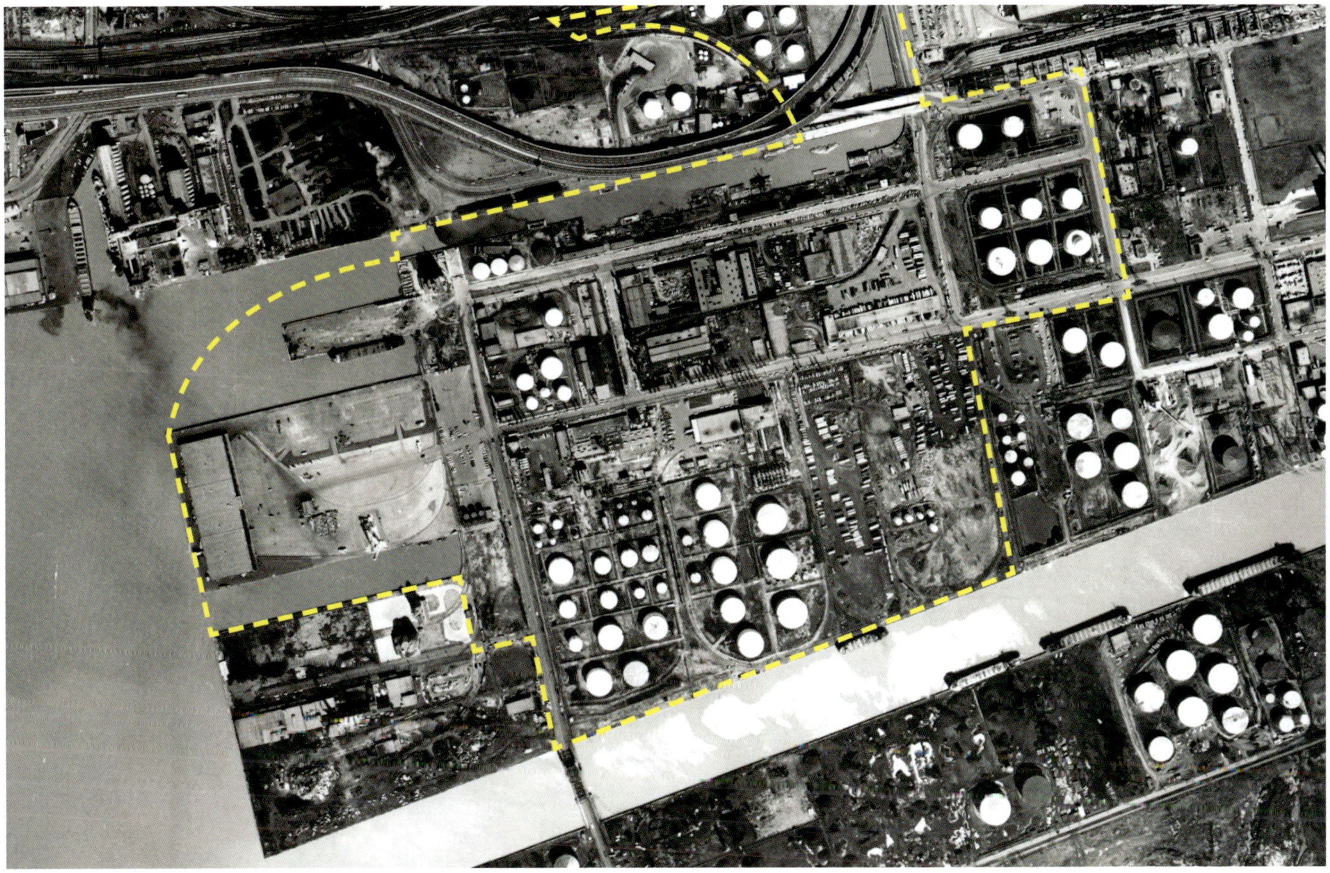

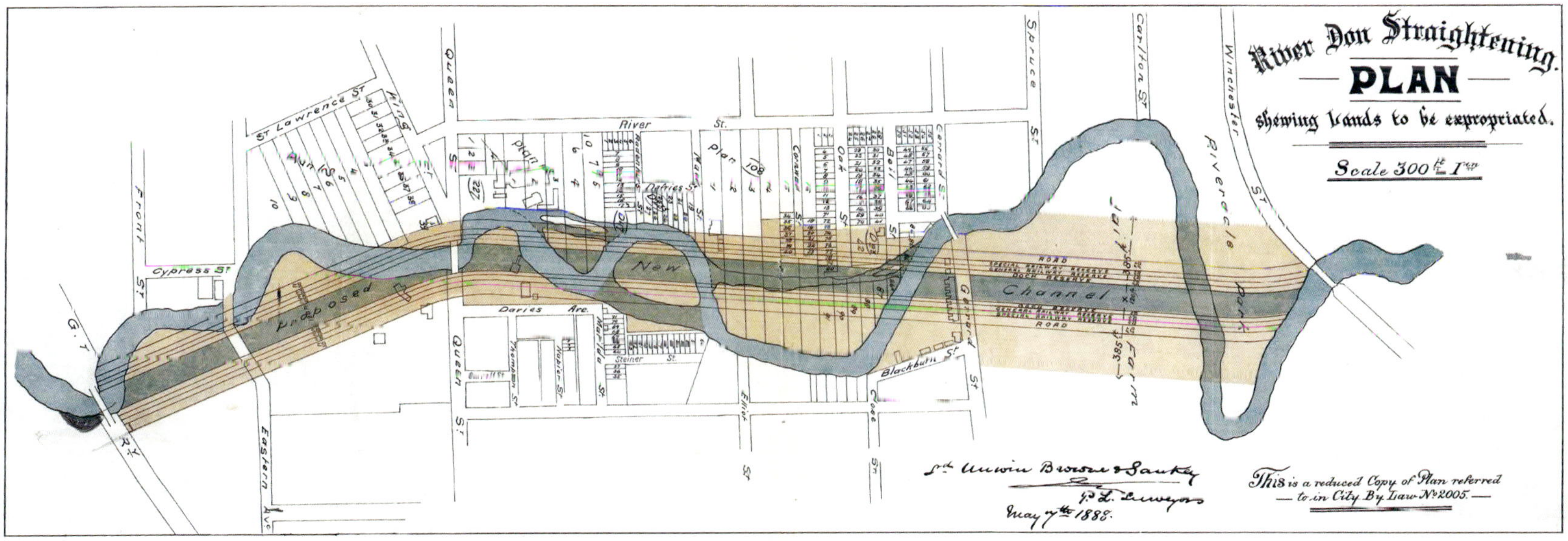
River Don Straightening.
PLAN
shewing lands to be expropriated.
Scale 300 ft = 1 inch
This is a reduced Copy of Plan referred to in City By Law No 2005.
May 7th 1888.
Proposed
New
Channel
Front St
Queen St
Spruce St
Carlton St
Winchester St
River St
St Lawrence St
King St
Cypress St
Davies Ave
Eastern Ave
Gerrard St
Riverdale Park
G.T. Ry

Gardiner Expressway
Lake Shore Blvd East
Keating Channel
Villiers St
Villiers Park
Don Roadway
Toronto Inner Harbour
Polson Slip
River Valley Park
Don River
Don Greenway
Ship Channel

Although many parts of the river were affected by industrialization, it was the filling of the Don River's mouth, once a 1,300-acre wetland called Ashbridges Bay Marsh, that proved catastrophic. The marsh's mouth was originally broad and shallow, a graceful slide into Lake Ontario that contributed critical ecological elements to the functioning of the upstream Don River Valley system, a 90,000-acre watershed. The marshy banks helped reduce the impact of floods on the upland and maintained water quality. Infilling the marsh began in earnest around 1880, and by 1910 the Keating Channel operated as the sole outfall for the Don, anticipating building ports for a burgeoning shipping industry [13-6]. Alterations to the Port Lands continued for the next eighty years, and today 2.8 miles of dock walls contain the site. With the completion of the Keating Channel, the flooding of adjacent neighborhoods became a frequent nuisance, but until 1954 no one imagined that blocking the mouth of the Don River would lead to flooding on 525 acres of the city—as it did when the torrential rains of Hurricane Hazel stalled above Toronto for two days.

For MVVA, the Port Lands project began in 2007 with a design competition to renaturalize the mouth of the Don River and end urban floods. The competition was held by Waterfront Toronto (WT), an agency created by federal, provincial, and municipal governments to oversee the transformation of Toronto's waterfront. Although the Port Lands project has a fundamental public-safety agenda, flood control comprised only a portion of the goals that instigated the competition. The Port Lands is a civic-minded infrastructure-enabling project for solving intractable engineering problems while delivering a physical transformation for the public good.[3] The full program, which was achieved by the MVVA team's winning entry, will reverse the damages to the Don's mouth, ameliorate upland flooding; create new landscape-centric neighborhoods set safely above the flood plain; as well as address related challenges of stormwater runoff, water quality, contaminants, ecology formation, and accessibility [13-7]. This will require the excavation of an astounding 1.65 million cubic yards of soil needed to create a mile-long river and three parks, to be completed by late 2023 [13-8].

13-6
The Port Lands.
Toronto, Ontario, 1914.
Following dock-wall construction, Keating Channel became the sole outlet for the Don River.
[Toronto Public Library Archives]

13-7
Michael Van Valkenburgh Associates.
The Port Lands.
Toronto, Ontario, 2017–23.
The proposed plan for transforming the former industrial site.
[MVVA, 2020]

A Vanished Landscape

Ashbridges Bay Marsh, today buried below the Port Lands, was once one of the largest wetlands in the Great Lakes, supporting biodiverse flora and fauna. Formed by lake currents and erosion from the sandy Scarborough Bluffs to the east, the marsh was situated at the confluence of the mouth of the Don and Lake Ontario's inner harbor. The 1837 writings of English writer, poet, and art historian Anna Brownell Jameson catalog this fertile environment:

> *[T]his marsh, intersected by inlets and covered with reeds, is the haunt of thousands of wild fowl, and of the terrapin, or small turtle of the lake; and as evening comes on, we see long rows of red lights from the fishing boats gleaming across the surface of the water, for thus they spear the lake salmon, the bass and the pickereen* [sic].[4]

MVVA's first visit to the Port Lands was at once exhilarating and jarring. On the one hand, the boundlessness of Lake Ontario and the expansiveness of the sky captivated the team [13-9]. The immediate context was far less poetic yet still attention-grabbing. Scattered throughout the site were remnants of its industrial past: features such as refinery tanks, repurposed and empty buildings, thick slabs of pavement, and defunct maritime machinery.

An unnatural and unrelenting flatness was one of the oddest things about the site. The base topography of the Port Lands was created by the tops of the dock walls, set at the same level for offloading cargo ships and extending inland to fulfill the imperatives of industrial efficiency; unfettered vehicle movement; and large, open work areas. The site felt a bit sinister: seemingly abandoned, but still bearing the imprint of frenzied industrial development. Any elevational variety currently on-site was limited to structures: the remaining low buildings, tanks, warehouses, silos, and some maritime features. Blocks of scrappy volunteer trees somehow managed to establish themselves. In short, with a few exceptions the possibilities for change were limitless, a true tabula rasa.

However awful the visible parts of this depleted ecosystem were in 2007, those hidden from view were even worse and less understood. Ashbridges Bay Marsh had not disappeared, but its soft, peaty soils were trapped beneath the Port Lands, its sand outwash contaminated by industrial waste laden with chemicals couched in acronyms such as "PCB," "PAB," and "NAPL" [13-10]. Intermingled with the contaminated soil were urban fill and debris, oil

(above left) **13-8** The Port Lands. Toronto, Ontario. Construction of the River Valley. [Ellis Don, 2021]

(above right) **13-9** The Port Lands. Aerial view of the Port Lands looking west to Lake Ontario. [Waterfront Toronto]

(right) **13-10** Michael Van Valkenburgh Associates. The Port Lands. Toronto, Ontario, 2017–23. Leapfrog Model showing expected subsurface contamination. [Jacobs, 2019]

Downtown Toronto
Lake Ontario
Toronto Inner Harbour
Promontory Park South
Cherry St.
Wetland
River Valley Park South
Wetland
Don River Corridor
River Valley Park North
Marsh

Lake Ontario
Downtown Toronto
Toronto Inner Harbour
The Port Lands
Keating Channel
New Don River Corridor
Don River

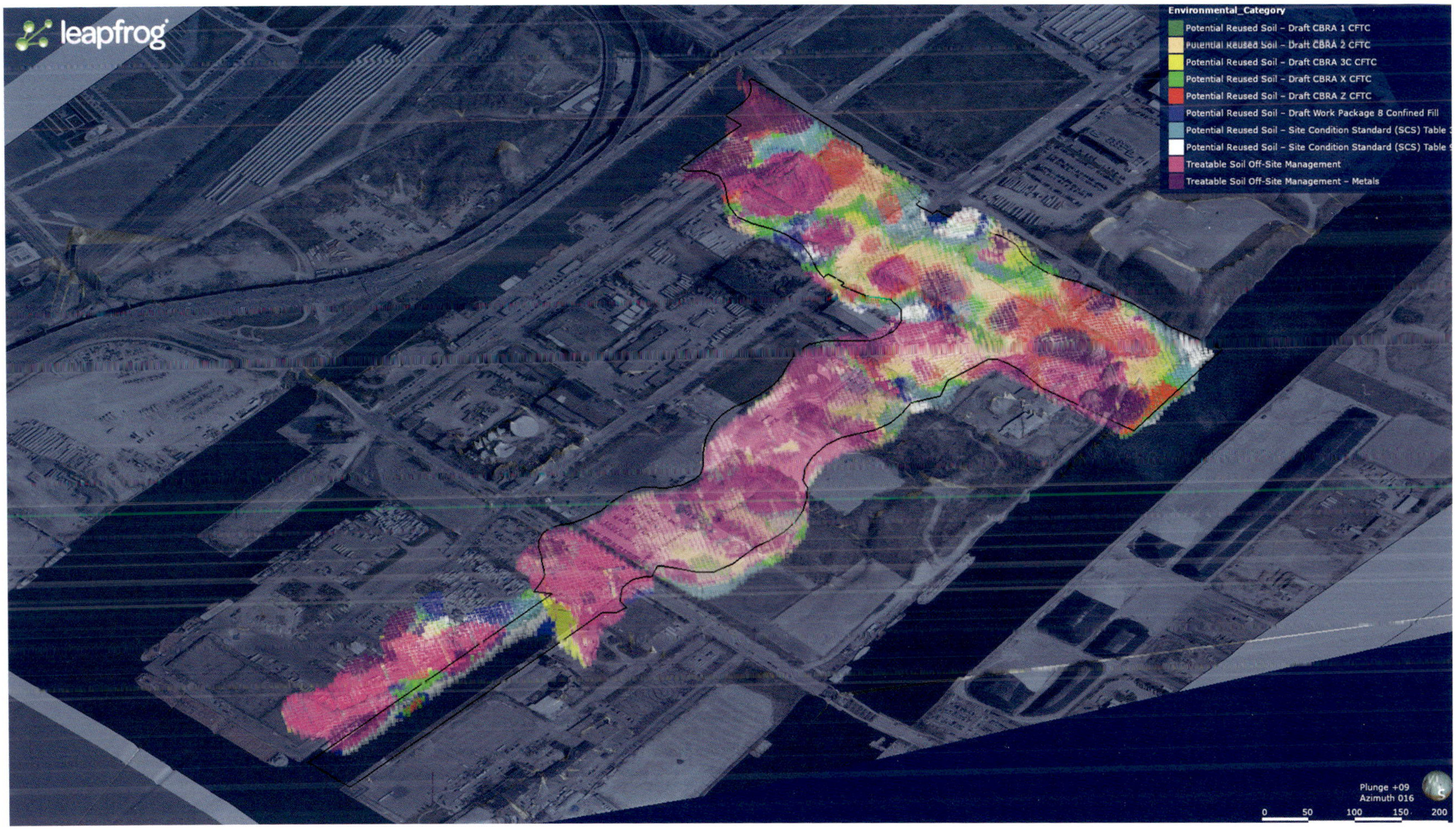
leapfrog
Environmental_Category
Potential Reused Soil – Draft CBRA 1 CFTC
Potential Reused Soil – Draft CBRA 2 CFTC
Potential Reused Soil – Draft CBRA 3C CFTC
Potential Reused Soil – Draft CBRA X CFTC
Potential Reused Soil – Draft CBRA Z CFTC
Potential Reused Soil – Draft Work Package 8 Confined Fill
Potential Reused Soil – Site Condition Standard (SCS) Table
Potential Reused Soil – Site Condition Standard (SCS) Table
Treatable Soil Off-Site Management
Treatable Soil Off-Site Management – Metals
Plunge +09
Azimuth 016
0 50 100 150 200

tanks, uncharacterized fill, and other evidence of past sins. Prior attempts at cleanup had failed. Although the problems were all too clear, the tools and the technology necessary to correct these matters were not yet available in the late twentieth century.

Topography as an Agent of Change

MVVA's scheme for the Port Lands solved flooding with a three-tiered approach: keeping but improving the existing Keating Channel; creating a second outlet to Lake Ontario by extending the Don River through the docklands to a new, naturalized mouth; and making a large wetland with an emergency overflow spillway for high-water storm events [13-11]. In arriving at the solution, it was clear that dramatic topographic change was going to drive much of the design as the MVVA team answered two fundamental questions:

First: "Where should the mouth of the Don River be, and how can its relocation help reassert nature on this vast site?" In modern memory, the edge of the docklands had obstructed the way in which the water travelled between city and nature. Hydrologic modelling confirmed a commonsense analysis that a full river's mouth should be located generally where it once was, at the edge of the city next to Lake Ontario, where it would be physically and functionally engaged. Ultimately the new mouth of the Don was not re-created in exactly the same location, but instead one mile to the west, which rerouted the river valley through the middle of the Port Lands, placing landscape, and specifically topographic expression, at the center of redevelopment.

Second: "How can the reenvisioned river give form to the future neighborhoods?" The MVVA team had noticed that in Toronto two basic park types prevail: those formed to fit within the city grid and those shaped in response to natural features. Between the two, the latter did a better job of offering an experiential escape from the urban environment. The boundaries between the new riverfront parks and the urban development of the Port Lands would be shaped by river morphology rather than an urban grid. MVVA's landscape-centric scheme was a powerful model for sustainable city living and offered economic value, by lengthening the especially valued waterfront adjacencies by an additional 30 percent.

While perhaps unremarkable that a landscape architect won the design competition, it might have surprised some that MVVA continued to lead this enormous geotechnical, environmental, and hydrological engineering project through its documentation and construction. The credit goes entirely to the client. WT understood that while the project's execution was technically complex, the realization of the vision required a designer's sensibilities. A highly seasoned client with experience building along the waterfront, WT also knew that inevitably site and technical problems—as well as the flow of updated information—would arise throughout the process, potentially conspiring to weaken the promises of the original vision and strain the budget. With MVVA as project designer and coordinator, the project benefits from the problem-solving skills of our discipline and our expertise in uniting living systems and the built world.

Forming the River

The river formation in the Port Lands is the driving force of the design, with topography as its expression. Its running course and fluvial cross section are determined by capacity, velocity, and sheer stress, and calibrated by hydraulic modeling [13-12]. River morphology is normally defined by geology formed through collective and naturally produced energies that operate over the course of thousands of years. By contrast, the fluvial morphology of the Don River will be achieved almost instantaneously, constructed in four years and delivered to operate stably as a continuum of upstream forces. The river had to be reverse engineered, guided by the upstream flows and watershed; the elevation of existing and new bridges; the regulatory high-flood stage of storm events; and the new designs for the parks, roads, and future development.

Designing a river and determining how it fits and functions in the landscape is a highly complex modeling exercise that begins humbly with grading plans and cross sections. The mandated high-level flood stage (the "regulatory" flood line) establishes a continuous datum where the river's bathymetry and the park's topography meet. This line is fastidiously tracked during design, but the final transition is meant to look and feel seamless as it shifts between river corridor and park space. The footprint of the river bottom reflects its mean level, narrowing on straight stretches and broadening as it turns a corner to absorb energy and slow flow. To carry the regulatory flood in the river valley, existing grade was excavated more than twenty feet. This vertical separation between the river valley and the new parks is further emphasized by raising the

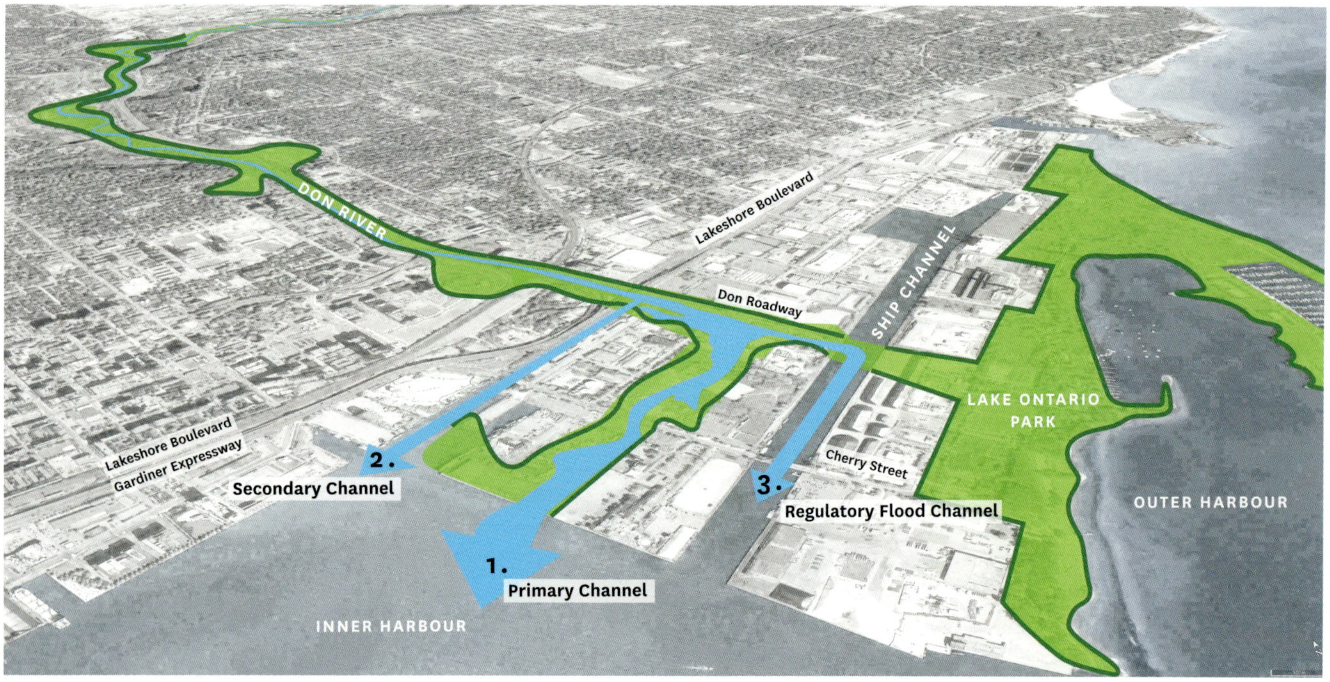
DON RIVER
Lakeshore Boulevard
Don Roadway
SHIP CHANNEL
LAKE ONTARIO PARK
Lakeshore Boulevard
Gardiner Expressway
2.
Secondary Channel
3.
Cherry Street
Regulatory Flood Channel
OUTER HARBOUR
1.
Primary Channel
INNER HARBOUR

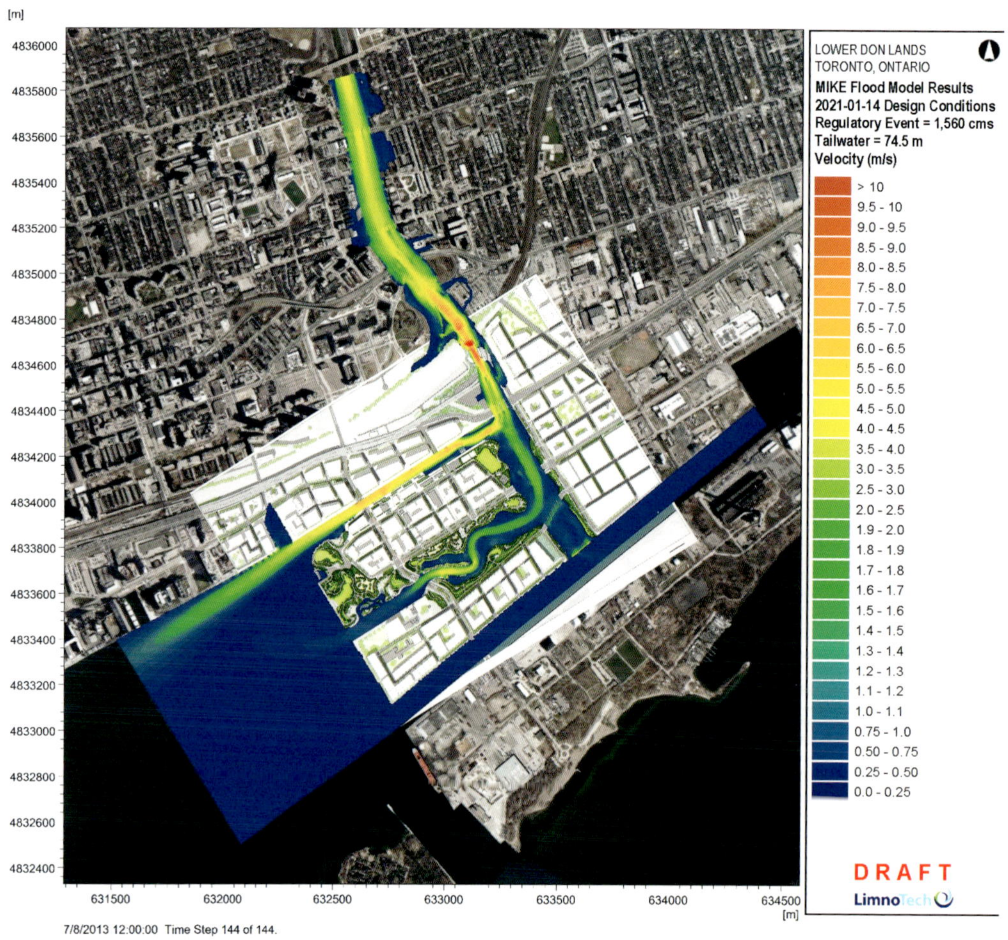
LOWER DON LANDS
TORONTO, ONTARIO
MIKE Flood Model Results
2021-01-14 Design Conditions
Regulatory Event = 1,560 cms
Tailwater = 74.5 m
Velocity (m/s)
> 10
9.5 - 10
9.0 - 9.5
8.5 - 9.0
8.0 - 8.5
7.5 - 8.0
7.0 - 7.5
6.5 - 7.0
6.0 - 6.5
5.5 - 6.0
5.0 - 5.5
4.5 - 5.0
4.0 - 4.5
3.5 - 4.0
3.0 - 3.5
2.5 - 3.0
2.0 - 2.5
1.9 - 2.0
1.8 - 1.9
1.7 - 1.8
1.6 - 1.7
1.5 - 1.6
1.4 - 1.5
1.3 - 1.4
1.2 - 1.3
1.1 - 1.2
1.0 - 1.1
0.75 - 1.0
0.50 - 0.75
0.25 - 0.50
0.0 - 0.25
DRAFT
[m]
4836000
4835800
4835600
4835400
4835200
4835000
4834800
4834600
4834400
4834200
4834000
4833800
4833600
4833400
4833200
4833000
4832800
4832600
4832400
631500
632000
632500
633000
633500
634000
634500
[m]
7/8/2013 12:00:00 Time Step 144 of 144.

parklands a minimum of five feet to cap contaminated soil and as much as fifteen feet for park features. During the design process, these relationships were tested in models and then finalized in grading plans for construction [13-13].

The cross section of the river has three topographically defined corridors: the central body of the river, averaging 100 feet in width at mean level; flanking wetlands that collect the upland stormwater; and walkable levees that separate the river from the wetlands [13-14]. Storm events will produce a sliding bathymetry that can alter the design and feel of the river. When the water rises, the footprint of the river and wetlands widens and the levees narrow, connecting them spatially if not physically [13-15, 13-16, 13-17]. Ecologically, the levees separate river waters from the wetlands, keeping upstream river water out and allowing upland drainage from the parks to settle and cleanse before it joins the river. The levee paths, raised above the 100-year flood, swing beyond the parks into the river valley for a unique sensory connection to the river through varied seasonal and climatic conditions.

The sinuosity at the Don's elbow is designed to slow and direct flow as it courses toward Lake Ontario. These bends form the widest part of the river, while also providing sensory movement from almost every aspect of the Port Lands. Sometimes the topography withholds views; at other moments it opens and frames the prospects up- and downriver. The cross section of the river changes here, which plays out in the beds of the river corridor. The gravelly river bottom is shaped to allow accumulation of sediment in specific areas that in the future will spawn new plant communities; some sections of the banks are armored by stone to withstand scouring from ice floes and other debris arriving from upstream; and the water sheet spreads out and thins to show the river bottom.

Establishing the stability of the valley is essential and must be done before the river is commissioned, using plant palettes that are calibrated by elevation, flow rates, and aspect. During construction, water will be pumped into the valley to simulate final conditions. Habitats cover nearly 75 acres, with requirements for conditions (plants, refuge, food, materials, aspect, breeding grounds) that attract aquatic, terrestrial, and herbivory species. Habitats must be sized to perform over time, and the topography that forms the container is critical. Slopes must be appropriately inclined to allow plants to establish, stabilize their environments, and allow animals to glide into the water. Micrograding had a role here, too; aquatic animals need small pockets on wetland floors to collect fallen

13-11
Michael Van Valkenburgh Associates.
The Port Lands.
Toronto, Ontario, 2017–23.
Three-tiered scheme for flood protection.
[MVVA, 2007]

13-12
Michael Van Valkenburgh Associates.
The Port Lands.
Fluvial morphology model, Regulatory High Flood Stage Velocity.
[LimnoTech, 2018]

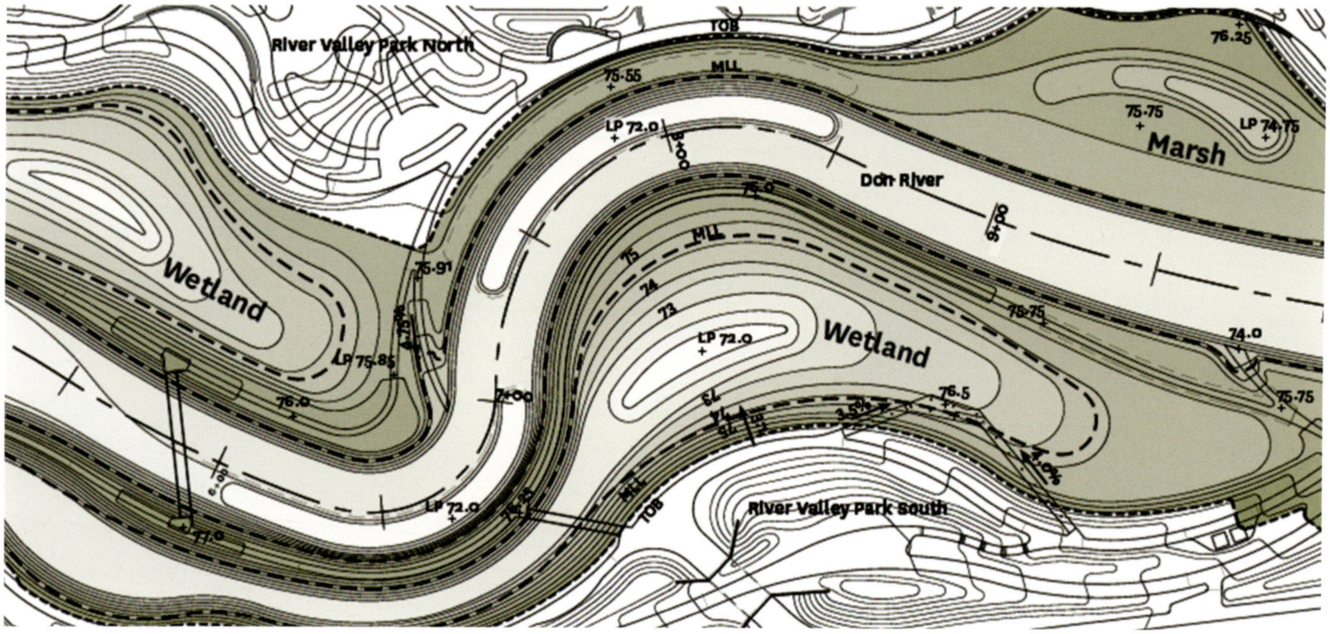

13-13
Michael Van Valkenburgh Associates.
The Port Lands.
Toronto, Ontario, 2017–23.
New river grading plan.
[MVVA, 2019]

13-14
Michael Van Valkenburgh Associates.
The Port Lands.
The three topographically defined corridors in the valley: river, levees, and wetlands.
[MVVA, 2019]

13-15
Michael Van Valkenburgh Associates. The Port Lands. Toronto, Ontario, 2017–23. Base-level river flow. [MVVA, 2018]

13-16
Michael Van Valkenburgh Associates. The Port Lands. Twenty-five-year storm event. [MVVA, 2018]

13-17
Michael Van Valkenburgh Associates. The Port Lands. Regulatory storm event (High Flood stage). [MVVA, 2018]

particles of food upon which to feed. In all, to be a successful landscape design the topographic expression needs to operate at a gradient of scales from the macro to the micro, creating a dynamic presence and stable river valley, an immediately functional ecology, and a condition that is stable by river standards.

Shaping the Parks

After the spatial and performance dimensions of the Don River were addressed, the remaining land was assigned to the delivery of three parks and parcels for future development. The Port Lands include Promontory Park South (PPS) as well as River Valley Parks North and South (RVPN, RVPS). While creating the river corridor was an act of cutting into earth, making the parks was done by filling, sustainably limiting the need for soil disposal as well as lifting the public realm safely above existing subsurface contamination. Soft subsoils directed locations for programmed uses and set maximum heights of new topography. A give-and-take process colored all phases of park design. Updated regulatory requirements and hydrologic and subsurface data affected the river's engineering and sometimes caused its envelope to shift. Almost every boundary movement of the river required adjustments to the park's grading plans, sections, and 3D digital models. Every foot of space was important to effectively locate program facilities, shape the land, and meet universal accessibility goals, especially within the intensely programmed and relatively narrow river parks.

At twenty acres, PPS, including Canoe Cove to its south, is the largest of the three parks and the only one that overlooks the lake and the city. Here, topography is the most varied, working hard to both vertically separate and unify functions [13-18]. PPS is organized around a central terrace, the highest point of all the parks, offering sweeping views and winding paths. The stone walls supporting the terrace are the only constructed elements, made more visually dramatic by lowering the base of its façade so that it appears higher from elsewhere. PPS's varied topography also accommodates the widest range of uses, with tilted lawns, stone tumbles for climbing and sitting, an event space, a destination playground, a dockside promenade, and varied ecologies. Small beaches descend into Canoe Cove and connect the park with the river and Lake Ontario. Intentionally shallow for increased safety, the cove was made by scooping out earth and reusing it to create small, pillowed, and planted islands to paddle around. The islands shape views, making the cove seem bigger than it is [13-19].

13-18
Michael Van Valkenburgh Associates.
The Port Lands.
Toronto, Ontario, 2017–23.
Promontory Park South.
[MVVA, 2020]

Promontory
Park
South
Canoe Cove
Promenade
Toronto
Inner Harbour

River Valley Parks North and South run parallel to the river's flow and are inwardly oriented to it. PPS and RVPN are connected by a wide, long sidewalk dubbed the "Hallway." Sloped at less than five percent, below the accessibility threshold that triggers the use of ramps and handrails, the path is the unofficial river promenade. The rooms off the Hallway include intensive nature play for all ages (with specific micrograding for each activity) and bermed lawns for picnicking and passive recreation. By contrast, RVPS, which is across the river, is the most willfully wild space connecting the Port Lands to the Don Valley Trail that links bikers, joggers, and walkers to downtown Toronto and upstream public trails. The path divides into two terraces, the lower one adjacent to the river and the upper one above the high-stage flood level to ensure that the route is always accessible [13-20].

A Post-Postindustrial Site

At the start of the project, the Port Lands legacy was one of artificial flattening (of ecology, of experience, of topography) that could only have resulted from human intervention in the guise of economic development, ultimately enabling environmental recklessness; a hundred years of raw-sewage disposal had further stifled the river's ability to repair itself. In the late twentieth century the river was often described by such pejoratives as "fetid," "filthy," "smelly," "disease-ridden," "life-less,""noxious," "offensive," and "pestilential." The last inhabitants to experience the natural splendor of the Don River have been gone for generations. Despite such a thorough erasure, the Lower Don still brings out a longing in people, perhaps passed down as a memory of a long-gone topophilic response.

The future Port Lands topography will be almost as different from its industrial state as the industrial Port Lands was from Ashbridges Bay Marsh. No memory will remain of the monumental technical efforts and years of design work that went into envisioning, tending, and shepherding a new neighborhood and reconfigured river mouth from conception to reality. Instead, the landscape will be judged by its management of floods and the topophilic response elicited from those who will use it. Topography plays an explicit role as both the foundation and backdrop for every aspect, both experiential and operational, of the living landscape that will continue to evolve over time.

13-19
Michael Van Valkenburgh Associates.
The Port Lands.
Toronto, Ontario, 2017–23.
Canoe Cove.
[MVVA, 2018]

13-20
Michael Van Valkenburgh Associates.
The Port Lands.
River Valley Park South.
[MVVAA, 2018]

Notes

1 Yi-Fu Tuan, *Topophilia: A Study of Environmental Perception, Attitudes, and Values* (1974; repr., New York: Columbia University Press, 1990).

2 Charles E. Beveridge, "Olmsted: His Essential Theory," National Association for Olmsted Parks. https://www.olmsted.org/the-olmsted-legacy/olmsted-theory-and-design-principles/olmsted-his-essential-theory.

3 The years after the competition were spent on master planning, securing city approvals, an environmental assessment, and fundraising $1.25 billion (CAD) with contributions from Canada'sfederal, provincial, and city governments. In 2016, MVVA preparedina due-diligence report to verify feasibility, process, and costs.

4 Anna Brownell Jameson, *Winter Studies and Summer Rambles in Canada* (Toronto, Ontario: New Canadian Library, 2008), p. 190.

14. CONTOURS WITH AND WITHOUT LINES

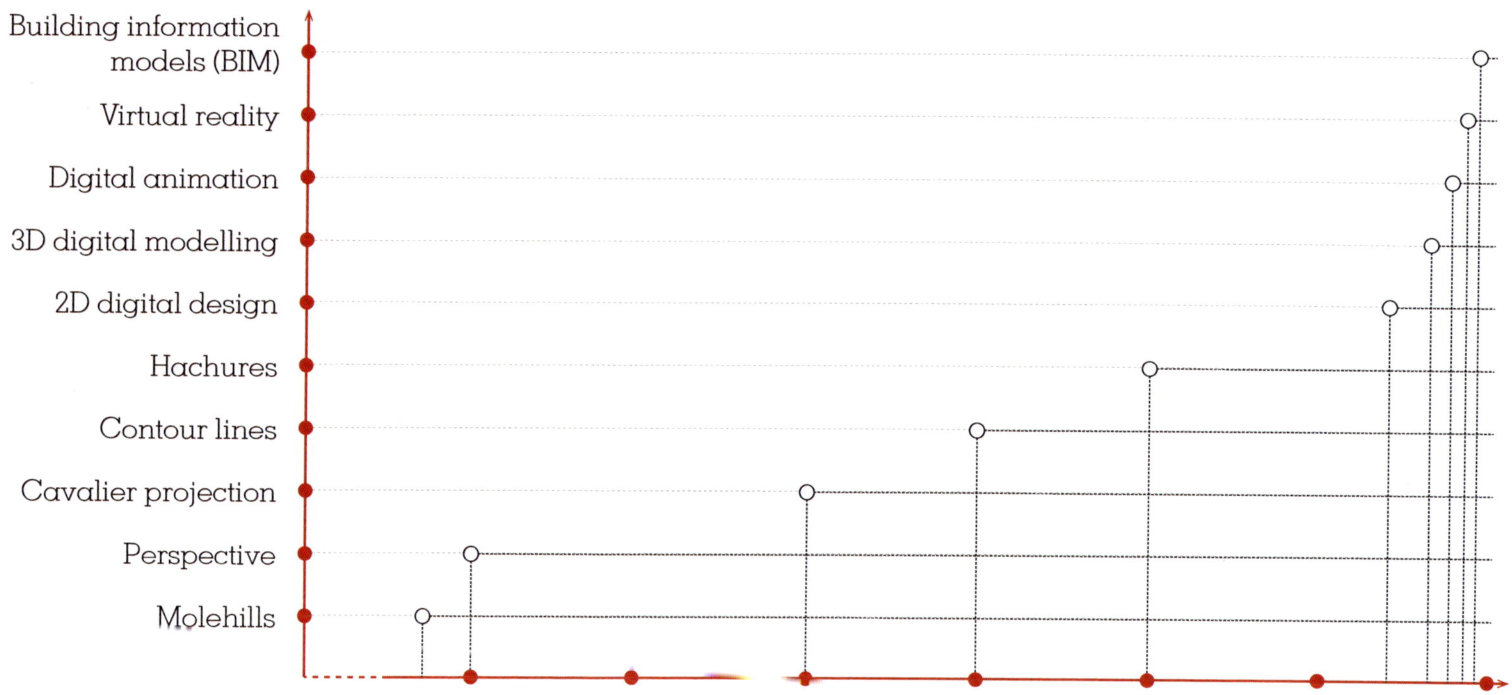

JOSÉ MIGUEL LAMEIRAS

Among the many human actions that modify the landscape, grading is possibly the most fundamental—and consequential. Whether for building, agriculture, or the circulation of human populations, grading structures the site and shapes both its horizontal and vertical dimensions, whether with a smooth, rugged, or convoluted profile. Grading is hardly a simple matter; it is a multidimensional, at times complex effort that embraces considerations of function, aesthetics, and ecology. In recent decades, the field of digital design has changed not only the methods of landscape representation but also the automation of tasks such as information gathering and the design process itself. New analytical methods, paired with three-dimensional and component-based modeling tools, today offer the technical means to enrich and expedite the processes and materials used in terrain design.

The techniques for representing landform have been a product of their times and available technologies [14-1]. The digital revolution of the last half-century has provided designers with scores of new possibilities for producing three-dimensional methods for modelling the land. These include models used for design representation (photos, videos, interactive models, virtual reality), design development (carving and sculpting by means of digital models), and design validation (form and function simulation).

Unless otherwise credited, all images are by José Miguel Lameiras.

14-1
Chronology of techniques for representing terrain form and the time of their application.

History

The earliest representations of the land were closely linked with major breakthroughs in cartography made principally during the fifteenth century—the so-called era of discoveries [14-2]. At that time, forms resembling molehills achieved a sense of height and depth on orthographic projections, portraying the complexity and relative elevations of rises and depression in the land. During the Renaissance, linear perspective added the dimension of depth to representations of terrain form, resulting in a richer portrayal of proportion and height. Together, these tools provided augmented fields of data while capturing the perceptual qualities of the land. Perspective views lack scale and measure, however, and as such lack the precision needed for study and execution in the field. More pictorial than metric, they nonetheless contribute information more closely related to daily human experience than orthographic projections. All systems of representation, whether metric or pictorial, contribute information in their own ways, and therefore all available projections and tools must be considered and used in combination.

Over the centuries, military demands, shipping, and trade called for increasingly accurate and realistic graphic representations of the land and sea. In the seventeenth century these led to the development of the cavalier projection, which offered a more comprehensive means of representing landscape and landforms by using oblique lines projected at a forty-five-degree angle. These techniques added the precision, scale, and measure missing in perspective views. Two centuries later, hachure—a graphic technique employing sets of lines to create the visual impression of shading—provided a plan view with an illusion of depth. With its emphatic rendering of the topography on-site, hachure was quickly and widely adopted, and remains in use even today. A mastery of light and shade is critical for the success of a method that is part pictorial, part metric, and many beautiful maps have resulted from the use of hachure to represent surface complexities. In 1730 the Dutch cartographer Nicolaas Cruquius employed the new technique of contour lines to represent the depths of rivers and is credited with their earliest recorded use. Only later were contour lines applied more broadly to represent landform. As an accurate and relatively simple system for delineating in two dimensions the three dimensions of terrain, contour lines became an essential method for plotting and grading the land—and, in addition, have served as a creative tool for the study and representation of proposed as well as existing conditions.

Similar to the course of historical cartography, digital representations of landform have followed an evolutionary development, propelled by several landscape architects at the forefront of digital design [14-3]. In the late 1970s, Massachusetts landscape architect Bruce MacDougall created a digital model for use in site analysis that employed symbols such as #, *, +, to depict elevations in terrain, slopes, and profiles. In the early 1980s, at

14-2
Historical evolution of techniques used to represent landform.

14-3
Historical evolution of digital techniques used to represent landform.

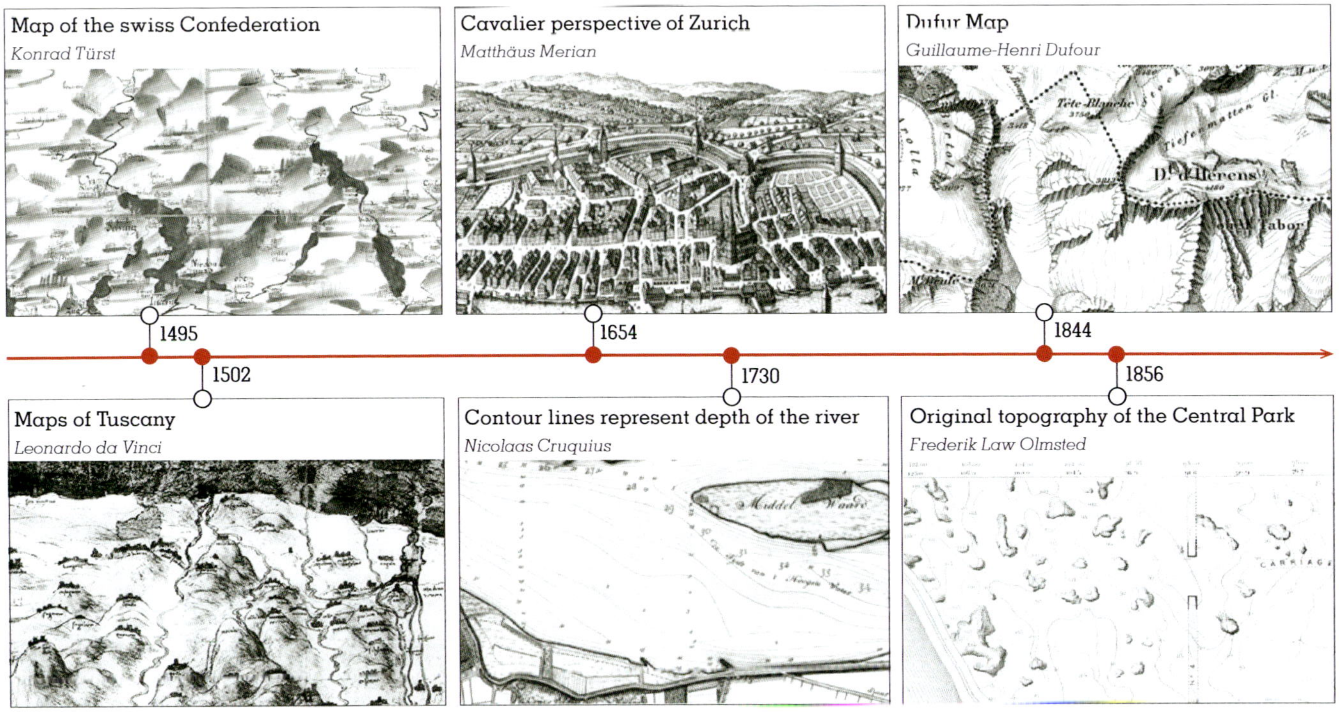
Map of the swiss Confederation
Konrad Türst
1495
Maps of Tuscany
Leonardo da Vinci
1502
Cavalier perspective of Zurich
Matthäus Merian
1654
Contour lines represent depth of the river
Nicolaas Cruquius
1730
Dufur Map
Guillaume-Henri Dufour
1844
Original topography of the Central Park
Frederik Law Olmsted
1856

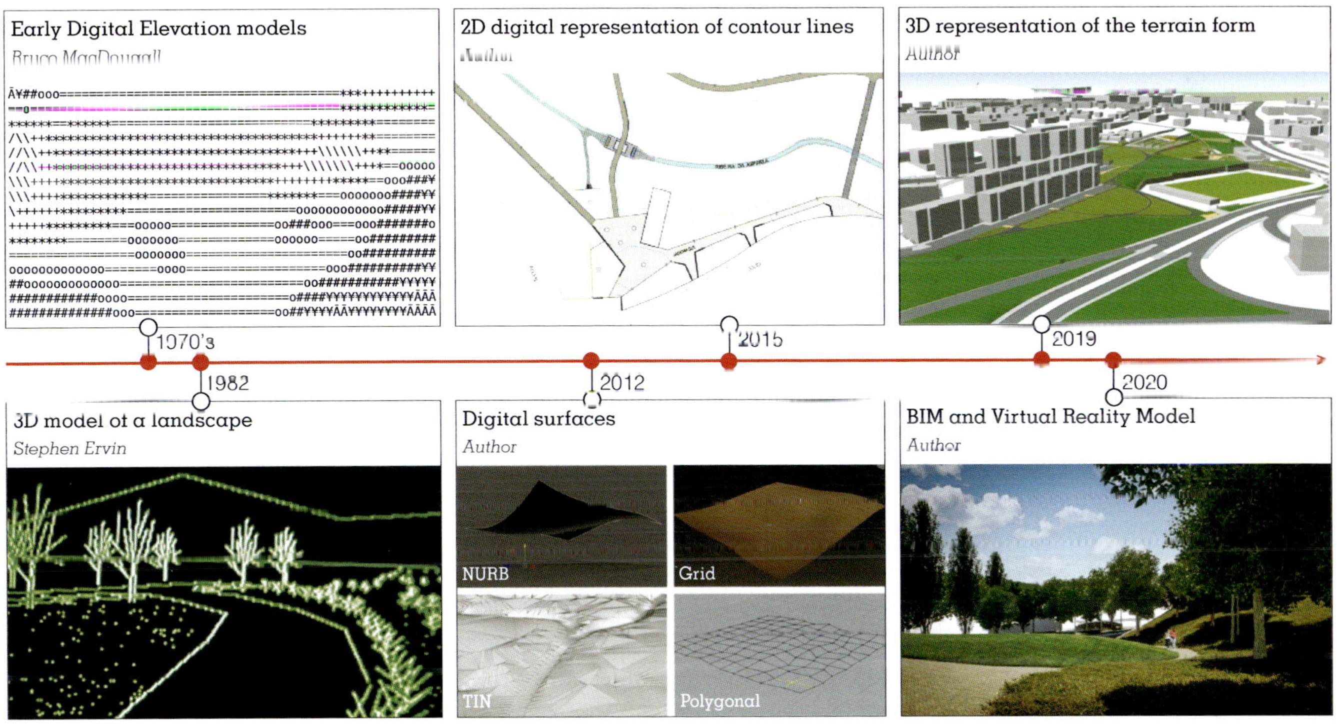
Early Digital Elevation models
Bruce MacDougall
1970's
3D model of a landscape
Stephen Ervin
1982
Digital surfaces
Author
NURB
Grid
TIN
Polygonal
2012
2D digital representation of contour lines
Author
2015
3D representation of the terrain form
Author
2019
BIM and Virtual Reality Model
Author
2020

Stephen Ervin developed the first three-dimensional model for representing and analyzing three-dimensional landscapes. These two breakthroughs offered a wealth of new tools useful not only for grading, but also for landscape design more broadly. Through digital technology, landscape designers can now adapt existing procedures to address more complex sets of factors, and in some instances, arrive at a solution more rapidly. Two-dimensional design using AutoCAD was among the first examples of this type of program. In time, however, completely new processes were developed and implemented that relied on the computer: processes that constituted the true achievement of three-dimensional modeling. In 1958, at the Massachusetts Institute of Technology, C. F. Miller used digital surfaces as representations of an infinitely thin plane able to adjust to the terrain at selected points. This technique made it possible to depict complex landscapes in digital form. Building on Miller's initial work, various programs using digital surfaces have furthered the effort to represent landform. The approach most applicable, and most commonly used today, is the Triangulated Irregular Network (TIN), although other surfaces, such as those based on NURBs (Non-Uniform Rational B-Splines), as well as regular and irregular polygons, are also employed when suitable.

At present, most landscape architecture firms still favor two-dimensional AutoCAD design, suggesting that the profession is not yet fully profiting from all the potential benefits of digital design. Although these designers could be using the computer as a more effective three-dimensional tool, they are in fact restricting its application to only two dimensions, losing one dimension of reality. However, given the rise of easier, more widely available, and more comprehensive modeling tools, landscape architects could be gaining broader access to new ways to study and express their ideas. These recent developments in computer graphics and digital rendering exploit a three-dimensional model to visualize landscapes in a more realistic manner, for example, by positioning the designer at normal eye level to experience the landscape design from a user perspective. With future advances in virtual reality and a corresponding ease in access to it, we can anticipate that this tool will also become an integral medium for landscape design.

The state of the art in digital modeling has been furthered by the implementation and widespread adoption of Building Information Models

(BIM) in architecture, engineering, and construction. BIM design is not developed solely through the use of geometric data, but also utilizes information about its components. These can be used to represent not only objectifiable realities such as trees and urban form, but also complex sufaces such as terrain and paved surfaces. This enhanced three-dimensional model can be used later for design development, construction, management, and even demolition.

The BIM system also allows architects and engineers to collaboratively simulate and test the efficiency of their design in three dimensions, at least in model form. Designers can now add a form into the digital model to convey a design intention—a three-dimensional model of a tree, for example—instead of drawing its more abstract representation, such as a circle. This component can, in turn, be enriched with specific technical data, augmented by its interaction with components inserted from other fields such as engineering, and tested directly by using the model. Applying this method a potential collision between tree roots and a gas pipe, for example, could be prevented.

Unfortunately, landscape architecture lags well behind other fields, engineering among them, in embracing the full range of possibilities offered by BIM. At one time, landscape design stood at the forefront of digital development, applications, and design. But no longer. BIM is already used by 95 percent of the major construction firms in Great Britain and has been widely adopted all over Europe; its presence in the United States is minor, however, especially in landscape architecture. Whether or not to use BIM is no longer the question: rather, the question is which form of BIM to use. To better suit the needs of the landscape architect, the most appropriate form of the BIM method should be adapted and/or developed by those in the field. This seems obvious. In addition, there should also be more landscape architects doing research in these areas and shaping the tools already developed to better suit the needs of the landscape designer, which are necessarily different from those of the engineer.

Digital Terrain-Design Research

In response to a current project and available technology, a research group at the University of Porto has developed applications using both two- and three-dimensional models that better address the actual process of landscape design.

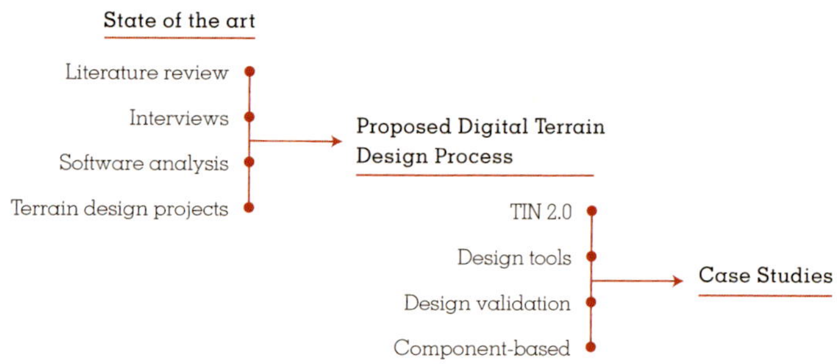

As research, it was structured in the standard way: first by identifying the problem and then proposing, testing, and developing possible methods for its solution [14-4]. To assess the specific needs of landscape architects, we interviewed practitioners in Portugal, the United States, Britain, and Canada. We also analyzed existing software and studied representative terrain-design projects with related issues and challenges, focusing on how these had been resolved. This research led to the development of a method for digital terrain-modeling; to test its viability, we then applied the method to selected case studies. After the research phase was successfully concluded, we validated the method and applied it to our own projects. Throughout the course of our work, we kept in mind that terrain design must blend art and science, employing both a sculptural sensitivity and technical understanding. Any hope of producing viable and beautiful landform must address both demands and value systems. We encountered numerous challenges during the development of our method. In landscape architecture, the starting point always resides in the existing landscape and its contours. Design never begins with an empty canvas, and design decisions must address the existing terrain, whether ultimately to accept it or to modify it, to a lesser or greater degree. Of the available options, we found the TIN surface model to represent the existing contours with the greatest accuracy and therefore to be the most useful approach. Yet, due to the structure of its internal geometry, TIN surfaces are incompatible with the free-form digital sculpting tools used to push and pull the digital surface material. Employing these tools with a TIN surface produces an irregular pattern that precludes the control of form, limiting the possibilities for creative solutions. This problem was at least partially, if not entirely, resolved with our proposal for TIN 2.0, which not only provides greater flexibility than its predecessor but also allows the landscape architect to determine the specific area to be modified [14-5]. A regular mesh over this area could then be developed, granting the designer greater control over the designed terrain form and opening the possibility to use free-form design tools—thus providing the means for more interactive sculpting using the digital representation of landform.

Another issue concerned the quality and accuracy of topographic representations in three-dimensional models. How can we improve these models and use them more effectively? Contour lines are a valuable design

(left above) **14-4** Outline of the research.

(opposite above) **14-5** Application of free-form digital sculpting tools *(left)*: to a standard TIN surface. *(right)*: using TIN 2.0.

(opposite center) **14-6** Digital terrain surfaces created from three-dimensional lines.

(opposite below) **14-7** Decomposition of terrain form into digital components and their interdependencies. When the geometry of a component is modified, neighboring components react by adjusting their geometry.

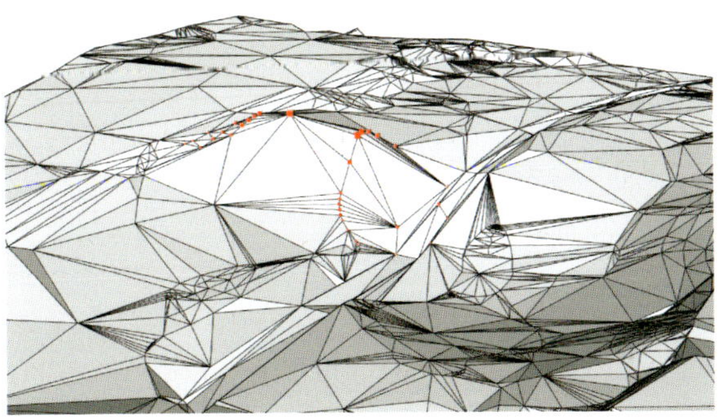

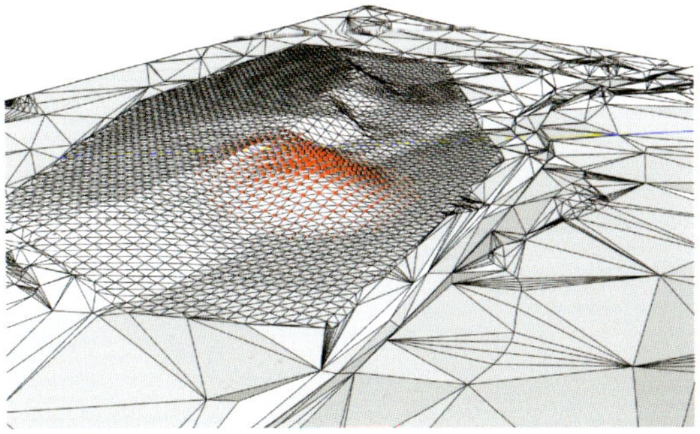

three-dimensional lines to create landforms

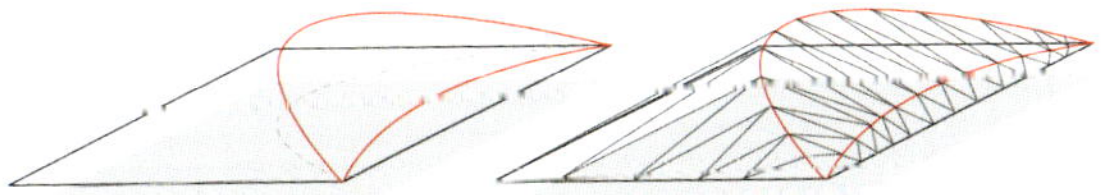

three dimensional lines to model retaining walls

three dimensional lines to create complex paths

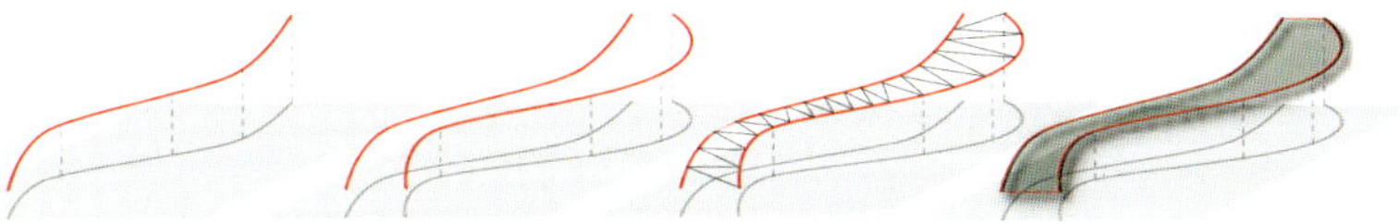

terrain forms modelled with three dimensional lines

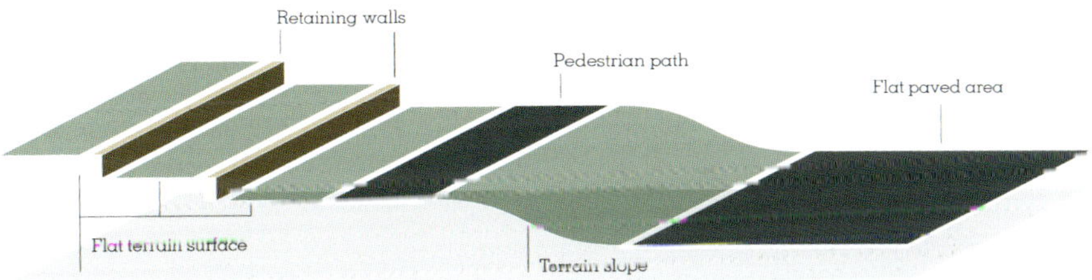

when the geometry of a component is changed, neigbouring components react by adjusting their geometry

resource, at least when used in plan. To address the issues of quality and accuracy, we proposed a three-dimensional model without the restrictions imposed by contour lines, which, after all, are excessive simplifications of the actual conditions. Using contour lines to create a digital terrain model is an impossible task, as it leads to surfaces that do not represent the intended form, even for a simple situation like a path with two neighboring surfaces [14-6]. Therefore, making such models based on contour lines not only creates difficulties—often they just don't work.

From an analysis of the design processes employed by several landscape architects, we derived digital design methods that rely on three-dimensional lines to depict the intended landform—replacing the two-dimensional contour line. After testing, we determined that describing the same landform with the new three-dimensional methods produced a far more accurate depiction of the conditions on-site. The new methods also better represented the contours of slopes, including those shaped with S-curves. Perhaps most beneficial was the program's ability to address other constraints that shape the landscape's design, among them the volume of soil to be displaced, the wind speed, and even auditory factors like noise. The feedback provides the designer with information about the efficiency and performance of the design.

As noted above, BIM uses components. In architecture and engineering these units are familiar, including standard elements such as walls, windows, and pipes. Yet, what constitutes a component in terrain design is not as obvious. How could we identify the landscape components and incorporate them into the design, truly benefiting from the use of BIM? Although this proved to be a difficult and challenging task, we identified those aspects common to most designs as well as unique design situations. From this study, we identified a set of terrain components directly linked to the way in which landscape architects work with landform [14-7]. These include soft components such as graded slopes and hard components such as walls, paths, and pavement. From these we devised a viable palette of terrain components, as well as a table of all the possible interactions among them. What happens if the slope of a path or the geometry of a wall is changed, and how will all the neighboring slopes adapt to the changes made to the path? Answering questions such as these is one of the many benefits BIM will bring to modeling for landscape architecture.

Case Studies

Theory and seemingly effective models and programs are one thing; functioning methods and easily usable software are another. To establish the validity of the new digital-design process, we applied it to several test cases. With the contour map as our point of departure, our challenge was to revise the topography by employing the specific terrain modeling components of TIN 2.0, tools using three-dimensional lines. The initial task was to design the site according to the components previously identified and then proceed to model the form of the terrain with the new digital toolset. No contour lines were used to create the three-dimensional model.

Employing the new design methods, we regraded the terrain for two university campus parks in Porto—their landscape design co-ordinated by Paulo Farinha-Marques—and used them to implement earth movement. A major consideration involved advanced stormwater management using landform to control water at times of peak rainfall. The work on the Parque da Quinta de Lamas featured the daylighting of a stream previously directed into a subterranean culvert [14-8]. As the area is subject to frequent flooding, sustainable stormwater management was a core design issue. The topography was modeled using three-dimensional lines and free-form design tools. The efficacy of the recontoured land was evaluated throughout the design process and continually revised to ensure that the retention basins were sufficient to accommodate the water collected from their catchment areas. Earthwork calculations were made throughout the entire course of design and construction in an effort to balance the soil excavated to construct the watercourse with the amount deposited in areas where the grade needed to be raised. This process provided the opportunity to test and determine whether the design performed as intended by the designers.

The construction of the Asprela Central Park began in 2020 with the primary design goals being an accessible network of paths and the modeling of an effective and attractive watercourse [14-9]. The designers faced the serious challenge of collecting and retaining water from a highly impervious watershed during a 100-year storm—a total of 10,000 cubic meters of water, a large volume relative to the size and scale of the project. We determined the best solution to be an earthen retention dam given a smooth serpentine profile with a sluice to control the passage of water. In the event of a large storm, the limited

Contour plan

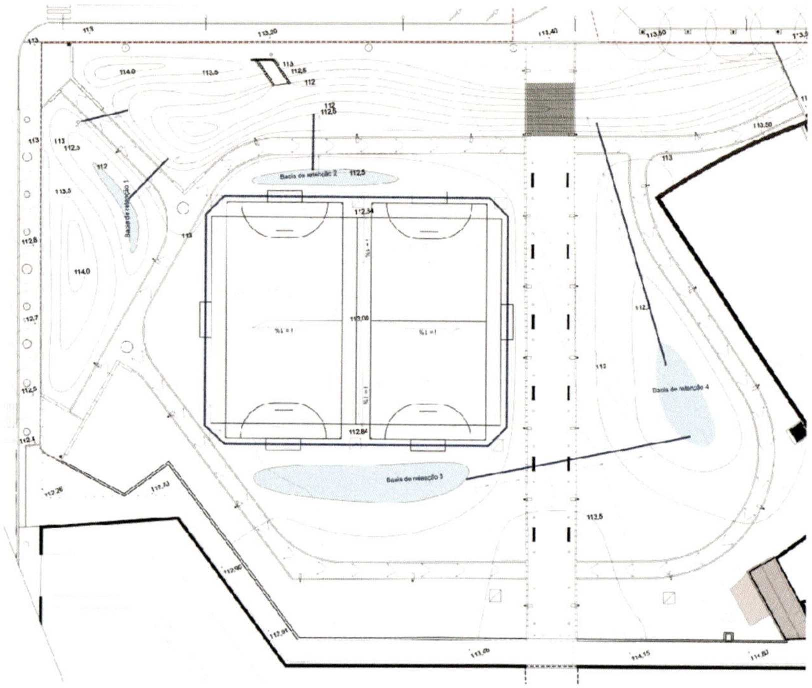

Digital terrain model (three-dimensional lines and components + TIN 2.0 surface)

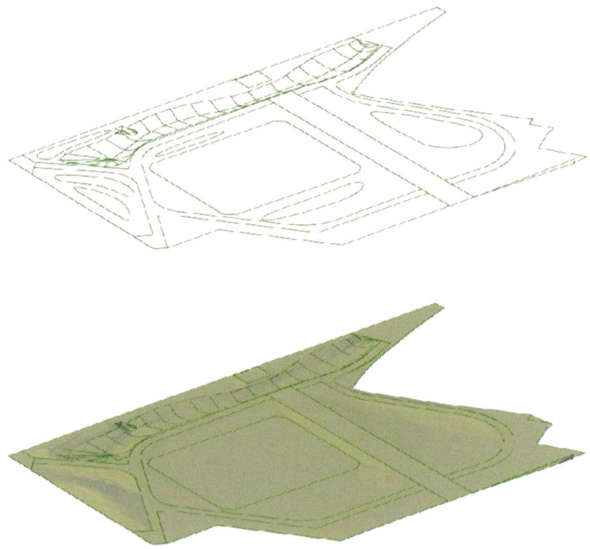

Case study Asprela Central Park

Master plan

Digital terrain model

opening of the sluice will raise the water level behind it. By reshaping the landscape alone, the dam is able to accommodate the target amount of water. The design process allowed for an interactive model that provided the landscape architect an immediate report on the performance of the design: a conversation regarding the idea, its digital representation, and the assessment of its performance. For each change in the terrain, its visual representation could be used to test its aesthetics, while at the same time receive feedback on the new water-retention capacities, the degree of slope—for pedestrian accessibility—and the calculation of earth to be modified, all of which allowed for a truly iterative and interactive design. This digital design process enabled the fine-tuning—in real time—of the height and storage capacities of the earthen dam and the supporting landforms.

Future Trends

In my opinion, landscape architects should be at the forefront in rethinking and developing new digital design processes and tools related to topography. To date this has been far from the norm, whether due to lack of interest, lack of knowledge and technical expertise, or the sheer number of hours required to achieve facility in the use of the current digital design tools. In all probability, however, it is mostly due to the inability of current digital programs to meet the requirements and needs of those involved with terrain design. Whenever a landscape architect is commissioned to undertake a new project, the materials at hand—the topographic survey or available satellite imagery, for example—may not be up-to-date. At times updating the survey may itself require several months, although the landscape architect may be required to start design immediately. Today, however, with the use of photogrammetry and drones, it is possible to obtain an updated three-dimensional model in only a few hours. In the design of the parks described above, these tools allowed us to produce an updated model of the existing site for use in the studio in a relatively short period of time. The three-dimensional model and accompanying aerial photographs provided a realistic representation of the project area and data sufficient to allow digital modeling and begin design almost immediately. In all, with this new technology it is relatively easy to create a "digital twin" of the project area, allowing the landscape architect to initiate design while offering access to the information at any point in the design process–to guide, challenge, or confirm its path.

14-8
Paulo Farinha Marques, José Miguel Lameiras, Gonçalo Andrade, Luís Guedes de Carvalho. Quinta de Lamas Park. Porto, Portugal, 2014. *(above left)*: Contour plan; *(above right)*: Digital terrain model. [Farinha Marques et al.]

14-9
Paulo Farinha Marques, José Miguel Lameiras, Gonçalo Andrade, Luís Guedes de Carvalho. Parque Central da Asprela. Porto, Portugal, 2021. *(left above)*: Master plan; *(left below)*: Digital terrain model. [Farinha Marques et al.]

Virtual reality (VR) offers state-of-the-art simulations of the proposed design and as such provides a useful complement to other, traditionally used models and media. Employing a VR headset, the designer can walk through the digital twin of the landscape to develop and test design decisions based on how they would be perceived on the ground. Recent developments allow for three-dimensional sketches to be made directly in VR, possibilities currently being explored primarily as three-dimensional tools for making conceptual sketches. Of course, the design still requires more technically oriented computational solutions to validate the design proposal, and if validated, to bring it into construction. VR also allows for real-time rendering and testing, encompassing grading, planting design, ambience, and social dynamics, among other factors. As a result, it affords a richer comprehension of the landscape design as an integrated system—one that can be modeled and designed digitally without contour lines.

The tools already discussed have been introduced in the curricula of many landscape-architecture programs internationally as a way to provide students with the means to better analyze, design, and assess the complexities of their designs. Hopefully, the use of this technology by the profession will become more widespread, leading to landscapes that perform more completely and offer richer aesthetic experiences. Landscape architects should be at the forefront of computational design as they once were, to aid in the development of the tools that better suit the specifics of their profession.

4-10
Complete VR model (*above*): showing terrain form; (*below*): with planting design.

ACKNOWLEDGMENTS

The Shape of the Land: Aesthetics and Utility, the symposium that provided the basis for this book, took place on the campus of the University of California, Berkeley, in March 2020, three days before the university closed in response to the outbreak of Covid-19. Unfortunately, because of the disease's rapid and widespread impact on both professional and personal lives, and subsequent travel restrictions, three of our speakers were unable to attend. For different reasons, Georges Descombes and Jennifer Guthrie faced travel issues and could not; Elissa Rosenberg was hampered by quarantine restrictions but participated using Zoom—in my own experience, the earliest use of a program that would govern many of our lives in the years that followed. Fortunately, although missing the symposium, all three would-be speakers have contributed essays to the book.

The planning of the symposium was co-curated with Louise Mozingo, chair of the Department of Landscape Architecture and Environmental Planning, which sponsored the event. The program was a true collaborative effort, and I thank Louise for her support. Her input, and that of the departmental staff and students, was critical for the successful mounting of the symposium and the making of this book, which follows two years later. In addition, Louise's Richard and Rhoda Goldman Distinguished Professorship provided a generous subvention for this publication. I am most grateful to departmental staff Jessica Ambriz and Sue Retta, who played crucial roles in handling travel arrangements, logistics, and financial matters, and could not have been more effective or pleasant to work with. In addition to processing the videos of the presentations and putting them online, Jeff Allen handled a myriad of other conference details, including—also unprecedented at that time—the installation of hand-sanitizer stations throughout the symposium site; to our knowledge, no one at the symposium fell ill. I thank them all.

Of course, I must also offer thanks to all the speakers, now authors, some of whom traveled to Berkeley across thousands of miles of land and sea, and for their efforts in providing or reviewing texts, as well as the visual material used to illustrate their ideas and works. As noted above, the impact of Covid-19 on the initial symposium and on the lives of the speakers thereafter made producing the book a considerable challenge. Given the chaos in everyone's lives caused by the pandemic, my appreciation is even greater than it would have been under more normal circumstances.

I thank Jane Friedman for her excellent and expeditious copyediting of texts by those who hail from many different landscapes and who typically write in languages other than English. Alicia Moreira provided insightful proofreading, precisely noting those slips of the mouse or cursor. And lastly, I must thank, once again, ORO Editions publisher Gordon Goff for his support of our work, and Jake Anderson for his skillful and efficient management of the production process. Our relationship in publishing a number of books together has been ideal.

I am again most grateful for the substantial financial support for the publication of this book provided by the Hubbard Educational Trust and the Richard and Rhoda Goldman Distinguished Professorship, University of California, Berkeley.

All involved with The Shape of the Land. Topography & Landscape Architecture sincerely hope that the substantial time and effort spent in its writing and production has resulted in a book that readers will find informative and a catalyst for their own thinking and work.

MT

CONTRIBUTORS

Marc Treib, Professor of Architecture Emeritus at the University of California, Berkeley, is a historian and critic of landscape and architecture who has published widely on modern and historical subjects in the United States, Japan, and Scandinavia. Recent books include *The Landscapes of Georges Descombes: Doing Almost Nothing*; *Thinking a Modern Landscape Architecture, West & East*; *The Aesthetics of Contemporary Planting Design*; and *Serious Fun: The Landscapes of Claude Cormier*.

Stephen Daniels is emeritus professor of cultural geography at the University of Nottingham, a landscape historian, and a fellow of the British Academy. His numerous writings include the coauthored *Iconography of Landscape*, which broke new ground in cultural landscape studies, and *Art of the Garden*. Well versed in numerous landscape subjects, he is also known as the leading authority on Humphry Repton, his theories, and landscapes.

Georges Descombes is an architect, landscape architect, and emeritus professor of architecture at the University of Geneva, whose work has been widely published and awarded. He has undertaken numerous projects both within Switzerland and abroad, including the Jardins d'Éole in Paris and the Parc de Lancy in Geneva. His decades-long project for the renaturalization of the River Aire outside Geneva has become a model for all design work in this arena.

Adriaan Geuze is a founding principal of West 8 Urban Design and Landscape Architecture, based in Rotterdam, the Netherlands, with numerous works there and in Britain, Europe, and Asia. Recent projects include the Rotterdam railroad station and its environs, Governor's Island in New York, and the water garden at Longwood Gardens in Pennsylvania.

Jennifer Guthrie, FASLA, is a founding partner of the Seattle-based Gustafson Guthrie Nichol (today GGN)—the recipient of the 2017 American Society of Landscape Architects' National Landscape Architecture Firm Award. GGN's work ranges broadly, encompassing urban districts of green streets and mixed-use housing, public squares, rooftop gardens, urban farms, and cultural institutions.

Kathleen John-Alder, FASLA, is Associate Professor of Landscape Architecture at Rutgers University, a practicing landscape architect, and scholar who explores the interplay of environmental perception, representation, and design. She holds degrees in environmental planning and landscape architecture from Rutgers, Pennsylvania State University, and Yale University, and has received numerous awards, including those from the National Park Service and the American Society of Landscape Architects.

Ana Kučan is Professor of Landscape Design and Theory at the Biotechnical Faculty of the University of Ljubljana, Slovenia. She holds an MLAUD degree from Harvard University and a PhD from the University of Ljubljana, and is a principal in the landscape architecture and urban-design studio Studio AKKA, which she founded with Luka Javornik in 2007. Her landscapes and urban-design projects have been exhibited in Slovenia and abroad, and have received national and international awards.

Karl Kullmann, Associate Professor of Landscape Architecture and Urban Design at the University of California, Berkeley, teaches design studios and digital representation, and maintains a selective design practice. His research and publications have addressed the cultural agency of complex topography as well as issues of representation and those facing landscape-architectural practice and education.

José Miguel Lameiras is Professor of Landscape Architecture at the University of Porto, Portugal, and a researcher in the university's Research Center in Biodiversity and Genetic Resources. He holds a PhD from the University of Porto; his dissertation explored the use of digital terrain design incorporating state-of-the-art developments in Building Information Models.

David Meyer was a senior partner at Peter Walker Partners before establishing Meyer Studio Land Architects in Berkeley. In addition to practice, he serves as Adjunct Professor of Landscape Architecture at the University of California, Berkeley. A fellow of the American Academy in Rome, he credits his Iowa origins with his love of simple, sensual, deliberate designs that judiciously employ nature's palette.

Elissa Rosenberg, Associate Professor at the Bezalel Academy of Arts and Design, Jerusalem, studies the ways in which topography has been used as a generative idea and expressive medium in landscape design, and how the shaping of the ground is bound up with ways of seeing, moving, and knowing the world. Her research has focused on contemporary landscape architecture and urban design, including postindustrial landscapes and urban infrastructure.

Bas Smets is the principal of Bureau Bas Smets, based in Brussels, Belgium, a practice whose work spans the small scale of the garden to large-scale infrastructure and territorial visions. Recent projects include the Tour & Taxis Park in Brussels; the landscape for the new motorway between the ports of Antwerp and Zeebruges; and the memorial for the victims of the 2016 terror attacks in Brussels.

Laura Solano is principal at Michael Van Valkenburgh Associates (MVVA), where she oversees the firm's projects in the Cambridge office, and has played a significant role in MVVA's award-winning projects for Teardrop Park in New York and the Jefferson National Expansion Memorial in St. Louis. She also serves as Associate Professor in Practice at the Harvard Graduate School of Design, where she has taught grading for many years.

INDEX

Notes and images have not been indexed.